THE ROAD TO
ARMAGEDDON

THE ROAD TO
ARMAGEDDON

THE LAST YEARS OF THE
CRUSADER KINGDOM
OF JERUSALEM

W.B. BARTLETT

SUTTON PUBLISHING

First published in the United Kingdom in 2007 by
Sutton Publishing, an imprint of NPI Media Group Limited
Cirencester Road · Chalford · Stroud · Gloucestershire · GL6 8PE

British Library Cataloguing in Publication Data
A catalogue record for this book is available from the British Library.

Hardback ISBN 978-0-7509-4578-3
Paperback ISBN 978-0-7509-4579-0

Typeset in Sabon.
Typesetting and origination by
NPI Media Group Limited.
Printed and bound in England.

*To Garry and Julie, with happy memories of
Middle Eastern adventures together.*

Contents

Acknowledgements

I would like to thank all those who have made this book possible. My particular thanks to Christopher Feeney, whom I wish all the best of fortune in the future. I am grateful, too, for the advice and support of Nick Reynolds, with whom it has been a pleasure to work.

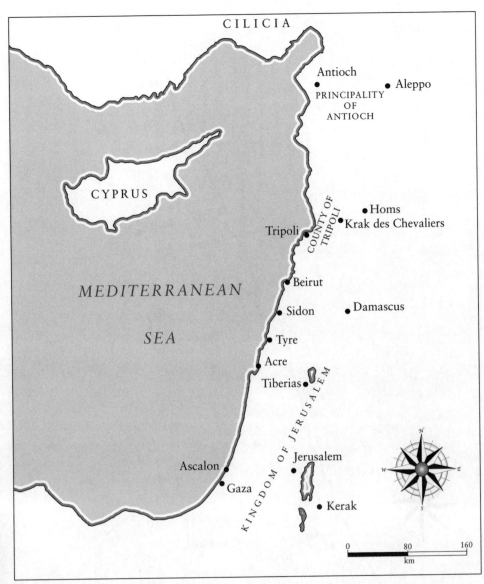

The Crusader States in 1187.

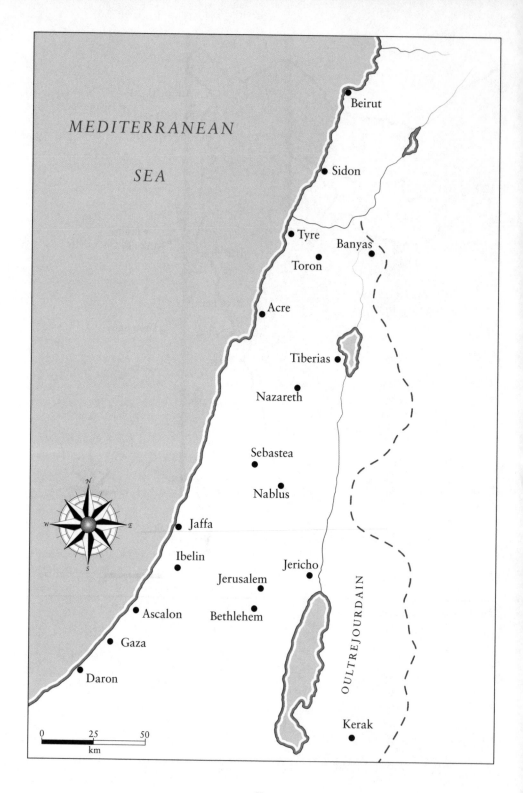

MEDITERRANEAN

SEA

Beirut

Sidon

Tyre

Banyas

Toron

Acre

Tiberias

Nazareth

Sebastea

Nablus

Jaffa

Ibelin

Jericho

Jerusalem

Ascalon

Bethlehem

Gaza

Daron

OULTREJOURDAIN

Kerak

0   25   50
km

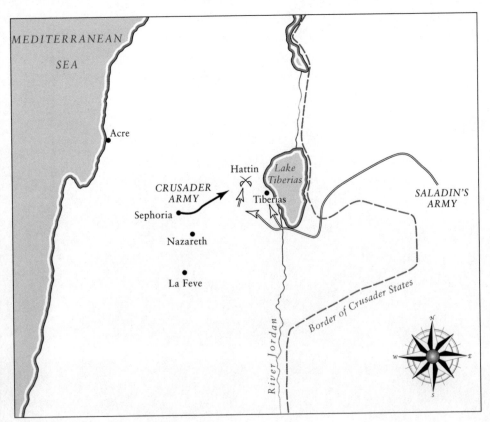

The Hattin Campaign, 1187.

Opposite: The Kingdom of Jerusalem in 1187.

Prologue

For nearly 100 years, Christian settlers from Western Europe ruled a kingdom on the far shores of the Mediterranean. Jerusalem was the heartbeat of this realm, the spiritual centre of the Christian world. It was always unlikely that the Westerners would hold on to this distant land forever. They had taken it when the Muslims who had held Palestine for centuries had been too busy fighting each other to notice that a greater danger was at their backs. By the time that they realised what was happening it was too late, and Jerusalem had gone.

But once the Muslims reunited they held all the trump cards in their hands. They had far greater numbers of warriors available to them and, unlike the Christian kingdom of 'Outremer', 'the land beyond the sea', which relied on reinforcements from Western Europe hundreds of miles away, short lines of supply. Should they ever stop fighting each other then the interlopers from the West were living on borrowed time.

Unity, though, was an elusive quality in the Islamic world. Bitterly divided by theological division, particularly between the Shi'a and Sunni branches of Islam, it would take something, or someone, special to cement together the factionalised Muslim lands around Palestine. The mortar that managed to do so had two vital constituents. The first of these was intense religious fervour, fuelled by the loss of one of the most spiritually significant cities in Islam, Jerusalem. The second was an extraordinary man by the name of Saladin.

It was ironic that, just as Saladin and his predecessor as ruler of Syria, Nur ed-Din, were bringing the Islamic world closer together, contrary pressures were dividing the Christian Kingdom of Jerusalem.

For the plain fact was that Outremer was no heaven on earth. The men who ruled in this unique kingdom were flawed, as most men are. They were driven by greed and ambition, they acted with rashness and self-interest, they were men of quick temper and doubtful judgement. And just as the Muslims had lost Palestine to a Crusader army because they were too preoccupied with their own petty squabbles, so did the settlers in Outremer fail to notice that their enemies were growing stronger because of their internecine and bitter feuding – a neat mirror image in fact.

During the latter decades of the twelfth century, Outremer was sleepwalking to disaster. Seemingly oblivious to the dangers of a resurgent Islam, the kingdom began to split apart. The nobles who governed with the king sought to outmanoeuvre one another, seeking to raise themselves up and bring their political opponents down. It was a persistent and sometimes brutal power struggle that did little credit to any of the parties involved.

All this came to a head on 4 July 1187, on two small hills above Lake Tiberias. Here, trapped, outfought and outthought, the largest army Outremer ever raised was obliterated by Saladin. It was a terrible defeat because it consigned the whole kingdom to oblivion. Nearly all available men had been called up and there was no one left to man the castles and cities of the realm. Jerusalem had mortgaged everything on one spectacular throw of the dice. And Jerusalem had lost.

But the great battle at Hattin was the culmination of a series of events, though it was not quite the end, which came when Jerusalem itself fell shortly afterwards. Hattin was part of a bigger story. The cast included some larger-than-life characters: a boy king who suffered the terrible blight of leprosy, a rogue baron who would stop at nothing to expand his influence, an adventurer from across the seas who saw himself as the future monarch and a Templar Grand Master who was driven by delusions of self-aggrandisement and vengeance for a personal slight. At times the storyline reads less like history and more like a previously undiscovered novel by Sir Walter Scott.

At the outset, a note on terminology is important. A 'Crusader' was, simplistically put, an armed pilgrim who took solemn vows that could only be fulfilled by visiting a holy place, often the Church of the Holy Sepulchre in Jerusalem. In return, they gained spiritual benefits that would ease their way into the Hereafter. These privileges were granted by the Pope through a mechanism known as an 'indulgence'. Therefore, most of the Christian participants in the great Hattin campaign were not 'Crusaders', there on a specific, 'one-off' mission to fulfil a vow; they were rather settlers in the Kingdom of Jerusalem.

The Muslims gave the men from the West a generic name, 'Franj', which is normally translated as 'Franks'. This is what I will in the main call the Christian participants in the story that follows. Only those seeking to redeem pilgrim vows on a papally sanctioned crusade will be termed 'Crusaders'. Occasionally, I will also refer to the settlers as 'Latins', another name that has sometimes been given to them by the indigenous population.

It is also important to consider briefly the status of Outremer and in particular the vexed question of whether or not it was a 'colony', as historians have debated over the years. Taking as a standard definition 'a body of settlers living in a new territory but subject to control by the parent state'[1] the answer is an emphatic 'no'. For although this was a new territory, there was no control by any parent state. There was indeed no clear parent state. The settlers came from many parts of Western Europe and if any body had nominal control over the territory, it was the Papacy. But despite this influence, the Papacy never exercised any degree of control in practice, nor did kings from Western Europe, though they were important. No, this was a unique state, subject to very strong influences from the West, but in no way under the control of any other. This was therefore not a 'colony'.

Such academic abstractions are subsidiary to the rich drama of the fall of Outremer. What follows is the story of flawed men and women, the tale of King Baldwin, the leper, Reynald of Chatillon, the rogue baron, Guy of Lusignan, would-be king and Gerard of Ridfort, Grand Master. It is also the story of Raymond of Tripoli, avowed enemy of Gerard; of Balian of Ibelin, inaccurately portrayed by Orlando Bloom in the Hollywood epic *Kingdom of Heaven*; of

Sibylla and Isabella, Baldwin's sisters and powerful pawns in the kingdom because of their royal status. And it is the story of Saladin.

But more even than stories of people this is the story of an ideal. For this was no ordinary kingdom. And, most of all, Jerusalem was no ordinary city. St Bernard of Clairvaux, greatest of all twelfth-century clerics, wrote of Jerusalem in awed tones:

> Hail then, holy city, sanctified by the Highest as his own temple so that this generation may be saved in and through you! Hail, city of the great King, source of so many blest and indescribable marvels! Hail, mistress of nations and queen of provinces, heritage of patriarchs, mother of apostles and prophets, source of the faith and glory of Christendom![2]

Jerusalem was held in reverence by Christendom and possession of the city was its greatest glory. By the same token, losing it was the most awful disgrace imaginable. Although the kingdom stumbled on in an emaciated state after Hattin, the ideal was lost. Men had lost faith in the concepts that the state had enshrined. Confidence and belief were shattered along with the Christian army, and nothing would ever be quite the same again.

What follows is an account of how Jerusalem fell, of all the twists and turns down the road to Armageddon. Within the text, there are frequent references to the Book of Revelation. Their presence is more than an attempt to adopt a clever literary device: they are included because this was a biblical age in the sense that the words of the Bible were often accorded literal meaning. Scholars scanned its pages in an effort to read hidden meanings into world events. To some of them, no doubt, the days just before and after Hattin seemed like the end of the world. And in many ways it surely was.

ONE

In the Beginning

For I saw a new heaven and a new earth: for the first heaven and the first earth were passed away . . .

Revelation 21: 1

On 7 June 1099, a Crusader army arrived outside the walls of Jerusalem, following a nightmare journey that had lasted for four years. The city was in the hands of a Muslim garrison, as it had been for over four centuries, but the Christians moving menacingly towards the walls had no intention of letting it stay that way. For this was the city of their God, the place where Jesus had been crucified. Jerusalem belonged to Christ, not to the Infidel.

A major problem was that the city was holy for Muslims too. From the rock over which the dome that is still one of Jerusalem's greatest treasures had been erected, the Prophet Mohammed had ascended into heaven. The Prophet's followers did not recognise the name 'Jerusalem': to them, it was never known as anything except al-Quts, 'the Holy City'.[1]

The garrison's desire to resist, no doubt built on genuine piety, was reinforced by the knowledge of what had happened to the Muslim defenders of the city of Antioch in the previous year. When the Crusaders had taken that city with the help of treachery from within, the result had been a slaughter of apocalyptic proportions. Jerusalem's defenders could expect little mercy from the ragged army that was approaching their city.

It was an equally worrying time for the Jewish population of Jerusalem. The city was precious to them also. Within its walls, centuries before Christ had died there, Solomon had erected his great

1

Temple, which would become the most revered of all Judaic sites. Destroyed long ago, it was still a place of sacred memory to the Jews.

The Jews lived in relative harmony with their Muslim governors, who generally respected the religious freedoms of Jews and Christians alike. The greater threat to their life and limb came from the army outside the walls. In the early stages of their pilgrimage from Western Europe to the Holy Land, many Jews had been slain, their perceived association with the death of Christ making them a target for the more fanatical elements of the Crusader army.

The Crusader host provided a strange spectacle, for in its ranks were many non-combatants, women, old men, children, priests and artisans as well as warriors. And they had suffered horrendous loss on their journey so far. Tens of thousands had died, some in battle, some of exhaustion, some of disease, some of starvation. Others had turned back long ago. So this was a moment of supreme spiritual euphoria for those who were left.

For many of the masses, people largely without the ability to read or write, meaningful possessions or hope, the Holy City had mystical significance. They only knew of Jerusalem through the mass teaching received from their priests, who extolled its virtues as a city above all others and through whom they came to believe they were like the Israelites of old reaching the Promised Land. The monk Robert, who wrote an early history of Jerusalem, called it 'the navel of the world, a land which is fruitful above all others, like another paradise of delights'.[2] Contemporary maps showed the city at the centre of the world, at the heart of their universe. It was a land of milk and honey, to some perhaps literally so, whose streets were paved with gold.

We find it hard to understand, from the standpoint of our increasingly secular society, how religious motivations can inspire ordinary people to undertake extraordinary actions. And yet even we can appreciate something of the mysterious and timeless lure of Jerusalem, if only because it continues to have a disproportionate impact on the affairs of our world even now.

One publication recently described the area around the al-Aqsa Mosque and the Dome of the Rock as 'the most explosive piece of real estate in the world'.[3] And so it was then. For the Crusaders, Jerusalem was the vision that enticed men, women and children to endure hardships of unbelievable severity, to live out terrible lives as slaves when they were captured in their droves, to die in their thousands by the roadsides of Europe and Asia Minor.

The reality of Jerusalem, an averagely sized, averagely wealthy city, was of no account to the humble pilgrims who fought their way across mountain, plain, desert and swamp towards their goal. It was, as one commentator has remarked, much more than a physical entity, it was 'before all else, a symbol. The Jerusalem of the Psalms, the celestial Jerusalem of the Apocalypse, lived in the heart of the faithful.'[4]

It was also a literal gateway to heaven. If pilgrims died in pursuit of fulfilling their Crusader vows, then they would be rewarded in the next life. In a world where death walked cheek by jowl with life, sickness with health, famine with plenty, the world yet to come seemed every bit as real as, and often much more attractive than, transient, day-to-day existence. The juxtaposition of these two concepts, the mystical magnetism of Jerusalem on the one hand and the promise of spiritual rewards on the other, formed the heady brew that gave life to the Crusading movement.

This was truly an apocalyptic era. In the year 1000, many believed the world was about to come to an end, a fear again prominent in 1033 when the millennium of Christ's crucifixion fell. Everywhere, the shadow of death hung over man. Even today, evidence of this can be seen. The quiet and half-hidden church of Tarrant Crawford in Dorset was once adjacent to a monastic establishment. Its chief glory is its fourteenth-century wall paintings, much faded now but still clear enough to see and 'read' some of the images. One in particular is striking. It is of three kings out hunting who stumble across three skeletons who have come to remind them that death is coming, that one day even the great will turn to bones and dust.

It is important to understand from the outset the vastly different view of the world that Christian Europe had in the medieval period from that we have now. Without such comprehension, the immense sacrifice involved in Crusading makes no sense. Men believed that this life was just a proving ground for the next, and in that world to come a man would be judged by, and punished for, his actions on earth.

This First Crusade had been summoned by Pope Urban II at Clermont in France in 1095. It was an armed pilgrimage, sanctioned – indeed called for – by the Church, and in return for their participation those who fulfilled their Crusader vows would receive spiritual benefits that would ease their passage from this world to the next. Those vows usually involved completing a pilgrimage to the Holy Sepulchre, supposedly erected over the site of Christ's tomb and the holy of holies for Christians.

The call struck a chord because many were fully aware of their sin and believed that they could only avoid the horrors of Hell with the help of the grace of God. Their participation in the Crusade would help them in this quest. The appeal of Crusading therefore reached out to a society as a whole, not just to warriors, and the expeditions that had made their way east (for there were a number, not just one army) therefore represented a microcosm of the Western world at that time.

Urban had not been slow to seize on the opportunity offered by the fascination exerted by Jerusalem. In August 1096 he wrote to the people of Bologna that

> we have heard that some of you desire to go to Jerusalem because you know that this would greatly please us. Know then that anyone who sets out on that journey, not out of lust for worldly advantage but only for the salvation of his soul and for the liberation of the Church, is remitted in entirety all penance for his sins.[5]

To a deeply religious Christian society these rewards were extremely persuasive. Men and women had responded to Urban's appeal in their droves and left the little that they had behind them in France, Flanders and parts of Germany. As they advanced, more joined them in Central and Eastern Europe but their losses along the

4

way had been immense. Those who were left, now ranged outside Jerusalem, were the chosen people from the waves that had set out, to whom God had awarded the greatest honour, that of recapturing His city for Christendom.

The masses assembled outside the forebidding city walls believed themselves to be the latter day Children of Israel. This was in every sense an exercise in religious expression. When early efforts to break through the walls were rebuffed, the Crusaders decided that they would march barefoot around the city, calling on God to help them. This was a revisiting of biblical episodes such as the procession of Joshua around the defences of Jericho, when his army had compassed the city daily until, on the last day that they did so, they let out a great shout and the walls fell down.[6]

But this would be no easy conquest. The walls were substantial and those inside were fighting for their lives. The initial attempts of the Crusaders to break into the city were driven back. The days that followed were trying in the extreme. There was no water for 6 miles and when it was ferried into the camp in ox-hide containers it smelt vile. Food was short and so too was timber, needed to construct the siege engines that had to be built if the city were to be taken. So this also had to be carried in from miles away.

But the Crusaders were nothing if not persistent. The siege engines were erected and the city tightly invested. On 15 July came the breakthrough. On that day, the attack was relentless, resistance desperate. Suddenly, a knight named Lethold jumped across from a siege tower onto the walls of the city. Terrified by the sight of this avenging warrior charging towards them the defenders fled for cover. Emboldened at the sight, other Crusaders followed Lethold and charged into the heart of the city.

An anonymous contemporary chronicle, the *Gesta Francorum*, takes up the story:

Our pilgrims entered the city, and chased the Saracens, killing as they went, as far as the Temple of Solomon. There the enemy assembled and fought a furious battle for the whole day, so that their blood flowed all over the Temple. At last the pagans were overcome, and our men captured a good number of men and women in the Temple: they killed whomsoever they wished, and chose to keep others alive.[7]

This fierce battle took place around the site of the Temple, holy for various reasons to Christians, Jews and Muslims. The battle here was not just one of survival but was also inspired by powerful religious emotion. Perhaps because of this, the resultant slaughter was awful. The same chronicler tells of soldiers wading up to their ankles in blood and of how men and women captured on the roof of the Temple were all beheaded. He talks of piles of the dead, 'as big as houses', of the terrible stench that hung over the city and almost exults over the extent of the massacre. The Kingdom of Jerusalem had had a violent birth, ushered in by a sea of blood.

The massacre was to have great repercussions, though not all were immediately apparent. It encouraged a desire for revenge among Muslims who saw the bloodletting as an awful stain on their reputation. Despite this thirst for vengeance, the perpetrators were able to find justification for their actions: for example when Joshua took Jericho then 'they utterly destroyed all that was in the city, both man and woman, young and old, and ox, and sheep, and ass, with the edge of the sword'.[8]

Other eyewitnesses recalled the End of the World, as foretold in the Book of Revelation. So vivid did these verses seem that some even quoted them in their accounts: 'the winepress was trodden without the city, and blood came out of the winepress, even unto the horses' bridles'.[9] In other words, the slaughter in Jerusalem was not without biblical precedent.

The Crusaders' victory in Palestine owed much to the disunity of the Muslim forces that had been arrayed against them. The Islamic world was split into two major camps, the Sunni and Shi'a. The eastern half of Islam, simplistically modern Persia, Iraq, Syria and Turkey, was primarily a Sunni sphere of influence. Egypt on the other hand was mainly in the hands of the Shi'a Fatimids. These two major divisions of Islam were constantly at odds with each other – a situation that, again, continues to play itself out in our own times.

One of the fault-lines where these two major Muslim groupings clashed was in Palestine. As a result, when the Crusaders marched through Asia Minor and down the Mediterranean coast of Syria, resistance to their advance, though on occasion fierce, was largely disjointed. Unbeknown to the West, their invasion had been launched at the perfect time, a moment of relative weakness among the Muslims. But this turned out to be a short window of opportunity because within a few years things started to change for the worse.

A perennial problem for the new kingdom which came to be called Outremer – 'The Land beyond the Sea' – was how to raise enough men to defend the lands that had been so dearly won. There were not enough settlers to fight off the Muslims, particularly if the latter ever managed to unite. As partial compensation for this deficiency, regular influxes of Crusaders from the West helped to boost the forces available on a short-term basis. Large numbers of new recruits made their way to Palestine to complete a pilgrimage to the Holy Sepulchre. Forced to make their way across Asia Minor, major expeditions that set out for Outremer in 1101 were cut to pieces by the Turks in the region, now reunited and determined not to let the Crusaders pass.

From the start it was clear that Outremer was in a difficult position. If the Muslims united then it would be very hard for the kingdom to resist. The Muslims far outnumbered the Christians and had the advantage of logistics on their side: reinforcements and supplies could be moved throughout Syria or Egypt whereas any such commodities for the Kingdom of Outremer would have to make a months'-long crossing over the Mediterranean. The only saving grace for the Franks as the twelfth-century began was that Egypt and Syria served different masters. The Turkish fightback in Asia Minor in 1101 was a short-term phenomenon which did not yet presage a complete resurgence in Islamic fortunes.

In the aftermath of the triumph at Jerusalem several separate Christian principalities were created. The Kingdom of Jerusalem formed the most important part of Outremer, but principalities were established in Tripoli and Antioch too. The rulers of the latter sometimes saw the king in Jerusalem as *primus inter pares* (though at others they did not), but in practice operated with a good deal of autonomy.

The Kingdom of Jerusalem was like no other on earth in the sense that it was based around a city that had unique symbolic pathos for Christendom. So unusual was the situation that the first ruler of the kingdom, Godfrey of Bouillon, refused to accept the epithet of 'king' and instead adopted the title 'Defender of the Holy Sepulchre'. He humbly refused to declare himself a monarch when this was God's city. This reluctance to take on all the worldly trappings that normally went with kingship, however, did not survive his death: his successor, Baldwin I, had no such problems in calling himself a king.[10]

In theory the King of Jerusalem was elected by his peers, but Outremer quickly developed many of the characteristics of Western monarchy. The crown partially became a hereditary possession, though there were certain crises that hit the realm when the absence of a suitable heir made this impossible, and on these occasions the expedient of election was adopted again. In theory, the barons of the kingdom were always required to elect a king, but in practice their choice normally fell on a close relative of the last monarch if there was a suitable candidate available.

While a series of laws was adopted to set the appropriate balance between king and state, and, initially, the monarchy was the pre-eminent institution, as the twelfth century advanced the nobility of the kingdom grew in power and the position of the king weakened in diametrical proportion. The change was to have profound results for the kingdom and would seriously undermine its foundations. Ambitious warlords were empowered by this shift in the balance of power to interfere much more in affairs of state, with unfortunate consequences.

In the early decades of the twelfth century the Kingdom of Jerusalem was lucky with its kings (or, as it would have been perceived at the time, it was protected by God, who ensured that the kingdom had a succession of capable monarchs). There were occasions when the monarchy was threatened, for example when King Baldwin II was captured in 1123 and spent years as a prisoner of the Muslims. But the strength of the new kingdom was evidenced by the way that the state managed to survive, and even to an extent thrive, while the king was out of commission.

Historians in times past have tended to see the kingdom as an extension of feudalism in Europe but this view is subject to increasing challenge and revision. Although the early settlers in Outremer inevitably brought with them their own paradigms of the world that influenced the design of the political structure they created, they also had their own vision that built in subtle variations from the institutions and norms they had left behind them in the West.

Neither was the state static. It evolved as it found its feet, as happens to any new frontier territory. To talk of the borders of the kingdom is an oversimplification if applied to anything other than a specific moment in time. They changed and metamorphosed, enclosing an amoeba-like political entity that shifted form with bewildering frequency. Outremer moulded and reshaped itself in response to internal pressures and external challenges.[11] The strength of the king and individual barons waxed and waned as a result – an important element that came into play in the events that led ultimately to the Battle of Hattin and the loss of Jerusalem.

In practice, the eastern borders of the kingdom can be thought of as three separate sectors. The northern sector, centred on the Litani valley, was notable for some of the strongest Frankish castles, imperious and imposing. The central sector ran roughly along the Golan Heights, in modern times, after the 1967 war, a depopulated buffer zone between Israel and Syria. Even then it was, in its own way, a no man's land or, to be more accurate, every man's land, for it was effectively a shared sphere of influence between the Kingdom of Jerusalem and Damascus. The southern sector, Oultrejourdain, was hostile terrain, dominating caravan routes between Cairo and Damascus, and often used as a toll road by avaricious Frankish lords.

Another significant element in the politics of the state was the position of the Church, which in Outremer was interesting, unusual and important. Throughout Christendom, this period of history is characterised by an ongoing battle between Church and State for supremacy. The Pope believed that all kings should be subject to him as their spiritual leader, an interpretation that most kings disagreed with. The situation was particularly complex in Outremer given its unique status to the Christian world. It was complicated still further by the status of the Crusade, which was summoned and approved by the Papacy.

When the First Crusade set out, it was unmistakably a religiously inspired, and partially controlled, enterprise in which the Pope's legate, Adhemar of le Puy, was the pre-eminent individual with the expedition. How long this position would have survived given the strong personalities of some of the secular leaders with the Crusade is a matter of idle speculation, for the legate died at Antioch before the army reached and took Jerusalem. As a result of his death, an important advocate of Church rights was removed from the scene at an inopportune moment. At the very beginning of the kingdom's subsequent history, the Church tried to hang on to a position of superiority over the secular powers in the kingdom. This did not last long before the latter claimed a tacit victory.

Despite the Church's failure to assert dominance over the secular, it was nevertheless the case that the leading churchman of the kingdom, the Patriarch of Jerusalem, was an important individual. To be the head of the Church in the Holy City was a rare honour and it brought with it a good deal of prestige as well as a significant store of wealth. The Patriarch's position was a much sought-after one.

The Pope was the ultimate ecclesiastic power in Western Christendom but the Patriarch was a crucial figure. It was he who crowned the King of Jerusalem, a symbolic act that attempted to demonstrate that no one could rule in the city without the Church's say-so. This was no mere symbolism. The Holy Roman Empire had been founded in AD 800 when Charlemagne had been ceremonially enthroned by the Pope. The coronation rites of a king in the city of God, the sacred site of such rituals in biblical times, assumed even greater significance.

If Islam was divided, so too was Christendom. The eleventh century had been a turbulent one, with ongoing disputes between the Western Church, headed by the Pope, and other Christian groups, particularly of the Orthodox persuasion. The latter, whose foremost leader was the Patriarch of Constantinople, adopted a number of different rituals, leading to heated theological debate. In addition, although the Orthodox faith recognised the Pope in Rome as being the most senior Church figure there was not the same recognition of his predominant authority as there was in the West.

Within the Holy Land, the situation was further complicated by the existence of adherents to other branches of Christianity, such as the Maronites. Again, rituals differed. There was a complex inter-relationship between these various strands of Christianity. Syrian Christians had been at odds with the Orthodox Church for centuries, and the newly arrived Latin clerics had little time for either. As Outremer became more established, there was frequent conflict between the Western 'Latins' and other groups of Christians as the former tried to install their preferred candidates into the key sees and bishoprics of the Holy Land, which had traditionally been held by Orthodox nominees.

To survive as an entity, Outremer had to establish itself economically. It was in a good position to do so, an entrepôt to the Middle East, which in its turn had strong links with regions much further east, such as China, from where highly valued spices came. Crucial to economic development were various Italian city-states, particularly Venice, Genoa and Pisa, which plied their trade back and forth across the Mediterranean as they had done for centuries. Unscrupulous and focused almost exclusively on commercial gain, these maritime powers showed little distinction between friend and foe: the highest bidder was their major concern. They nevertheless played a crucial role in creating a viable Christian kingdom, for without their ships Outremer could not have survived.

But Outremer was also reliant on developing links with its Muslim hinterland. The kingdom, despite some areas of fertile land, could not be self-sufficient and neither could it rely on the West to sustain it; so it was important to develop relationships with Muslim states. It is easy to imagine that Outremer was in a constant state of war: it was not. For much of the time, peace – sometimes uneasy, frequently breaking down – existed between Christian and Muslim. It was also true that there were many Muslims who lived with Christian masters, who continued to practise their faith even after Outremer had been established.

Relations with the West were, though, very important. It was not just supplies and provisions that ships carried with them. As the land routes across Asia Minor became increasingly dangerous, the use of the more expensive but much safer sea lanes assumed greater importance.

Jerusalem was the Christian world's leading pilgrimage destination, in terms of importance if not of frequency of visitation. The medieval era was the great age of relics and pilgrimage, and Jerusalem had plenty to commend it in both respects. The Holy Sepulchre in particular was the pre-eminent site for pilgrims to visit and great spiritual rewards were on offer for those who completed the trip.

The Holy Sepulchre had been the site of Christian pilgrimage for centuries. Christ's tomb, the remains of which were housed within its walls, had been discovered in the fourth century and detached from the quarry of which it had formed part. A small chapel had been built over it. Not far away stood Golgotha, the Place of the Skull, the site of Christ Crucified.

Close at hand was the spot where Helena, mother of the Emperor Constantine, had found a fragment of the True Cross. Miracles attended the discovery. Three crosses were found and it was not clear which belonged to Christ. To find out which it was, the body of a newly deceased youth was placed over them. When the body was laid over the True Cross, the corpse came back to life as a result of the resurrecting power of Christ.[12] It was from the Holy Sepulchre that another piece of this precious relic had been seized by a group of triumphant Crusaders from the Greek monks who held it. By 1140, the site of both crucifixion and burial had been brought together under a great roof. No wonder this was Christendom's foremost place of pilgrimage.

A pilgrimage to Jerusalem was a dangerous undertaking. If the pilgrim journeyed by land, then he was at risk from bandits. If he went by sea, then he was still vulnerable, either because of pirates who patrolled the Mediterranean looking for prey or from the hostile seas that could all too easily overwhelm the fragile craft of the times. The latter was a particularly terrifying prospect for a Christian should not be drowned and his body accordingly deprived of the benefits of a Christian burial.[13] Whatever route was chosen, there was also the ever-present threat of disease, far more destructive than any human enemy.

There were other hardships. The diet would be frugal and boring, the journey full of discomforts. Seasickness was a constant companion of the medieval traveller: contemporary records note that kings of England paid a fee to an individual from Dover whose job was to hold the monarch's head while he was vomiting when crossing to France. The pilgrimage necessitated a long period away from home and any creature comforts. It was an expensive enterprise too, and if a pilgrim had dependants then these had to be provided for in the traveller's absence.

Despite these travails, the spiritual rewards were worth it. There were other, far more worldly compensations too. The Muslims were shocked at what they saw as the promiscuity of Latin women in contrast to the much more modest behaviour of their own. Even Jerusalem had its whorehouses, with a surprisingly large number of loose women keen on plying their trade. In 1191, shortly after the momentous events we are about to consider, Saladin's secretary Imad ad-Din, waxed lyrical about the athleticism of these ladies in language that would surely make a bishop blush:

> Tinted and painted . . . desirable and accommodating – bold and ardent, with nasal voices and fleshy thighs . . . they offered their wares for enjoyment, brought their silver anklets up to touch their golden ear-rings . . . made themselves targets for men's darts, offered themselves to the lance's blows . . . made javelins rise towards shields.[14]

The historian went on with a series of increasingly appalling *double entendres* that left little to the imagination. But if he was shocked by the brazen sexuality of the Franks, theologians were equally worried. The Church believed that sexual misbehaviour was one of the surest roads to sin and did its best to discourage it. In fact, it was widely believed that after the Day of Judgement, when God returned to judge all mankind, Heaven would be home to those who were free of sexual drive.[15]

Religious motivation was the main inspiration for the pilgrim, though there might be subsidiary reasons for a pilgrimage too: criminals, aiming to escape the consequences of their actions, undoubtedly had an alternative motivation. So too did those desiring to gain money, power or land (though few men ever made their fortune by their participation and more typically ended up substantially in debt as a result of their actions). As the Crusading era advanced, chivalry and thoughts of glory also played their part to an increasing extent. But for most these were secondary motivations far behind those of a spiritual nature.

Having arrived in Outremer, a Crusader was still in danger. If he (or she) arrived by sea, typically through the port of Acre, he then had to make his way across country to Jerusalem. Even when Outremer had been established, the roads were still dangerous places to travel. The Crusaders took advantage of the strong walls of the major cities such as Jerusalem and Acre and also built castles, but the countryside remained a dangerous place where the unprotected traveller was open to the threat of robbery, rape and murder. Many of the pilgrims were without any means of defending themselves, often being poor, travelling in small groups and without weapons and/or the skills to use them effectively.

It was to meet this very real need that a crucial event took place in Jerusalem in 1118. Conscious of the risk that pilgrims took when they made their way overland to Jerusalem, a small group of knights established an Order with the aim of protecting them. Because their base was in the al-Aqsa Mosque, built on the site of Solomon's Temple, they took the name of Templars.

Their initial impact was minimal. That all changed however when, a decade after their formation, they were taken under the wing of Bernard of Clairvaux, the foremost churchman of his day.

Bernard, later canonised, is one of the great ecclesiastical figures of medieval history. Passionate in his advocacy of his religious beliefs and possessed of a sharp mind with a visionary view of the world, his impact on the Church was immense.

He was not a strong man physically and could not take an active role in a Crusade to the East. Instead, he turned his attention to the Templars. His masterstroke was to give them their own monastic rule book. A strict set of regulations was imposed on members of the Order, who were required to take vows of chastity when they joined, were to have no personal possessions and were to obey their leader, the Grand Master, without hesitation.

The Templars were part of the Church: they were 'warrior monks'. Their rules governed their lives, both in peace and war. They could not seek ransom when captured and were only to retreat in battle when the odds were overwhelmingly against them. Their religious standing was reinforced by the fact that they were to be answerable to no earthly ruler bar the Pope. No secular king could tell them what to do or bring them to account.

Formal confirmation of Templar privileges by Pope Innocent II in 1139 strengthened their position. Innocent outlined their purpose in a Papal decree. Particularly telling is his explanation that the creation of the Order has transformed secular knights into 'true Israelites' fighting 'divine battles'. Many privileges were granted them: in particular, any material gains made from defeating Muslim enemies were to be preserved for the Order and were protected from forfeiture to secular authorities. But the benefits awarded came accompanied by a heavy cost. A Templar took solemn vows when he joined the Order, from which he could not be excused. Once he took these vows, he would remain subject to the regulations of the Order and its officers until the day he died.

Bernard's sponsorship proved to be a seminal event in the life of the Templars. Adopted by the greatest cleric of the age, the Order, and its fortunes, prospered. Knights from around Europe were attracted to join its ranks, not only allowed to fight for their faith but positively encouraged to do so. Strict training regimes were developed so that their fighting skills could be kept well honed.

Inspired by their example, other orders mushroomed in their wake, most notably the Hospitallers. Originally set up before the Crusader conquest as a hospital to provide medical and hostel facilities to pilgrims, they also took on the mantle of warrior monks with enthusiasm. Smaller groups would develop in their wake, such as the Knights of St Lazarus (a leper order) and, much later, the Teutonic Knights. But the Templars and Hospitallers would always be the most influential.

Few can have envisaged how these Orders would evolve from initially humble beginnings. The concept of these warrior monks touched a deep chord somewhere in the psyche of the times. Some were attracted to join the Order to utilise their martial prowess in the cause of their religion, others made generous grants to them to fund their activities. Although sometimes in the form of cash, these were often grants of land that would generate significant incomes for the Templars.

In a society where land was the principal source of revenue, be it through taxes from those who lived on it and worked it or from goods produced from it, this was an immense source of wealth. Across Europe, the new military orders and the Templars in particular obtained properties the income from which underwrote dazzling and spectacular fortunes.

This led to an unforeseen side effect, superficially contradictory. Although individual Templars were allowed no property of their own, the Order itself became immensely rich, owning vast amounts of lands in both Europe and Outremer. This wealth was under the control of the Grand Master who, through his officers, was able to exercise great power and influence.

In part, this wealth was needed to maintain the Order as a fighting force. A Templar knight took four horses with him on campaign. These were expensive commodities, first to buy, then to keep. Members of the Order needed to be fed and housed and would also need to be provided with armour and weapons. The cost of all this was exorbitant but, to the Orders themselves, was justified in terms of both the crucial part they played in affairs of state and also in terms of increasing their status.

The Orders effectively became the standing army of Outremer and, in a region where warriors were always in short supply, this gave them considerable influence over the government of the kingdom. Their numbers might not in modern terms appear to be great – typically the Templars and Hospitallers might each have about 300–400 knights in Outremer – but this is deceptive.

The manpower of the Orders cannot be measured in knights alone, although these were undoubtedly the shock troops of the Christian armies. The knights would be accompanied by squires and infantrymen – this was no meritocracy and to become a Templar or Hospitaller knight one had first to be a secular knight. There would also be a number of local troops recruited – Turcopoles as they were known – who would accompany them on campaign. Many of these were converts from Islam and so particularly detested by their enemies as traitors to the cause. They often served as light cavalry with Frankish armies.

The Templars also had many non-military duties to attend to. Farms had to be managed and income from a variety of sources looked after. In this latter field, the Templars in particular made significant strides. They developed an early form of banking system, where pilgrims travelling over thousands of miles could exchange their cash for letters of credit at the start of their journey that could later be redeemed in Outremer. The Treasurer of the Temple therefore carried onerous responsibility on his shoulders. So rich would the Templars become that they would attract the envy even of kings.

As the twelfth century advanced, the influence of the Orders grew. The King of Outremer was hugely dependent on their military support. Outremer was a feudal society where military service was owed to the king by his vassals but the limits of this service were well defined and restrictive. The Orders provided a crucially important 'top-up' to the forces available to the king: equally importantly they were not under his direct command.

Short-term increases in numbers from groups of pilgrims arriving from the West helped, but created their own problems as the participants were hard to control and often looked for trouble with the kingdom's Muslim neighbours. Neither local feudal sources nor pilgrims from the West provided the king with the wherewithal he would need if faced by a major Muslim assault. There was therefore a vacuum which the Orders filled readily.

This was all well and good. The Orders garrisoned a chain of castles that could not have been manned by the king's own resources, though it is important to note the presence of a number of castles housing secular lords too. Sometimes, royal castles would be given to them to man when the king was either short of manpower or felt that they would be safer in the hands of military experts. The Orders therefore formed a part of the kingdom's defensive network that was indispensable, as well as providing a crucial part of the kingdom's offensive capacity.

But this indispensability brought with it its own problems, since the Orders' independence and their state of being literally above the (secular) law meant that they did not always act in the manner that the king would have desired. This did nothing to discourage the view, which quickly took root, that the Orders were arrogant and selfish. For a time, the Orders were a necessary evil, vital to the defence of Outremer. But in the process they made many enemies, a state of affairs that would have disastrous long-term results for the Templars in particular.

The emergence of the Orders both strengthened the kingdom but also helped to unsettle the balance of power in the infant state. At first, the King of Jerusalem was in a pre-eminent position, the head of the feudal tree, below which were the barons, the lower branches so to speak. However, the fragile framework of the new kingdom did not lend itself to strong centralised control. Although not covering a large area in terms of square miles, the long but narrow enclave formed of the Kingdom of Jerusalem, the County of Tripoli and the Principality of Antioch was constantly under threat.

The frontier status of Outremer encouraged local barons to be strong and independent, an independence they increasingly asserted as the twelfth century advanced. In this ever more decentralised environment, the Orders were able to tilt the balance still further against the centralising authority of the king. In considering the reasons for the ultimate decline and fall of Outremer the importance of this increasingly unbalanced political equilibrium should not be underestimated.

For much of the time, a state of uneasy peace existed between Outremer and its Muslim neighbours. This was sometimes disturbed by pilgrims from the West who knew little, and cared less, for the *realpolitik* of the region. They would arrive in Outremer and quickly launch themselves into raids on Muslim territory, with frequently unfortunate results. The lack of a shared understanding and view between the permanent settlers in Outremer and the temporary arrivals from the West would lead to immense difficulties.

The early days of Outremer, when Antioch and Jerusalem had fallen to the armies of Christ, would appear in retrospect like a golden age. As the forces of Islam grew stronger those of Outremer became weaker. For a while, Outremer managed to hold its own. But the loss of the city of Edessa, in the north-east corner of the Christian territories, was a major blow that marked an important deterioration in Outremer's position.

Edessa had been one of the first conquests of the Crusaders. It was an important city and frontier post and the headquarters of an independent county. In 1144 Zengi, the Emir of Mosul, launched an attack on its substantial walls. The ruler of the city, Joscelin of Courtenay, sent for aid to Raymond, Prince of Antioch, but the two men were at odds with each other and no help came.

On Christmas Eve 1144 Muslim miners tunnelled away beneath the foundations of the city walls. Large wooden props were put in place to hold up the roof of the tunnel. When the sappers were happy that the tunnel had reached far enough under the walls, they set light to the timber and ran for their lives. The flames took hold of the props, which were soon ablaze. As the timber was incinerated, the roof of the tunnel collapsed, bringing down the walls with it. A huge breach was opened in the defences of the city through which the Muslim forces streamed. Hopelessly outnumbered, the Christian defence collapsed.

A terrible massacre followed in which the entire Frankish population was either taken into captivity or slaughtered. The loss of the city exposed a gap in the defences of Outremer, but other effects were even more important. The failure of the Franks to cooperate in its defence revealed the divisions that existed within Outremer. The taking of the city also caused shockwaves in the West. If the initial conquest of Jerusalem revealed divine approbation of the Crusaders and their enterprises, then the loss of Edessa was equally suggestive of divine displeasure. For the past four decades most Crusading expeditions had been relatively small-scale. The loss of Edessa was so great a shock that it demanded a massive reaction.

The Pope, Eugene III, was not slow to take advantage of the opportunity. He offered an indulgence to all who took part in the Crusade and promised that their dependants and property should be protected while they were away and ordered that no interest should be charged on loans made to finance their expedition. He also asserted that Edessa had been lost because of the sinfulness of Christendom. To expunge their sins, the Christians of the West needed to purchase their redemption with a journey to Outremer, their blood and quite possibly their lives. It was a call that would find an urgent echo forty years later.

The First Crusade had involved none of the kings of the West, but the Second, which was launched in response to the fall of Edessa, included two rulers, Conrad, the Holy Roman Emperor and King Louis VII of France. The two men were hostile to each other and their armies journeyed separately. Both took the land route across Asia Minor, Conrad arriving first, and both armies were badly cut up by the Turks. As a result, the armies were radically reduced in size by the time that they arrived in Outremer in 1148, although the remaining forces were still sizeable.

But, difficult though the journey had been, those who had survived it were now faced with another kind of conundrum: what to do next? It had soon become obvious that there was no clear strategic objective for the expedition to aim for. Edessa was one possible goal; but it had not been chosen. After a great deal of debate and soul-searching, a target was finally selected for the army that assembled at Antioch: Damascus.

This was a strange choice indeed. Everywhere Outremer was surrounded by Muslim enemies – or, to be precise, almost everywhere, because Damascus was the home of just about the only significant Muslim ally of Outremer in the region. It was an independent and powerful city, coveted by other local Muslim powers, particularly a rapidly emerging threat in the shape of Nur ed-Din, ruler of much of Syria. To counteract this, the Emir of Damascus, Unur, had formed an alliance with Outremer. Now, unbelievably, this was about to be torn asunder.

Unur had at first been incredulous when he heard that his city was the target of this new Crusade, but he soon realised that the rumours were all too accurate and he set about organising a vigorous defence. Short of manpower to fight off the Crusaders, he had no option but to search out every available ally, including Nur ed-Din, who was naturally enough very eager to help. So it was that Nur ed-Din, who for so long had been kept at bay by the political acumen of Unur, was invited into the city.

The Crusade fell apart soon after it arrived. The army had at first established itself in the lush orchards that stood outside the city. However, the dense undergrowth here provided perfect cover for guerrillas who launched increasingly fierce counter-attacks on the Christian army. The besiegers for their part were soon forced to move to a much less salubrious camp, which, unfortunately for them, was far removed from any water supplies. The siege disintegrated after just four days.

The problems that led to this debacle presaged the years ahead for Outremer, with differing objectives between newcomers arriving from the West and those who had spent much of their lives in the kingdom. King Louis in particular had been a prime mover for the attack on Damascus. Local barons, conscious of the importance of the truce they had made with Unur, were much more reluctant to engage in the assault on the city. This reluctance became more noticeable during the very short course of the siege and it was dissension from local barons that was one of the main causes of its abandonment.

Louis, an exceptionally pious but not very worldly-wise ruler, clearly struggled to understand the nature of the rapprochement between the Frankish colonists and local Muslims like Unur. But then again such matters were of little concern to him. He was a short-term visitor to Outremer, no doubt sincerely inspired by winning a great victory for Christ but equally likely to return back to his own kingdom soon after.

The local barons and the King of Jerusalem (at the time Baldwin III), on the other hand, were in a far more difficult position. Their state was small when compared with the vast Muslim territories that surrounded it, a tiny island in the middle of a huge Islamic sea. The Franks were good fighters but the mathematical equation was essentially very easy to understand: there were simply far more Muslims than there were Franks.

The emergence of Nur ed-Din marked an important staging post along the road that led to Hattin. He not only had the vision to see that Muslim unity was the way to destroy the Kingdom of Jerusalem but he also had the requisite skills to make that ambition a reality. Time was not on his side and he would die before he could see his dream fulfilled, but he laid the foundations for the ultimate defeat of Outremer.

A devout Muslim, he perceived the Christian enclave of Outremer as an outrage against his religion. Jerusalem was sacred to Muslims, third in importance only after Mecca and Medina. Christian ownership of the city was an abomination. He therefore sought to destroy the Franks. But before he could do so he had to unite Islam. During his lifetime he consolidated much of Syria and, in later years, added Egypt to his empire. His legacy to his heir, Saladin, was a Muslim Middle East that was well on the way to unity.

The strengthening of Nur ed-Din's position was one significant effect of the failure of the Second Crusade. Equally damaging was the fact that a great expedition, raised by the West at the cost of great effort and considerable financial resources, had achieved nothing. It would be extremely difficult to persuade other Western rulers to commit themselves to such an undertaking in the future. The credibility of Crusading had suffered a major reverse.

There was one other reason for concern, much less obvious at the time. In the dejected ranks of the Crusade was a little-known knight from the West. His name was Reynald of Chatillon. Most of the knights who had accompanied Louis and Conrad on their expedition would, if they survived, have expected to return back to their lands in the West. Reynald would prove an exception to that general rule. He was destined for great things but his future lay here, in Outremer, not back in France.

The career of Reynald of Chatillon would be shrouded in controversy, and he would not have far to seek to find an enemy, be they Muslim or Christian. He was a man of remarkable talent and energy without a doubt, but he was also someone who sought out trouble with the experienced nose of a connoisseur. He would climb great heights during his extraordinary life, but his greatest achievement of all would be truly dramatic – Reynald of Chatillon, this unsung knight from the West, would be the man who would be, as much as any other, responsible for the loss of the Kingdom of Jerusalem.

TWO

Hawks and Doves

Repent, or else I will come after thee quickly . . .

Revelation 2: 16

Nations and empires rise and fall for a number of reasons. The gains made from initial, seemingly relentless releases of energy are often dissipated later in life by exhaustion. States and their ruling elites become complacent, unaware of the nature of the threats that are rising to overpower them. Past triumphs lead to overconfidence and future defeats: initial victory in battle against an enemy can lead to an assumption that such an outcome will always be the case. At the heart of many of these problems is one constant factor: human fallibilities. And the leadership of Outremer was to exhibit such failings in abundance.

Timing plays its part too – some may call it fate. It was an unfortunate coincidence for the Kingdom of Outremer that, just at the time that the Muslim world was about to unite itself, the leadership of the Christian state began to fragment. Partly this was because the monarchy weakened and the power of the barons grew correspondingly stronger. While Outremer had strong kings on the throne, they could arrest this pattern to a certain extent; but the later decades of the twelfth century were notable for the fact that, at the very moment that a strong king was needed, there was an unmistakable decline in the abilities of the various rulers who sat on the throne.

The Kingdom of Outremer would begin to factionalise between those who sought some kind of accommodation with the Muslims in the region and those who pursued a more aggressive policy towards them. It would be too simplistic to group these 'doves and hawks' into two distinct groups. Inevitably there were those at the margins who were opportunistic and moved with the tide in a way that seemed to best suit their interests at a given moment in time. But there were some prominent characters in each party who did more than others to shape the course of events.

Changes in society also played a part. In its early days, Outremer was characterised by a number of small fiefdoms, allowing the monarch to become an all-powerful figure at the head of the realm. But over the course of the next fifty years, the situation changed. In particular, there was a move towards a sharp division within the knights themselves. Within this social class, two distinct categories developed. One of these was a class that may be defined as the 'high nobility'[1] – powerful, in control of relatively large fiefdoms and an increasing threat to the dominance of the monarch. The members of this class were distinct from the hundreds of knights who had relatively small landholdings and as a result much less power and influence.

The king was in a unique position among his contemporary Christian rulers. His kingdom was unusual as it was literally regarded as the Kingdom of God, where Christ Himself had walked. He did not render homage to the Pope for his land, although for the pontiff it was undoubtedly a place of special interest given its unique spiritual connections. The Pope was too far away to intervene effectively in the government of the country. But the nature of the special relationship did allow the kings of Jerusalem to approach the Pope for help in raising troops in Western Europe when required – a most valuable arrangement in theory but of limited use because Western interest in Crusades to the East declined after the debacle of the Second Crusade.

The king was also short of money. This reflected to an extent the insufficient amount of land that he held. In many ways in the medieval period, land equalled money. The king received income from the land that he held and from the produce that it brought forth. But successive monarchs had been forced to give out some of the land that they held to cement the support of the nobility. By the middle of the twelfth century, the king's lands consisted primarily of Jerusalem, Acre and Nablus. A clue as to their relative importance in practical terms to the kingdom was the fact that Acre was required to supply eighty soldiers to the king, Nablus seventy-five and Jerusalem only sixty-one.[2]

There were four other great fiefs in the Kingdom of Jerusalem. These were the County of Jaffa, the Principality of Galilee and the feudal Lordships of Sidon and Oultrejourdain (Transjordan). Jaffa and Sidon were both coastal areas, giving them strategic importance of one sort, while Galilee and Oultrejourdain were both frontier territories bordering onto Muslim territory, giving significance of a different kind altogether. The Count of Jaffa, the Lord of Sidon and the Prince of Galilee each owed the King of Jerusalem 100 knights in time of war, while the Lord of Oultrejourdain was pledged to give him sixty.

Behind these great fiefs were a number of secondary landholdings varying significantly in size and resources. Some were held by the Church and others by the military Orders such as the Templars. They were scattered widely, meaning that the power of the individuals who held title to the land was less influential at a state level than that of the holders of the great fiefdoms. But land was in short supply and as a result a far higher proportion of the knightly class resided in cities rather than the countryside, a direct opposite to the situation in Western Europe at this time.

The development of powerful barons was a fundamental sea-change in Outremer that would cause great damage to the kingdom. The high nobles began to play an increasingly influential role in government. They resented new arrivals from the West who sought to advance their interests and, by so doing, challenge theirs. Tension smouldered between these two groups in particular.

It was possibly a faction in the middle ground that posed the greatest difficulties. Short-term visitors to Outremer were problematic but they came and went and any damage they caused could be smoothed over. But a number of men decided to build a life in Outremer after arriving from the West. Some historians have accused them of being hell-bent on confrontation, but the truth was more complex than that. They were aggressive because they felt that they had to challenge the 'natural order' of those who governed in Outremer. No doubt they felt a strong degree of antipathy towards their Muslim neighbours but that was not the primary point of their tactics, which was to advance their own ambitions within the kingdom itself.

Sweeping generalisations about 'newcomers' and 'old blood' should be avoided in seeking to understand the ultimate loss of Jerusalem. The events leading up to Hattin should be seen as nothing more complicated than a battle for power, to decide who would govern in the most unique state in Christendom, and to confirm the policies that Outremer would adopt with regard to its Muslim neighbours. Greed and selflessness, cowardice and bravery, pride and humility all came into play. Factions did emerge but they were not exclusively based around the longevity or otherwise of the families involved in the region. Rather, they were based around individuals.

New arrivals did shift the balance of power in Outremer, however. One of them, Reynald of Chatillon would, perhaps more than any other individual, make confrontation with the Muslim powers surrounding Outremer inevitable. He was a man of relentless determination, driven on by ruthless selfishness. Nothing, and no one, would be allowed to stand in the way of his best interests. Reynald erred by failing to appreciate the unifying effect that some of his more extreme actions would have on the Muslim states surrounding Outremer. He failed to understand – and this would not have worried him in the least – that his actions towards Muslims in the region would generate an unstoppable momentum towards a *jihad*, or holy war, that would engulf the nation.

It is, as the saying goes, an ill wind that blows nobody any good and the death in battle of Raymond of Antioch in June 1149 was to give Reynald a marvellous opportunity to advance his fortunes. Antioch, after Jerusalem, was the most important city in the Frankish territories hugging the Mediterranean shoreline. It was ringed about with massive walls that snaked up and down mountainsides for miles.

It was important on several fronts. It was a major trading link, being adjacent to the Mediterranean coast thanks to the nearby port of St Symeon, and also a crucial staging post between Anatolia and Asia Minor in the north, as well as the Kingdom of Jerusalem and Egypt to the south. It was also a link to the Muslim hinterland, particularly with major cities such as Damascus and Aleppo.

As a result of its strategic position, Antioch played a very important economic role in the life of Outremer (for example, it was particularly important in the textiles trade).[3] Its population was large, and the surrounding countryside relatively fertile. It was also possessed of symbolic significance. It had been a major city even in the time of Christ and St Paul. In short, whoever possessed Antioch held in his hands a great deal of power and influence.

Raymond's death presented an opportunity for a variety of suitors to try to claim the hand of his widow, Constance. The political position of Antioch was somewhat complicated. Both Antioch and Tripoli were separate from the Kingdom of Jerusalem, though the king of the latter was normally held in high regard by the rulers of the former and was sometimes asked to intervene, for example as regent in the case of a minority, when the occasion demanded.

To complicate the situation, Antioch had for centuries been part of the Byzantine Empire, though it had been lost to the Turks just a few years before the First Crusade set out. In strictly legal terms, the Crusaders were required to return the former lands that they conquered to the Byzantine Emperor, but they rarely did, even though they had taken a solemn vow to him to do so. Between the city and the Emperor in Constantinople were hundreds of miles of territory that was now in the hands of Turks, and Byzantium was therefore unable to re-establish its control over cities such as Antioch. This ambiguous position was something that could easily be exploited by an unscrupulous prince.

There was no shortage of suitors for the hand of Constance. Any new husband should officially have been sanctioned by the Emperor but the King of Jerusalem too would have an important say in the agreement. When Raymond was killed, King Baldwin III was installed as regent pending the remarriage of Constance. When he arrived in Antioch in 1151, he included in his retinue Reynald of Chatillon. Both King and Emperor suggested potential husbands for Constance but none of them was acceptable to her.

It must have come as something of a surprise when, in 1153, Constance married Reynald. The famous chronicler William of Tyre suggested that the marriage was performed in secret before the consent of others had been obtained. William deserves to be discussed, as his chronicle is the major source of information on Outremer at this time. His narrative is fresh, lively and informative; but it is not unbiased. William was not just an onlooker, he was a major player in the politics of the region as one of its foremost archbishops. He was largely supportive of the party of Count Raymond of Tripoli, whom we will discuss shortly, and as a result antagonistic to his opponents, of whom Reynald was assuredly one.

Nevertheless, it cannot have appeared to many to have been a good match. Reynald, a younger son of Geoffrey, Count of Gien, brought with him a good family name but no great fortune. There would have been many prominent citizens of Antioch who felt that they offered a much more prestigious catch for Constance.

Medieval chroniclers did not write biographies of their contemporaries, or at least not in a fashion that we would understand, and we are therefore forced to read the actions of men as a way of obtaining a hint or two as to their character. In Constance's surprise decision we may glimpse something of the powerful charisma of Reynald (he would repeat the trick with another wealthy heiress later on in life). We should not equate 'charisma' with 'charm' in the modern sense of the word. Reynald did not sweep Constance off her feet, for she herself was a strong-willed character. But she had to be a politician, particularly with regards to her spouse, because she could not rule in her own right and must govern through her husband. It is not too fanciful to speculate that she saw in Reynald someone of exceptional character: she certainly did not choose him for his status. And, if this were indeed the case, her assessment was entirely accurate for, if nothing else, Reynald had character in abundance.

Although irritated by her failure to ask his permission for the match, the Byzantine Emperor, Manuel, did not push the point but instead sought to take advantage of the situation by offering to recognise the marriage if Reynald would fight alongside him in a forthcoming campaign. The suggestion was readily complied with: it offered a good opportunity for Reynald to enhance his reputation and position and thereby strengthen his credibility.

Reynald fought well in the subsequent campaign, driving an invasion force of Armenians back from Alexandretta, close by Antioch. Reynald was clearly an able soldier and leader who, nevertheless, would demonstrate in time clear weaknesses as far as his strategic sense was concerned. His courage was never in doubt but his judgement was, which he was about to demonstrate with a spectacular lack of acumen.

The island of Cyprus, just a few miles off the Mediterranean coast, was at the time part of the Byzantine Empire. It was in a prime strategic position, an important maritime link between the Levant and Western Europe, and Reynald coveted it for himself, even though it was owned by his overlord. Before he could do anything to satisfy his lust for the island, he sought to protect his back. He made generous grants of land to the Templars in the region, a particularly prescient sign of things to come.

Reynald then prepared an invasion force for Cyprus. However, he was short of money both to provision his fleet and also the army that he would need to subdue the island. A ready source of cash was at hand in the form of the Patriarch of Antioch, Aimery, a wealthy man who had been an outspoken critic of the marriage of Constance to Reynald.

The position of the Patriarch of Antioch was, after that of Jerusalem, the most important ecclesiastical post in the Frankish territories. Whoever held it was deserving of great respect from the secular authorities, even a prince like Reynald. Such considerations counted for little with Reynald though, who, infuriated by the Patriarch's obstinacy in refusing money to support his planned expedition, flung him into prison – another insight into the inner workings of his character.

31

It took a strong man to imprison a patriarch; it would take a ruthless one to torture him into compliance as Reynald now proceeded to do. Aimery was badly beaten up: he was then tied to a tree, his wounds open and untreated. Exposed to the searing Levantine heat, as well as the torments of hungry insects that he could not drive away with his bonded hands, the Patriarch's resistance collapsed in a day. Reynald could have everything he wanted as long as the torment was stopped.

Buoyed up by this successful conclusion, Reynald launched the invasion soon after, in the spring of 1156. The island was governed by Manuel's cousin, but the Byzantine troops were unable to resist. Cyprus fell after a brief resistance. An orgy of rape and pillage followed: old men and children were not spared their lives, nor nuns their honour – the people were after all Orthodox Christians, poorly regarded by some of the Latin Christians who governed Outremer. Hearing that a Byzantine fleet was en route to drive out the raiders, Reynald's fleet sped away, the gunwales of its ships weighed down low in the water by the abundance of loot that they carried.

The raid offered Reynald enormous short-term gain but only at the cost of huge long-term risk. The Byzantine Empire may have been in decline but it was still very powerful. Further, the Emperor valued his honour very highly and the rape of Cyprus was a terrible slur on this. Reynald could only have managed to pull off this great coup if the Emperor did not, or could not, react.

But Reynald had miscalculated. An emperor of Byzantine was in a very vulnerable position, sustained only by the support of the army and the dubious protection of the mob in Constantinople. Intrigue, coup and counter-coup were key elements in Byzantine politics. If an emperor showed any sign of weakness, then the vultures would quickly gather in anticipation of his demise.

Well aware that this was the case, Baldwin III, King of Jerusalem, weighed up his options: should he support his vassal, Reynald, or the Emperor to whom even he theoretically owed a form of allegiance? It was an easy decision to make. Reynald was in a highly dubious moral situation: he had assaulted a patriarch and ravaged a Christian island that formed part of the Emperor's inheritance.

In the process, he had ignored Baldwin's injunctions not to do so. Further, the resources of the Empire were great. After what seems to have been a very short period of reflection, Baldwin decided that, should the Emperor choose to punish Reynald, then he would not seek to interfere.

For a time, it seemed that Reynald would get away with his outrageous breach of trust. But, in 1158, the Emperor Manuel launched a spectacular surprise attack through Cilicia and up to the gates of Antioch itself. Reynald may have been brave but he was not stupid: the Emperor's army was much more powerful than his and the only hope of survival was instant submission, which duly followed. Reynald dressed himself as a penitent and, resplendent in his sackcloth, walked barefoot into Manuel's camp. Manuel kept him waiting: for some minutes Reynald lay prostrate in the dust before the Emperor deigned to recognise him.

The end result of this act of submission was that Reynald was pardoned, but at a price that would hit him hard. The citadel in Antioch was to submit to a Byzantine garrison, Reynald was to provide troops for Manuel's army and the Latin Patriarch was to be replaced by an Orthodox nominee. However, the outcome could have been much worse for him. He held on to his position and most of its attendant benefits. He was lucky: but he was not to learn from his mistakes. On the contrary, this was just the first of many major incidents in which Reynald would exceed his authority and show a terrible lack of discretion, a series of misjudgements that worsened in severity over time.

Nor was Reynald slow to make enemies of his Muslim neighbours, and it was this unfortunate talent that would, for the time being, prove to be his downfall. Although Nur ed-Din's position grew more powerful he could not eject the Franks from Outremer until he had conquered his enemies within the Islamic world. When Nur ed-Din's back was turned, Reynald took advantage of the opportunity to launch raids against weakly defended Muslim caravans and herdsmen that passed too close to his powerbase in Antioch.

In November 1160, he launched such a raid against large herds of cattle, camels and horses that were being driven to Aleppo, passing close to Antioch. Unable to resist the temptation, he led a raiding party out to seize the livestock. This was achieved without much difficulty, but the ease of the victory made him complacent. Hampered by his slowly moving booty, Reynald was attacked as he made his way back to Antioch by a force sent out by the Emir of Aleppo. Unhorsed and captured, he was presented to Nur ed-Din and flung unceremoniously into prison. He would not taste freedom again for sixteen years.

This prolonged absence would do nothing to improve his temper. Much changed while he was in prison. In 1150, the Middle East was effectively locked in a tripartite equilibrium between Islam, Byzantium and Latin Outremer. The 1160s and 1170s were to see that balance change out of all recognition, with Islam becoming much more united, Outremer much more divided and Byzantium appearing to be just plain weak.

Baldwin III died in 1162 and was replaced by his brother, Amalric. The succession process is important in the light of later events leading up to Hattin as it gives an insight into the way in which kings were chosen in Outremer. Baldwin was childless and so his obvious heir was Amalric, Count of Jaffa and Ascalon. However, there were some doubts about the legitimacy of Amalric's marriage to his cousin, which was theoretically forbidden by the Church and expressly criticised by the Patriarch of Jerusalem at the time. The barons therefore demurred before agreeing to Amalric as Baldwin's successor. The point they wished to make was that the crown was given by election, not by hereditary rights of succession – a point that would come home to roost with a vengeance twenty years later. They insisted on a divorce as the price for their support, with important consequences.

This electoral process emphasised the limits of regal power. The king of course had greater status than any other secular person in the country and to do him harm was to commit high treason. He presided at the High Court and appointed the chief officials of the kingdom. He also had the right to choose husbands for the heiresses of the kingdom, a helpful political benefit. But his lack of money restricted his influence and his barons' insistence on electing him acted as a reminder of the limits of his power.

Amalric's reign saw significant developments in Egypt. The country was perceived to be wealthy but weak and decadent, and as a result inviting to avaricious neighbours. It was still Fatimid and as a Shi'a state inimical to the Sunni Syrians. Outremer saw no easy means of expansion to the east, where Syria, now largely united behind Nur ed-Din, presented a formidable defence. The natural inclination was therefore to gravitate towards Egypt, a country rich in agricultural produce and with major ports, such as Alexandria and Damietta, which could be used by the Franks to strengthen their grip on the Mediterranean sea lanes.

A threat by the late King Baldwin III to attack Egypt in 1160 had been bought off by the promise of a tribute. However, the tribute had not subsequently been paid and Amalric took advantage of this as an excuse to launch an invasion of the country in September 1163. But his timing was inauspicious: the Nile was in full flood and the puncturing of a few strategically placed dykes caused the area around the besieged town of Pelusium to disappear under water and left Amalric with no option but to raise the siege. In the meantime, Nur ed-Din was able to attack Outremer, which was relatively undefended. However, an impressive display of unity, whereby the Franks left in Outremer united with the Byzantines, enabled an army to be raised that forced Nur ed-Din back.

In the meantime a deposed Egyptian vizier, Shawar, presented himself before Nur ed-Din in Damascus and attempted to buy the Muslim leader's support to restore his fortunes in Egypt. In an unusual display of hesitation, Nur ed-Din took some time to make up his mind. Eventually he sent his most able general, Shirkuh, across the desert to Egypt, accompanied by some of Nur ed-Din's best troops as well as Shirkuh's young and as yet unproven nephew, Saladin.

The fortunes of the Franks and Shirkuh's armies ebbed to and fro over the next few years in Egypt. However, by 1169, the Muslims were in firm control of the country. But this was not all. By the time that the extended war was over, Egypt was no longer in the hands of the Fatimids, it was firmly in the grip of the ostensible supporters of Nur ed-Din.

This was a matter of the gravest significance for the Franks of Outremer. They were now surrounded, with hostile Sunni states both to east and west. From this point on, Outremer would be under increasing pressure as the Sunni states in the area sought to squeeze the life out of the kingdom like a python constricting its prey.

There were other negative outcomes, too. The treasury of the Kingdom of Jerusalem was badly depleted after the failed expeditions to Egypt. The Hospitallers, too, had thrown in the largest part of their resources in an attempt to conquer the country. It was an all or nothing throw of the dice and the gamble had not come off. The Master, Gilbert of Assailly, was forced to resign and the Order teetered on the brink of collapse.

Worst of all though was the strengthened situation of Nur ed-Din. The unification of Islamic power in the region coincided with a decline in the fortunes of Byzantium. This deterioration was not a new phenomenon. The catastrophic defeat of Byzantine armies by Turkish forces at Manzikert in 1071 heralded the loss of Asia Minor. But the Turkish conquest of the region – an area that was crucial to the Empire in terms of both manpower and natural resources – was not a cause of the Byzantine malaise, it was a symptom.

The emergence of several outstanding emperors since Manzikert had, superficially at least, arrested the decline. But the day of reckoning could not be put off forever. This was a crucial factor in the weakening of Outremer, too. A strong Empire acted as a buffer against Muslim ambition in the Middle East. Not that the Latin Franks of Outremer and the Orthodox Byzantines worked tirelessly together, inspired by mutual interests. On the contrary, ever since the First Crusade relationships had been characterised by suspicion and intrigue. Open warfare between the two was rare: surreptitious political manoeuvring was at this stage the more common manifestation of the mistrust. But whereas in theory the introduction of a vibrant Frankish state into the region offered Byzantium an opportunity for renewal, in practice this could never happen. Divided by their common faith, the closer contacts forged between Eastern and Western Christendom as a result of the Crusades only served to accelerate the decline of the former.

The underlying mistrust had revealed itself particularly strongly in Amalric's campaign in Egypt where a Byzantine force had been sent to assist in his attempts to conquer the country. The catastrophic finale to the campaign, which had seen the Byzantine fleet sail back towards Constantinople in ignominy only to be crushed by a heavy storm that caused many ships to be lost, left a sour taste in the mouth. During the Egyptian campaign it proved impossible for the Byzantines and the Franks to work together but, despite the truly disastrous conclusion to the operation, there was at least a recognition that both Byzantium and Outremer needed each other.

Amalric resolved to do his utmost to maintain good relations with the Emperor, planning to head a delegation to him. But before he could set out, he received worrying news from the south. The approaches to Outremer from Egypt were protected by the fortress of Daron and the town of Gaza. Daron was not in a strongly defended position, perhaps because in the past Fatimid Egypt had not generally proved itself to be a great threat to the Franks. The changing signs of the times were demonstrated clearly enough by the arrival of Saladin with an army at his back, clearly determined to capture the fortress.

This is an important moment in the life of Outremer, the first time that the kingdom's downfall, Saladin, led an attack on it. The loss of Daron could not be countenanced, though the poor state of repair of the defences did not seem to hold out much hope of successful resistance. Amalric responded with alacrity. He called on the support of the Church, in the forms of the patriarch and the important relic of the True Cross, both of which would accompany him as he counter-attacked. This latter object was a small portion of the Cross on which Christ was crucified (there were many such relics liberally spread across Christendom.

Following its discovery by the Empress Helena, the True Cross quickly established itself as the most eminent of all relics. An elaborate ritual was developed for its use in divine services. This included a number of priests watching it closely – a crucial role following the stealing of part of it by a pilgrim who, pretending to kiss the relic, bit a piece off and took it away! The Cross had been lost when the Zoroastrian Persians had captured Jerusalem early in the seventh century and unleashed a wave of destruction that exceeded in ferocity even that visited on the city by the First Crusade in 1099.

In the expedition led by the Byzantine Emperor Heraclius that followed the loss of Jerusalem in 638, the quest to restore the True Cross to the Holy City was a key motivation. Heraclius, called by some the first Crusader,[4] won the war against the Persians that followed, but for a time the fragment of the Cross could not be found. When it was at last restored to Byzantine hands, Heraclius had brought it back to Jerusalem in a show of great humility, dressed as a pilgrim. In one of those strange ironies that history sometimes offers, on the way he stopped at the town of Tiberias, on the shores of the Sea of Galilee, a place that was to play an altogether less glorious part in the history of the True Cross half a millennium later.

Subsequently, Jerusalem fell to the rising tide of Islam, then a new religion. The fragment was taken back to Constantinople so that it could be kept safe. Other fragments of the supposed 'True Cross' were also regarded as relics – knowing which were genuine was a common problem in an age where, for example, more than one skull of John the Baptist was declared to exist.

The relic of the True Cross held by the Franks had a totemic significance. It was regularly taken into battle, its presence signifying that not only were the Franks fighting on behalf of Christ but that He was in a sense accompanying them in their campaign. It was natural enough that the Patriarch of Jerusalem should go too, not just as the guardian of this precious relic but also as a way of providing a spiritual focus for the expedition. This was after all the Holy Land that was under threat, God's own kingdom. And the patriarch's presence was an extension of the same kind of spiritual sanction that underpinned the whole concept of the Crusading phenomenon.

Armed with the most important churchman in Western Christendom (the Pope excepted) and the fragment of the True

Cross, Amalric set out to face off the Muslim threat with a small but well-equipped force. Saladin had no siege engines with him and was not therefore well placed to take full advantage of his strong position. Daron continued to resist. Amalric moved to Gaza, where there was a Templar fortress. At his side rode Miles de Plancy, his seneschal. The Templars had already gained for themselves an impressive martial reputation and the garrison of the Gaza fortress would be a welcome addition to the relieving force, which duly set out with them towards Daron, a few miles to the south.

Daron was finally relieved when Amalric managed to break through Saladin's siege lines. But this merely swapped one problem for another as Gaza was now denuded of its garrison and exposed as a result to Saladin's forces. For his part, Saladin was quick to spot the opportunity and, decamping from Daron, moved to Gaza. The town itself was taken, though its fortress held out. Many of the inhabitants were massacred or taken away to a life of slavery. Pleased with this successful outcome to the raid (for this was not yet an army of conquest), Saladin took himself back to Egypt.

The role of the Templars in this expedition demonstrates the important contribution that the Order now made to the Kingdom of Jerusalem. Since their adoption by St Bernard, and the official formulation of their Rule at the Council of Troyes in 1129, the Order's significance had expanded at a rapid rate, though it was its rival, the Hospitallers, who had first been given (in about 1136) formal responsibilities for defence of the kingdom when awarded the castle of Bethgeblin. It was not until fourteen years later that the Templars were given a similar honour at Gaza.[5] However, in the north of the region the Templars assumed importance much earlier, and by 1136–7 were in charge of the defences of the mountain passes that led to Antioch from Cilicia.

There are early mentions of Templar involvement in battles against Muslim enemies in Outremer, accompanied by sizeable losses. It is interesting that the concepts espoused by the Templars became so well established that, even by the 1130s, the much smaller Order for those unfortunate enough to be lepers, the Order of St Lazarus, had probably been established in Jerusalem.[6]

The Second Crusade had marked an important point in the development of the Templars, as they played a prominent role in the events of that expedition. Their involvement began even before the armies of the West left Europe: 130 Templar knights stood at the side of King Louis before he left Paris.

It was Everard of Barres, Master of the Temple in France, who was to become the leading adviser to King Louis during the Crusade, and the Templar knights acted as the armed escort protecting the flanks of Louis's army. Although severely depleted by the losses sustained during the campaign, the Order emerged with its honour and prestige enhanced. Everard himself played a key role in achieving this outcome. He organised his forces into units of fifty, each under a Templar knight, with a supreme Templar commander, introducing an element of order that was not generally characteristic of Christian armies of the time.

Equally impressive when Louis arrived in Antioch was Everard's ability to replenish the King's denuded funds from the Templar treasury in Acre. King Louis was later to tell Abbot Suger in Paris that it was only the financial support of the Templars that enabled him to stay in Outremer. However, not all impressions were positive. In particular, the Templars were blamed by some for engineering the retreat from Damascus that marked the end of the Crusade. An anonymous chronicler from Würzburg in Germany wrote of their 'greed, deceit and envy' during the expedition, a view reinforced when a visitor to Outremer in the 1160s, John of Würzburg, explained that there were many locally who regarded members of the Order as treacherous.[7]

There is little evidence that accusations stating that the Order betrayed the expedition at Damascus are true, but they achieved wide circulation at the time. King Louis himself defended the Order stoutly, and the accession of Everard of Barres, a key supporter, to the position of Grand Master reinforced this solidarity. But the fact that such accusations could be made showed that the Templars were already inspiring resentment as well as respect, which hinted that they might become a convenient scapegoat should things go wrong. Unfortunately for the Order, it was a perception that would prove to be hard to shake off.

By the 1150s the rise of the Templars may be fairly regarded as meteoric. Already an integral part of the defences of Outremer, and also possessing major establishments all over Europe, they were a truly international Order. However, in the Holy Land their status was ambiguous. Although a core part of the defences of the realm, their lack of accountability to the secular authorities was already proving problematic. Their only earthly master was the Pope, thousands of miles and many weeks distant, and unable to exercise immediate control over their actions. This lack of direct accountability encouraged a fiercely independent streak to take root in the Templar psyche. The self-interests of the Order became more important than those of the kingdom. What started as a means to an end, a way of protecting poorly armed pilgrims, soon became an end in itself, the protection of the rights of the Order. Serious repercussions would ensue.

This penchant for independent action revealed itself in striking fashion at the siege of Ascalon in 1153. This was the foremost outpost of Fatimid Egypt at the time, dangerously close to Jerusalem and a good staging post for raids on important Frankish ports such as Jaffa. It threatened like a knife permanently pointed at the flanks of Outremer.

The situation could not be allowed to exist in perpetuity if the security of the Kingdom of Jerusalem was to be safeguarded. A substantial force set out to conquer Ascalon in January 1153, replete with great siege engines as well as large numbers of soldiers, including Templars and Hospitallers. The city was stubbornly defended, but the chance of a breakthrough presented itself on 15 August. The defenders had sallied out from the city to set one of the Franks' siege engines alight. They succeeded far too well for their own good, for although it went up in flames it then collapsed against the city. The intense heat cracked the walls, which then collapsed. When the flames died down, there was a large breach through which the attackers would be able to pour into the city streets and at last take the stronghold.

Or so it seemed. The troops next to the breach were Templars. They insisted that the right to take the city should be theirs alone, so while some of them rushed into Ascalon others stayed behind to prevent any non-Templars from joining them. But there were not enough Templars to take the city on their own and, as soon as the defenders realised this, they turned on the infiltrators and butchered them. The corpses of these misguided heroes were hung from the walls to mock the Infidel. So shocked was King Baldwin III that he contemplated raising the siege, but fortunately for him he desisted and the city fell soon afterwards.

These actions gave a worrying insight into the Templar psyche. It should be noted that medieval chroniclers are not renowned for providing accurate accounts of those they wrote about, and our understanding of the events at Ascalon is from the pen of William of Tyre, who was not an eyewitness.[8] However, whether true or not such accusations often stick and in such cases perception can be as powerful as reality. It became accepted in some quarters that these warriors of Christ had some rather un-Christian qualities. The allegations about their actions at Ascalon served to demonstrate two particular vices that would become associated with the Templars: pride as evidenced by their unwillingness to share the glory of victory, and avarice – it could be argued that their actions were inspired by a desire to claim as many material rewards for themselves as possible based on the terms of Pope Innocent's decree of 1139.

These allegations of Templar misconduct continued, again, often in the writings of William of Tyre, who was clearly no friend of the Order. He quotes a damaging incident in 1166,[9] when the Templars responsible for defending an outpost beyond the Jordan surrendered to Shirkuh before Amalric could hurry to its rescue. According to William, when Amalric arrived he hung a number of the garrison who had capitulated so easily. If this is true, it is evidence of some grave tensions within Outremer: Amalric had far exceeded his authority in acting in such a peremptory fashion and must have been livid with the garrison.

Another worrying incident occurred in 1173. The Nizari sect, better known as 'the Assassins', achieved a notoriety that is perhaps undeserved. While they were responsible for the deaths of a number of prominent enemies, an alleged responsibility for about fifty assassinations in 200 years is hardly prolific.[10] Their presence close to Tortosa, in the Principality of Tripoli, brought them into contact with Templars in the area. The Templars undertook to leave the Nizaris to their own devices if, in their turn, they would pay a regular tribute to the warrior monks.

For a while, this arrangement carried on with few apparent difficulties. The leader of the Nizari sect, a shadowy figure known to the West as 'the Old Man of the Mountains', preferred to avoid the tribute. He sought to enter into a treaty arrangement with Amalric and, in return for the offer of his cooperation, asked to be exempted from continuing the payments. Amalric therefore responded positively to the proposals.

The Nizari envoys set off back to their master with a promise that a Frankish delegation would be sent to him soon afterwards. On the way back the envoys were attacked by Templars led by Walter of Mesnil, a knight based in Tripoli, and killed to a man. Amalric was incensed and demanded that the culprit be handed over. The Grand Master, Odo of St-Amand, refused to cooperate, whereupon Amalric threw Walter into prison without the Grand Master's consent.

This story is once more from the pen of William of Tyre. While it is obviously imprudent to rely too much on the evidence of one man, particularly one with enemies in Outremer as we shall see, there may well be elements of truth in his accounts, even if they might be exaggerated. For example, consistent themes emerge from his accounts of Templar activity at Ascalon, in surrendering the castle across the Jordan and in their assaults on the Nizari ambassadors. The major theme is that the Templars were increasingly motivated by self-interest and paid limited regard to the wishes of the King of Jerusalem.

The Templars would eventually come crashing to earth when, in 1307, the Order was accused of heresy and immoral sexual practices. Soon after, it was disbanded and its last Grand Master was burned at the stake on the banks of the Seine. This sensational demise has helped to colour modern views of the Templars. Later literary mentions, such as the unscrupulous Templar in Sir Walter Scott's

Ivanhoe, have also helped perpetuate a semi-legendary view of a dark, sinister organisation. But it is worth remembering that the Templars inspired both apologists and critics from early on in their history.

For example, in the 1140s the Bishop of Angers wrote of the Templars that 'these are the messengers and officers and soldiers of Christ . . . whose militia is without doubt true and most pleasing to God', men who 'have chosen to fight against the enemies of God . . . nor do they hesitate to give their souls and to shed their blood'.[11] To him, these warriors were clearly dedicated to the service of Christ.

Contrast this view with that of John of Salisbury, writing in 1159. John was incensed that the Templars had assumed rights only previously held by the 'official' Church. With little subtlety, he declaimed that 'it is wicked that, enticed by the love of money, they open churches which were closed by the bishops. Those suspended from office celebrate the sacraments, they bury the dead whom the Church refuses . . .'[12]

The dangers posed by the Order largely emanated from its structure. The strict hierarchy brooked no democracy. The Master's word was, to Templar knights, law. His instructions must be obeyed without question: only the Pope could countermand them. This was all well and good if the Master were wise, but potentially catastrophic if he were not.

Enter then Gerard of Ridfort. Gerard, a Flemish knight, arrived in Outremer in 1173 and took service in the entourage of Count Raymond of Tripoli. His early career is that of a mercenary who caught the eye of King Amalric, but was not controversial. However, his relations with Raymond would put him, and Outremer, on a collision course.

Having established himself as part of Raymond's coterie, Gerard sought to advance his own interests. One way to do this was to marry the next available rich heiress. He entered into an arrangement with Raymond, who had power over such matters, to do this. Gerard waited patiently for his moment. Some time later, it came.[13] When Walter of Botron, which was a small coastal town, died, his daughter, Lucia, was left as heir. According to Raymond's agreement, she should have been married off to Gerard. But

Raymond, who may have been in debt to the Hospitallers, had a change of heart and instead offered her to a Pisan, Plivano. Gerard was outraged, even though Plivano had bid to buy the hand of the lady by offering her weight in gold.[14]

Gerard accused the Count of preferring a peasant to a man of nobility, his argument being reputedly that a Frenchman of however lowly a status was superior to an Italian, however great. He then took himself off in a fury to the Templars. He pledged himself to the Order but, rather than seeing the end of his earthly ambitions, his pledge seemed to advance them. He became the Order's seneschal (effectively the deputy Grand Master) and finally its Master.

Reynald and Gerard eventually became allies. As such, they would find themselves in opposition to Raymond of Tripoli, who became the prominent proponent of conciliation towards the Muslim states around Outremer. In contrast to them, Raymond was essentially a 'native' of Outremer, if a member of the ruling settler class can be so called.

The position of Tripoli was an interesting one. Although the kings of Jerusalem often attempted to exercise a degree of control over this territory, it was not legally explicit that they were entitled to do so. Their ability to do so in practice depended on their strength vis-à-vis the small state by the Mediterranean. The king's control over Tripoli was greater at some times than at others, notably when Raymond of Tripoli became ruler in 1152. As he was only a young child, successive kings of Jerusalem, first Baldwin III, then Amalric, became regent on his behalf. But Raymond would never admit later that the King of Jerusalem had authority over him as his ruler – significant in the light of subsequent events.

Raymond's parents had not enjoyed a happy marriage. His mother Hodierna was an impetuous woman. Her reputation was suspect and there were rumours that her daughter, Melisende, had not been fathered by Raymond. She quarrelled persistently with her husband, also named Raymond. So difficult did their arguments become that the Queen of Jerusalem felt constrained to intervene personally.

A reconciliation of sorts was achieved. It was agreed though that Hodierna should go to Jerusalem for a while. Her husband accompanied her for the first mile of her journey. Then he turned back. Re-entering Tripoli through its south gate, he barely noticed a small group lurking in the shadows. All of a sudden, this group fell upon him, knives flashing in the sun. They left him for dead and made good their escape.

Raymond's father did not survive the attack and his young son took his place as ruler of Tripoli. It was hardly an auspicious start to life and any sense of insecurity that he may have had would have been worsened soon after when Tortosa was briefly taken by Nur ed-Din. On its recapture, Hodierna realised that her son's county did not have the resources to protect itself on its own and the Templars were invited in to take over.

When Amalric was involved in a campaign in Egypt in 1164, Nur ed-Din led a raid on Outremer. The Franks who were left in the country raised an army, helped by a contingent from Byzantium. Raymond was one of these. The leaders of the Christian armies were no match for the Muslim warlord. Early on in the battle that ensued at Artah, Bohemond of Antioch led a rash charge on the Muslim forces, who apparently turned tail and fled – but this was a classic Muslim trick that, surprisingly enough, the Franks failed to spot despite having encountered it on a number of occasions in the past. They lured the undisciplined Christian cavalry straight into an ambush.

A massacre followed, and many of the Christian leaders were taken into captivity. Among their number was Raymond, who was taken to Aleppo. Nur ed-Din's jails were now awash with Christian prisoners. He was prepared to ransom a number of his captives, but he hung on to both Raymond and Reynald of Chatillon for the time being. Not until 1172 would Raymond be released on payment of a substantial ransom. The exorbitant fee could only be raised with the help of a significant donation from the Hospitallers, whom Raymond later rewarded with grants of land when he became regent. This should be borne in mind when considering his later good relations with the Order.

The product of an unhappy marriage, someone who ascended to the throne when his father was murdered and then spent eight years in a Muslim prison, Raymond could hardly be said to have had a happy start to life. But soon after his release he was to be propelled towards much greater things. This change in fortune came about with the demise of Amalric in 1174. His heir was a 13-year-old boy, Baldwin. An adolescent monarch was far from helpful in what was becoming a delicate situation. But the boy's tender years were not the greatest difficulty. The child king had an even greater handicap. He was suffering from that most terrible of all medieval maladies, leprosy.

Because of Baldwin's adolescence, there would need to be a regent but one was not appointed straightaway. Miles de Plancy coveted the role but he was not a popular man. The choice therefore fell on the closest male descendant of the boy king: Raymond of Tripoli. Miles did not take the rebuff quietly and continued to jostle for position. Shortly after Raymond's appointment, Miles was walking through the dark streets of Acre when he was set upon by a party of assassins and slain. It was not clear who was behind the assassination but his elimination certainly did Raymond no harm.

So the regency of Raymond of Tripoli began in blood, in the shedding of which he may of course have been innocent. It was an entirely appropriate start given what was to follow in the next thirteen years, a period that would see the gradual disintegration of Outremer. Raymond was now a man in the prime of his life. It is not surprising, given what had happened to him, that he has been described as cold, self-controlled and a little ungenerous. But he had not completely wasted his years in captivity, a period in which he had learned Arabic and studied the Muslim world closely. A tall, thin man with a large nose, dark hair and a swarthy complexion, he appears somewhat austere and intimidating, but in a much more calculating way than some of the enemies he would face from within such as Reynald of Chatillon.

In the wake of his appointment as regent, distinct factions began to form within Outremer. One of these wished to seek accommodation with the Muslims while the other sought to destroy and dominate them. Even the Orders were divided, with the Hospitallers generally siding with the former party, the Templars the latter. The doves and the hawks began to choose their sides.

It was a combustible situation that just needed a spark to ignite a great conflagration; and something was about to happen that would indeed light a slow-burning fuse. In 1175, after sixteen years of captivity, Reynald of Chatillon received good news: he was at last free to go.

It is tempting to speculate on Reynald's thoughts as he rode back towards the world he had left behind a decade and a half ago. He cannot have been unaware that much had changed in his absence, that Egypt had fallen into the Sunni camp and that a great new force in Islam, Saladin, had burst onto the scene like a comet of doom. Reynald would also have known that he had been a widower for many years, and that his position had suffered as a result.

Having been deprived of his liberty for so long, maybe his character had changed; but in what way? Had he mellowed through long hours of contemplation as he pondered on the transience of earthly wealth and status? Or had an already hot-headed man become enraged by all these years of captivity? The answer would soon become obvious. Reynald returned to Outremer infuriated by the frustrations of captivity and incensed by the thought of all that he had lost. Within his soul there burned an overwhelming desire for revenge that would stop at nothing. This bred in his character – never one that took much notice of authority – a complete disregard for the conventions of the state in which he lived. Nothing and no one would be allowed to stand in his way. The journey to Armageddon had begun.

THREE

Saladin

And I saw, and beheld a white horse: and he that sat on him had a bow; and a crown was given unto him: and he went forth conquering and to conquer.

Revelation 6: 2

While the enemies within the Kingdom of Jerusalem began to split into their various factions, the fortunes of Saladin, the enemy without, continued to improve. Saladin has gone down in history as a romantic figure, chivalrous even to his enemies. To Muslims, he is known as a religious man: Salah ed-Din means 'Protector of the Faith'. There is truth in this perception, but he was not quite the paragon that romanticists have made him out to be. He could be ruthless and was not afraid of eliminating those who stood in his way. Despite this, his positive press is broadly merited; in the main, he deserves his place in history.

So widely accepted did the myth of Saladin the chivalrous become that Westerners, keen to explain away how a non-Christian could be so noble, devised stories of his birth that helped to build the legend. These said that Saladin was the grandson of a beautiful French princess forced into marriage with a Turk named Malakin. They explained how their union produced the mother of Saladin who was described as 'an honourable, a wise and a conquering lord'.[1]

Saladin, despite becoming an Arab hero, was not an Arab but a Kurd, born in Tikhrit, in modern-day Iraq – the home in more recent times of Saddam Hussein. Therefore, to some extent he was an outsider, but any disadvantages that this may have given him only appeared to inspire him. His start to life was hardly auspicious:

49

his family were marked people in Tikrit and while just a newborn child Saladin was smuggled out of the city in the dead of night along with his father and his uncle, Shirkuh.

It was Saladin's good fortune to be the nephew of Shirkuh, a mighty warrior, much respected by Nur ed-Din. Shirkuh acted as Saladin's mentor, giving him much of his early training in warfare and politics. In both fields, he would be a sound, if not always a brilliant, exponent. Militarily, Saladin was no Alexander and tasted the bitter pill of defeat on more than one occasion. Politically, he did not win everyone to his side: but in both fields he was a more than capable operator and in politics in particular he showed himself to be adroit at handling some difficult situations.

What then would make Saladin great, a name so famous that, 800 years after his death, he is to the West perhaps the most famous of all Muslims from the past with the exception of the Prophet himself? There are two perspectives of Saladin. One, the Western view, is shaped around his confrontation with Richard the Lionheart. This is an encounter that became imbued with an almost mythical veneer, a story of great chivalry but one that also has layers of hyperbole obscuring the underlying truth. But it found a willing audience in the readers and listeners of Western Europe who thrilled to the accounts of the battles, intellectual and military, between the gracious and generous Islamic leader and the mighty warrior-king Richard.

This is not the view that seized the imagination of the Islamic world. Here, Saladin was a warrior who fought himself to a standstill in the cause of his faith. The story has all the classic ingredients of a young, worldly man who later turned to religion to find greatness. In his early years, Saladin was headstrong, ruthless and ambitious. But then, late in life, he was the victim of a potentially terminal illness. As he hovered in the shadow lands between life and death he took a solemn vow that, should he recover, he would devote himself to the service of Allah. When the recovery was granted, he sought to make good his pledge.

His timing was impeccable. His birth and meteoric rise coincided with a resurgence of the concept of *jihad* against the enemies of Islam in the Middle East. Such feelings had never gone away but the twelfth century had seen a re-emergence of the concept.[2] Saladin did not ignite the flame – it had sparked into life long before he emerged – but he seized the moment and the prize that went with it: an assured place of honour among the annals of Islamic history as a religiously inspired warrior who restored pride to the Muslim world by the recovery of lands sacred to the faith.

The conquest of the Holy City of Jerusalem by the Crusaders was an insult to Muslim sensibilities. The great slaughter that had attended the triumph of the First Crusade in 1099 also cut to the quick. The massacre of so many, regardless of age or sex, had horrified Islam. It also shocked because the Muslim world saw itself as culpable for the loss: its disunity at the time had allowed the atrocity to occur. Saladin, a devout Muslim, saw the continued Christian ownership of Jerusalem as a dark stain of dishonour that must be washed clean. He would devote his energies, and ultimately his life, to the recovery of Jerusalem, and it was for this that he is best remembered in Islam.

But commentators from both sides painted a portrait of Saladin that is far from black and white. Frankish chroniclers, although they might recognise some of his chivalric traits, also sought to blacken other elements of his character. An early thirteenth-century chronicle, *Itenerarium Regis Ricardi*, as well as describing him as 'this great persecutor of Christianity', also tells how he made his fortune by acting as a pimp for prostitutes in Damascus. He then bribed his way into the good offices of key men in the Islamic leadership at that time: 'the money he thus obtained by pimping he lavished on entertainers, purchasing the people's indulgence for all his whims by displays of generosity'.[3]

Islamic observers were not unanimous in their praise either. Some criticised him for his nepotism, although one could perhaps see this as an understandable attempt to secure his position in a very unpredictable environment. He was also believed to be a lover of the finer things in life, which marked him out in contrast to the austere Nur ed-Din. Nor was he without failures as a military leader, but the capture of Jerusalem would count for much and would compensate for many of these.

Yet some spoke in awed terms of his human qualities. One biographer, Baha al-Din Ibn Shaddad, who was part of the great Sultan's entourage, said that 'the purity of Saladin's character was always evident: when in company, he would allow no one to be spoken ill of in his presence, preferring to hear only of their good traits: when he himself spoke, I never saw him disposed of to insult anyone: when he took up his pen to write, he would never use words to harm another Muslim'.[4] The same writer spoke movingly of Saladin's concern for the orphan, backed up by gifts to enable the unfortunate to exist with a decent standard of living. He would hand these disadvantaged children over to other members of the family for adoption if such existed, and, if not, he would house them appropriately with another household. He also looked after the old, treating them with respect and generosity.

Saladin was a capable politician who used diplomacy as much as force in the advancement of his objectives. He was adept at exploiting propagandist opportunities. His political skills were crucial particularly as his military career was far from unblemished. He has been described as 'a good tactician but a bad strategist'.[5] He was not a gifted administrator and his government was consistently short of money. Given his military and administrative shortcomings, his political acumen was vital.

Every general needs capable lieutenants if he is to be successful and Saladin was no exception to this rule. His nephew Taqi al-Din was one such. Described by contemporaries as a deeply religious man, Taqi al-Din was also brave and led his troops by example, always in the thick of the fighting. He often took control of the Muslim right wing in battle. This was significant, since it was the right wing that normally took the offensive while the left held a defensive position.

But Taqi al-Din could also be impetuous, obstinate and politically ambitious. He was, in addition, an opportunist. He once held Egypt on Saladin's behalf but was dismissed because of his intriguing. On the verge of open rebellion, he held his hand and was restored to Saladin's good graces; but the breach with Saladin was never wholly healed. Nevertheless, Taqi al-Din played a key role in the Hattin campaign.

Muzaffar el Din Gökböri ('the blue wolf') was also important to Saladin. His father had served both Zengi and Nur ed-Din. When the time came and Saladin made his move for power, Gökböri was one of his key supporters, a position that would have cost him everything if Saladin had failed. So pleased was Saladin with Gökböri's support that he married off one of his sisters to him.

Gökböri's military skills were renowned. Al Isfahani, Saladin's secretary, described him as 'the audacious, the hero of well thought out projects, the lion who heads straight for the target, the most reliable and firmest chief'.[6] He lived to a good old age, dying shortly before the terrible Mongol hordes descended on the Middle East and destroyed the culture he had done so much to build. For not only was he a warrior but he was a patron of the arts, of scholars, of colleges and hospitals.

Another important commander was Hajib Husam al Din Lu'lu. The name Lu'lu means 'pearl' and suggests a slave origin. This was no ordinary slave though: his family would have been of Mameluke stock. The Mamelukes were groomed to be soldiers from birth. Recruitment took place from the furthest reaches of the Muslim world and was voluntary – at least on the part of their parents. Fathers were proud to sell their sons into the ranks of the Mamelukes. Ostensibly, this was slavery but families considered it an honour when their offspring were taken away to be trained for war. As for those enslaved as a result, they could later amass wealth, power and glory and would ultimately produce a dynasty that ruled Egypt.

Of Lu'lu, al-Isfahani would say that his 'courage was well known to the infidels, whose violence against the enemy was extolled. He was without equal when it came to raids with which none but he were associated', while another chronicler, Ibn al Athir, talks of him as 'a brave and energetic man, a naval and military expert full of useful initiative'.[7] It was as Saladin's admiral that he won his greatest fame. The Muslim fleet was in decline but he used the resources available to him with maximum effect. Lu'lu simply disappears from history without explanation, and it has been suggested that he may have been one of the victims of Richard the Lionheart's massacre of unarmed prisoners at Acre in 1191.[8]

The Muslim chroniclers' ambivalence towards Saladin can be partly attributed to ongoing schisms within Islam. Ever since Mohammed founded the faith in the seventh century, it had been riven by internal dispute. By the end of that century, not only had the amazing conquests that saw Islam dominate the Middle East, North Africa and parts of Europe begun, so too had the internal wars that would so weaken the Muslim world. A momentous battle near Karbala saw the slaughter of al-Husayn, grandson of the Prophet, and the establishment of the Shi'a branch of Islam. Even today, many adherents of that form of the Muslim faith wear black in remembrance of that fateful confrontation.

The subsequent centuries saw regular and fierce manifestations of this ongoing schism, with other elements – such as the Isma'ili Nizaris – adding to the complexities that differentiated these various strands of the religion. There is nothing so divisive and destabilising as the situation that occurs when adherents of the same faith choose to adopt doctrinal stances and beliefs that are diametrically opposed to each other. Saladin was a devout Sunni Muslim, and his beliefs would bring him into conflict with others, including Shi'a or Isma'ili supporters, in a literal as well as a metaphorical sense. In summary, not every Muslim chronicler who wrote about Saladin was a natural supporter of him.

Saladin came of relatively poor stock, and his prospects for greatness at the time of his birth in 1138 were limited. However, his relationship with Shirkuh stood him in good stead. When Nur ed-Din had seized power after the death of the victor of Edessa, Zengi, he was proclaimed sultan in Aleppo by Shirkuh. When Shirkuh set out on his first foray into Egypt in 1164, a seemingly reluctant Saladin was at his side. It is ironic that the young man, whose reputation, indeed whose entire career, would evolve because of his involvement with that country, was not happy about going there. It turned out to be the turning point in his life.

The campaign of 1164 ended in stalemate, and Saladin went home with Shirkuh a wiser but probably disappointed young man. In the event, the campaign had been a failure from Shirkuh's perspective. He had been besieged in the city of Bilbeis and only escaped by the payment of a large ransom to the forces of Amalric. When Saladin returned to Egypt in 1167, again alongside Shirkuh, it was to be an altogether different experience. After a terrible desert crossing, where a dreadful sandstorm almost put paid to Saladin's career – and his life – before it had really started, another campaign against Amalric's army took place along the banks of the Nile.

A battle broke out on 18 March when King Amalric, protected by the fragment of the True Cross that he wore around his neck, initially routed the centre of the Muslim army. This was unfortunate for Saladin, who was in charge of the centre, but good for Shirkuh, who managed to take advantage of the Franks' loss of discipline as they chased after the retreating soldiers to win the battle.

Although from Saladin's point of view his part in the battle had been inauspicious, his star was by now most definitely in the ascendancy. This particular campaign did not end with a Sunni victory, but when Shirkuh and Saladin returned once more to Egypt in 1169 the outcome would be very different. For years, the Shi'a vizier of Egypt, Shawar, had been playing a dangerous game trying to offset the Franks against the Sunnis. When Shirkuh returned at the head of another of Nur ed-Din's armies he had no intention of leaving empty-handed.

Shirkuh entered Cairo on 8 January 1169. Shawar greeted him warmly, hoping once more to run with both the hare and the hounds. But he had met his match. On 18 January, Shawar set out to visit the tomb of a holy man. En route, a group of Sunnis fell upon him and struck him down. They were led by Saladin, apparently the prime instigator of this action. Saladin the assassin is not someone who figures highly in romanticised views of history, but no one should doubt that he had a ruthless streak.

Shirkuh did not live long to enjoy his triumph, reputedly dying of overeating. Saladin was left to protect his newly won prize of Egypt against a Frankish counter-attack. Amalric could not countenance a Sunni government in Egypt and, with the assistance of the Byzantines, led an army into that country. Before facing them, Saladin had to destroy the enemy within. Prominent supporters of the deposed Shi'a regime were eliminated with ruthless efficiency.

In the campaign that followed, the incompetence of the Latin–Byzantine alliance[9] played into Saladin's hands and he was able to weather the storm. However, a new threat to Saladin's position was to emerge from a different direction. Saladin was ambitious, a fact that Nur ed-Din became acutely aware of. Nur ed-Din attempted to assert his authority. Although Sunnis now ruled in practice in Cairo, officially Egypt was still a Shi'a country and prayers were still said every Friday directed at the Caliph in Cairo rather than the Sunni Caliph in Baghdad. Nur ed-Din wrote to Saladin telling him to change this.

Saladin prevaricated until Nur ed-Din was so incensed that he threatened to personally come to Egypt to ensure that his wishes were complied with. Divine intervention then came to Saladin's aid: the conveniently timed death of the Fatimid caliph made an official change of regime more straightforward and the object of the weekly prayers in the mosques were in future to be directed to the Caliph in Baghdad.

The coup was handled with sensitivity by Saladin. It was not he who took the initiative in the disbandment of the Shi'a faith in Egypt but an imam from Mosul, in Sunni territory, who visited Cairo and took it upon himself to say prayers in the Great Mosque on behalf of the Caliph in Baghdad rather than the Fatimid alternative, al-Adid, the traditional recipient of such supplications.

Al-Adid was on his deathbed and Saladin gave express orders that no one should tell him of the change, marking as it did the destruction all that al-Adid stood for. And so the Fatimid Caliph passed into the world beyond unaware that his death coincided with the demise of something much greater and longer lasting, the Egyptian dynasty of which he was the spiritual head. It was an act of straightforward kindness and generosity on Saladin's part, for which he deserves much credit as a human being.

But Saladin was clearly a young man who was motivated by great ambition. He had threatened to overstep the mark with his actions in Egypt, and he now passed way beyond it. Without the sanction of Nur ed-Din, he attacked the castle of Montreal, a Frankish fortress to the south of the Dead Sea. This was far beyond his sphere of influence and his actions were tantamount to a declaration of independence towards Nur ed-Din, one that the latter could not possibly ignore.

Just as the castle was on the point of surrender, Saladin was mortified to see Nur ed-Din appearing at the head of a large army. This was a moment of both great tension and risk, a crossroads point in Saladin's life. The younger, more headstrong members of Saladin's entourage counselled that this was the time for open defiance. Older, wiser heads cautioned to the contrary. In the end, it was Saladin's father, Najm ed-Din Ayub, who won the day, berating his son for his excessive ambition. Realising that he had acted unwisely, Saladin offered his apologies to Nur ed-Din, which the latter warily accepted.

Chastened by the experience, Saladin for the time being decided to keep his ambition in check. Nur ed-Din was moving towards the end of his life and, although patience is not a virtue for which ambitious young men are renowned, Saladin realised that a waiting game might pay off.

In the meantime, the burgeoning Muslim superstate attempted to tighten its grip around the constricted Kingdom of Jerusalem. The process had already been started by Saladin in 1170 – a particularly notable year in the region in which a terrible earthquake caused immense damage to Antioch and Tripoli. This was an ominous portent for the Christians. Earthquakes were seen as evidence of God's displeasure: they were regarded as 'an instant and severe punishment for evil people'. A life of St Matthias told how when some people refused to listen to his preaching, he said to them, '"I give you notice that you will go to hell alive!" And the earth opened and swallowed them.'[10]

Such bad omens were well founded. Saladin also took Gaza and Aila (Aqaba), the Latins' outlet to the Red Sea. In addition, he attacked Arabia and Yemen. This potentially enabled him to exert further pressure from another direction, the south. Effectively, Outremer was now surrounded completely by land with Nur ed-Din's domains in the south, west and east and Turkish Asia Minor to the north. Only the Mediterranean gave the kingdom a lifeline along the lengthy, seasonal and risky road that stretched uncertainly across the ocean.

In 1173, Nur ed-Din attacked Oultrejourdain, the Frankish territories on the eastern side of the Dead Sea. He planned a pincer movement and, to effect this, instructed Saladin to bring his forces up from Egypt and attack Amalric from the rear. At first, Saladin complied with the request, attacking the grim fortress of Kerak, while Nur ed-Din moved down towards him from Damascus. But then Saladin called off the siege and returned to Egypt. He stated that his father was dangerously ill. This was true enough and indeed he would die shortly afterwards. But there were other reasons, too. In particular, the Christian territories acted as an effective protective buffer between Saladin in Egypt and his erstwhile master in Syria, and so from Saladin's point of view, at this stage they might be better off in Latin hands.

Nur ed-Din was enraged. He resolved to lead an army to Egypt and bring Saladin to heel. For a time, matters looked distinctly worrying for the ambitious Saladin, so much so that he sent his brother to the Sudan to identify a potential refuge should Nur ed-Din make his way to Egypt.

Napoleon, when asked what he most looked for in a general, replied that the supreme quality he valued more than any other was luck. And this was the quality (or to the more devout it was divine intervention) that aided Saladin now. Nur ed-Din had suffered a debilitating illness many years previously. It had taken its toll on him though he still strove to advance the cause of Islam. A pious man, who lived a simple life and had done much to espouse the cause of *jihad*, he was worn out by his exertions; and on 15 May 1174 he died.

This inevitably led to a succession dispute as would-be heirs apparent lined up to take over. The Franks must have thought that this was a propitious moment for them. With Nur ed-Din dead and no certainty among the Muslims concerning his successor, there was a chance that the kingdom could have embarked on some kind of recovery. Such hopes were soon to be dashed, however, with the death of King Amalric, on 11 July of the same year. Amalric was just

38 years old. He died after an attack of dysentery and an ill-advised attempt by his doctors to cure his illness by bleeding him. With a leprous child, his son Baldwin, earmarked as his heir, the future for Outremer suddenly seemed very uncertain again.

Amalric's death came at a crucial time. During his reign, relations with Byzantium had improved. Indeed, Byzantine influence was becoming increasingly obvious – a state of affairs that was certainly not welcome to all the Franks in Outremer. A community of Orthodox monks appeared at the Holy Sepulchre and, in a move of great symbolic significance, court dress at Jerusalem was remodelled on that at Constantinople.[11] With the demise of Amalric these closer links were threatened.

A further ray of hope for the Franks was soon to be extinguished. A Sicilian fleet appeared off Alexandria on 25 July, but failed to catch the garrison off its guard. Another campaign in Egypt would have kept Saladin occupied, but the raid achieved nothing and soon sailed away. This left Saladin free to turn his attentions to Syria, the real fulcrum of power in the Islamic Middle East at the time.

In order to rule Syria, Saladin had first to rule in Damascus. As his 'invitation' to do so was not unopposed, it was crucial that he struck quickly. Realising that time was of the essence, Saladin rode post-haste to Damascus accompanied by only 700 horsemen. Unmolested by the Franks when he galloped through Oultrejourdain, he arrived in the city in November and was welcomed ecstatically by the population. Showing much political acumen, he made generous donations to the Damascenes that further helped to cement his position.

Although this was a crucial step forward for Saladin, it did not mark the end of resistance to his rule. His major opponent was Gumeshtekin, who had installed himself in Aleppo. Saladin, after seizing the important city of Homs (though failing to take its citadel), laid siege to Aleppo. His attempts to capture it were cut short soon after when Nizari assassins were found in the camp and only killed following a desperate fight from Saladin's bodyguard. Shortly afterwards, a force of Franks laid siege to Homs: led by the regent, Raymond of Tripoli, the Franks had realised the threat posed by an Islamic state increasingly united under Saladin and had decided to do all they could to prevent such a union.

The distraction was enough to save Aleppo for the time being. In gratitude for the help of the Franks, all the Frankish prisoners held in the city were released by Gumeshtekin, including Reynald of Chatillon (a dubious reward for many in Outremer as it transpired). Soon afterwards, Saladin fell upon the forces of Gumeshtekin and defeated them roundly. The latter had so far pretended to support Nur ed-Din's young son, as-Salih, who was the late king's nominated heir. Claiming that the young ruler had been badly advised Saladin asserted that he could no longer stand idly by and see Nur ed-Din's legacy wasted. He now openly called himself King of Syria and Egypt and proceeded to perpetuate this claim in the most obvious way possible, by the issuing of coins in his own name. Seeing which way the wind was blowing, the Caliph in Baghdad accepted him as such.

This was not the end of the matter. In March 1176, the Emir of Mosul, Saif ed-Din, led a large army to join Gumeshtekin. At the end of April, Saif ed-Din, catching Saladin by surprise, fell on him. The battle was hard fought but in the end Saladin was victorious. In the aftermath of the battle, the many prisoners taken were not thrown into jail or slaughtered, but were well treated and released. It was a move that further enhanced Saladin's support. When he wished to unite rather than divide the Muslim world, such sensitive actions were, as well as being chivalric, both wise and expedient.

Aleppo still held out and Saladin accepted the status quo by agreeing to a truce with as-Salih's supporters. This left him free to deal with other enemies. The Nizaris had once more made an attempt on his life and his chainmail undercoat was all that had saved him. Determined that he would no longer tolerate their threat, he made his way into the mountains and laid siege to their great fortress of Masyaf.

The subsequent siege was short-lived. After a brief campaign, he agreed a truce with the Nizaris. It was rumoured that there were not just political reasons for this. It was said that Saladin, fearful for his life, had been surrounded by a much stronger bodyguard than normal when he had slept in his pavilion at night. One morning, he woke up to find, next to his bed, a Nizari dagger laced with poison and an ominous message along with a cake of the type that only members of the sect knew how to prepare. One of the would-be assassins had apparently breached the security screen and could easily have killed Saladin if he had been ordered to do so. The implication of all this was that the Nizaris could take his life any time that they wished to. Fearful of their power, according to the legend, Saladin decided to seek peace with the sect rather than persist in his attempts to destroy them.

In the previous year, 1175, Saladin had agreed a truce with the Franks of Outremer. However, the Franks found such agreements very hard to keep. In 1176, while Saladin had been besieging Aleppo, Raymond of Tripoli had raided Muslim lands in the Lebanon. Although this raid did not achieve all its objectives, Raymond heavily defeated Saladin's brother, Turan Shah, in battle and it was only when Saladin responded to the threat by leading a large force to meet it that the Franks withdrew. Satisfied with progress thus far, Saladin made his way back to Egypt to further secure his position.

For Outremer, a period of 'phoney war' existed. No one doubted the threat posed by the Islamic states grouped around Outremer, but for the time being the Franks did not have the resources to do much about this while Saladin had not yet achieved the stranglehold on Syria and Egypt that would be needed before he could be confident in his own situation. A restless peace therefore descended on the Kingdom of Jerusalem, an uncertain and potentially volatile state of affairs that could quickly be obliterated by the sudden threat of war.

But while Outremer might have appeared to be holding its own, momentous events further north were to shift the delicate balance of power in the region, with dramatic and permanent effect. It was not Saladin's forces that were responsible for this scenario but a much older Muslim power, the Seldjuk Turks in Asia Minor led by Sultan Kilij Arslan. No one could ever keep the Turks under control for very long. Tribesmen of independent spirit, fierce in battle and opportunistic in nature, their continuing presence in Asia Minor was a thorn in the side of the Byzantine Empire. In the aftermath of the death of Nur ed-Din, the Seldjuks took advantage of the free-for-all that followed to grab large chunks of land from their Danishmend Turk cousins.

Determined that the Seldjuk Sultan should be brought to book, the Byzantine Emperor Manuel led a vast army into Asia Minor in 1176. Manuel even wrote to the Pope encouraging him to launch a new Crusade. His intention was to clear Anatolia of the Turks and make the roads safe to travel once more. If the West had been interested in Crusading, then the offer would not be unattractive: opening up the Crusade routes across Asia Minor again would be a welcome boost. But the West was not interested, and no help came. Manuel's army was still impressive though. Seriously alarmed by the scale of the forces arrayed against him, Kilij Arslan sued for peace, but to no avail. Manuel set out with the aim of taking his capital, Konya.

With their backs against the wall, the Turks were ferocious fighters. The Byzantines found the campaign to be much tougher than they had anticipated. One of the foremost Byzantine generals, Andronicus Vatatses, cousin of the Emperor, was slain in battle and his head sent to Kilij Arslan as a trophy. But far, far worse was to follow.

The Byzantine war-machine was a cumbersome animal. Manuel's army was laden down with heavy siege engines and trundled slowly through the hostile Anatolian landscape, a parched, dry region with high hills dividing arid plains. On 17 September 1176, the vast Byzantine host lumbered into the head of a long and narrow pass at the far end of which was an old fort called Myriocephalum. Their way was barred by Turkish forces, but the powerful Byzantine army smashed into these and scattered them. The Turks fled before them, leaving the pass free for the Byzantines to enter with seemingly only light opposition ahead.

As the Byzantine force proceeded lethargically further into the valley, out of the blue Turkish cavalry swooped down from the hills and started to make inroads into the Greeks who did not have sufficient room to manoeuvre and organise themselves for a defensive action. The Turkish horse archers aimed in particular at the animals with the Greek army, unprotected against their arrows. The Greeks in the van found their problems were exacerbated by the huge masses behind them, attempting to force their way into the narrow pass. As the ferocity of the Turkish attacks increased, so too did the desperation of the Byzantines. An attempted counter-attack led by the Emperor's brother-in-law, Baldwin of Antioch, ended with Baldwin's death on the hillside.

Seeing what was happening, Manuel – who had not yet entered the death trap – panicked and fled. His actions seem almost a metaphor for the Byzantine Empire, living on past glories and unable to face up to the extent of the challenge before it. The Turks, inspired by the prize before them, fell on the Greek army. Many of the Byzantines lay dead by the end of the day.

Myriocephalum was the greatest defeat for Byzantine arms since the disaster at Manzikert a century before. Kilij Arslan was magnanimous in defeat and allowed Manuel to return to Constantinople with what were, in the circumstances, amazingly light terms. Perhaps he did not realise how complete his victory was. But for the Emperor the scale of the disaster was all too apparent. Only retrospect enables the observer to see historical events in their true context, but Myriocephalum was, with the benefit of hindsight, an act that symbolised the terminal nature of the malaise that now beset Byzantium.

The defeat of the Byzantines also exposed the Franks to a greatly increased threat. While Byzantium was a real power in the region, it acted as an invisible shield protecting Outremer. Despite frequent misunderstandings between Frank and Greek, on the whole recent years had seen a good deal of cooperation between the two. It is true that the end results of this had frequently been disappointing, but the Empire was still a menace to the emerging Islamic superstate in the region. But Myriocephalum showed how weak the Empire was becoming and in a few years such cooperation would be a thing of the past.

Not that this was immediately obvious. In the following year, 1177, hopes were raised in Outremer when Count Philip of Flanders arrived in the region. His father had been a great Crusader and the Franks hoped that he would be the figurehead of an expedition against Egypt. There was now increased urgency in their desire to subdue the Islamic kingdom. It was no longer just a question of wealth and glory but also of survival. With Egypt in Saladin's hands, they could be attacked from both east and west, and this threat had to be removed if the kingdom were to breathe more easily, free of his constricting grip.

The Byzantines, desperate to restore both pride and position after their catastrophic performance in the previous year, offered ships from their fleet – still a powerful weapon, even if their army was less so – in support. This would allow the Franks to launch a seaborne assault on one of the great ports at the head of the Delta, such as Alexandria and Damietta. But despite the opportunities offered by Constantinople's offers of help, Philip prevaricated.

His initial hesitation revolved around a suggestion made by King Baldwin that Reynald of Chatillon should be given joint command of the army. Such a suggestion was not without its merits, since Reynald was an experienced warrior with good knowledge of the realities of fighting in the East. But joint commands rarely work well and in this instance Philip protested that Reynald's morals made him an unworthy commander. It finally emerged that Philip had no real stomach for a fight and had come to Outremer largely to arrange for the marriage of the King's sisters, Isabella and Sibylla (who were his cousins), to two of his vassals.

When the barons uncovered the truth, they were outraged. Philip left shortly afterwards, having achieved nothing. The only outcomes of his visit were negative. The hopes of the Franks had been raised by his arrival only to be dashed again soon after. The Byzantines, realising that their efforts had been wasted, sailed back to their home ports, seething at the inconstancy of the Franks.

Philip did not return directly to the West but travelled north, first to Tripoli, then to Antioch. Despite his offers of support in expeditions against Muslim neighbours, both were desultory affairs that achieved nothing. There was no doubting that the expedition to Egypt had been a fiasco. It seemed to typify the lack of direction in Outremer and the sense of uncertainty that existed given the resurgent Islamic threat.

Like a predator sensing weakness in its prey, Saladin decided that the obvious weakness of Outremer meant that this was an ideal moment to strike against the kingdom itself. He crossed its vulnerable borders on 18 November 1177, knowing full well that the Greeks had gone back home and that Philip of Flanders was far away to the north. The Templars in the south hurried to Gaza, ready to repulse his attack. However, he neutralised them through the simple expedient of bypassing Gaza and moving straight on to Ascalon. In the process he chose to assume that the Templars in Gaza offered no threat to his rear, which was a catastrophic miscalculation.

Saladin's timing appeared perfect, as the Constable of Ascalon, Humphrey of Toron, was very ill and King Baldwin had also been sick recently. However, despite the awful leprosy that ravaged his body, Baldwin was a young man with great spirit and rushed off to Ascalon as quickly as he could. He arrived there in the nick of time, just before Saladin, and prepared to fight the Muslims.

Saladin now sensed that an even greater opportunity had appeared. The Franks had been caught off guard and there were no reserves left. He realised that Jerusalem stood naked before him with nothing to shield her from a head-on assault from his forces. A great prize beckoned, the greatest imaginable, and it seemed easily within his grasp.

It was a moment of destiny. The seizure of Jerusalem would secure Saladin's position, not only within Islam but within history. The twelfth century, as has been noted, had seen a revival in the concept of *jihad*, since the loss of Jerusalem in 1099 had fuelled a flame that ignited a Muslim fightback. Works of literature known as 'Mirrors for Princes' extolled the virtues of *jihad* in its wider sense, and men such as Saladin were caught up in the euphoria of the emotions generated as a result. Now he seemed to be on the verge of writing his name in history.

But the extent of the opportunity offered to Saladin turned his head and he forgot some basic tenets of warfare. His greatest flaw was to forget the maxim 'never underestimate your enemy'. Believing that the conquest of Jerusalem was a foregone conclusion, the discipline of the Muslim army broke down. Rather than maintaining their cohesion, the Muslims began to concentrate more on other distractions and plundered freely over a wide area.

Realising the desperate nature of the situation, King Baldwin sent messengers to the Templars in Gaza, telling them to abandon the city and rush to Ascalon. The Templars knew this was no time for prevarication and hurried as quickly as they could to Baldwin's side.

The situation was critical: if Saladin was not defeated quickly, then Jerusalem itself could fall. Baldwin gathered his commanders round him, Reynald of Chatillon, Reynald of Sidon and Joscelin of Courtenay among them, and prepared to set out with his hastily assembled army. Hotchpotch as it was and hopelessly outnumbered, the only hope of salvation would be if Saladin were so confident of success that he failed to make himself aware of their existence.

Oblivious to events in Ascalon, Saladin sauntered on towards Jerusalem, musing over the reactions he could expect to news of his inevitable conquest of the city. While he daydreamed of his imminent triumph, his men were dispersed around the countryside, more like picnickers on an outing than an army. On 25 November, he had reached the castle of Montgisard near Ramleh. All of a sudden, the distant horizon was obscured by clouds of rising dust, kicked up by the hooves of heavy horses charging towards him.

Saladin had managed to combine two of the most serious mistakes a military commander can make in one expedition. He had both underestimated the enemy and failed to post adequate scouts. The former was an unwarranted error of judgement. Whatever else one might say or think of the Franks, no one could doubt that they could fight. And they were cornered, with nowhere else to go. They would therefore fight hard and desperately.

The inadequate scouting too was a foolish error. When a medieval army marched, weapons and arms were carried in the baggage train, which was kept at the rear. This was so that the army could move more quickly, but the downside was obvious: if a surprise attack was launched, then the army would be virtually defenceless. And this is what happened at Montgisard. As the Franks came charging over the horizon, the Muslim army did not have time to react. Most of its weapons and armour were with the *thuql*, the baggage train. A chastening defeat was imminent.

The smaller Frankish force crashed into the rear of the unsuspecting Muslims like a wounded buffalo charging desperately in a last-ditch counter-attack to drive off the lion that had maimed it. The odds were still stacked against the Franks but they fought heroically, inspired by knights such as Balian and Baldwin of Ibelin, members of one of the oldest and most prestigious of Christian families in the region. The two stepsons of Raymond of Tripoli and experienced warriors like Reynald of Chatillon, frequently much maligned but at this time deservedly a hero, also battled bravely. The King, despite his malady and recent ill health, was inspirational, urging his men on. It was not just valiant men who were fighting with the Franks: at one stage, it was said that even St George was seen fighting alongside them.

In contrast, Saladin's army started to disintegrate even before that first seismic crash of the Franks into its rear. Terrified by the damage that they knew a charge of heavy cavalry could deliver, many of Saladin's troops ran away when they saw the imminence of the threat facing them. Most of them would probably have been unarmoured, unprepared as they were for battle. Those who remained were hacked to pieces by the Franks. Only the courage and tenacity of Saladin's bodyguard saved him. They bought his freedom with their lives. But there was no avoiding the defeat that loomed.

An eyewitness to these heroic events from the Christian side spoke of the glorious part in the battle played by the Templars and their Grand Master, Odo of St Amand. He had eighty-four knights with him. He

took himself into battle with his men, strengthened by the sign of the cross. Spurring all together, as one man, they made a charge, turning neither to the left nor to the right. Recognizing the body of troops in which Saladin commanded many knights, they manfully approached it, immediately penetrated it, incessantly knocked down, scattered, struck and crushed. Saladin was stricken with admiration, seeing his men dispersed everywhere, everywhere turned in flight, everywhere given to the mouth of the sword. He took thought for his own safety and fled, throwing off his mail shirt for speed, mounting a racing camel and barely escaped with a few of his men.[12]

The army fled back towards Egypt. So horrified was it by the turn of events that plunder, captives taken in the weeks before Montgisard and even weapons were abandoned so that they could flee more quickly. The horror did not end there. There was the prospect of a journey through the desert, for which the army was unprepared. Seizing on their vulnerability, Bedouin brigands constantly harassed them. Some of the survivors of the battle reckoned that slavery was preferable to the ordeals of a journey across the desert and surrendered.

Saladin sensed that even his position in Egypt was precarious as a result of this debacle. Not long installed there, and in effect a usurper, it was by no means unlikely that a rising against his rule might ensue. He was after all the champion of Sunni orthodoxy in what had for centuries been a Shi'a country. Rumours might even be spread abroad that he was dead. So he sent carrier pigeons ahead of him to tell his people that he was alive and returning to Egypt. Then he made his way pensively back to Cairo to face a future that suddenly seemed very uncertain.

For the Franks, it was a marvellous escape. Seemingly on the brink of disaster, the triumph of Montgisard appeared to show that the Kingdom of Jerusalem could still hold its own. For them, the victory was heroic. It had been bought at a high price, with perhaps 1,000 dead and 750 wounded.[13] Despite the element of surprise on their side, this was clearly a fierce and desperate fight. It is notable that those who fought and won at Baldwin's side were men whom later supporters of the cause of Raymond of Tripoli would castigate, in particular Reynald of Chatillon. None could underestimate the bravery and valour exhibited in this triumph. It was said that by this stage the King had the use of only one arm and steered his horse by the use of his knees while he held his weapon in his one usable limb.[14]

But this splendid victory was the result of two prime factors. The first was the ability to work together, so capably demonstrated by the way that Baldwin, the Templars and others had joined forces to counter-attack Saladin. But the second factor was Saladin himself. In the latter part of the campaign, he had led his army with extraordinary complacency, believing that the hard work had been done and that the greatest prize of all would fall obligingly into his lap. It had been a great error of judgement, to which Saladin was prone from time to time. But he had been taught a painful lesson and it was doubtful whether he would repeat his mistakes in future.

History is full of 'what if's, and one of them concerns these great events. If Philip of Flanders had arrived after Saladin had been defeated, and if the Greeks had sent their fleet to aid the Franks a year later, maybe the Franks would have launched their attack on Egypt when it was uniquely weak. But it was not to be. The Greek fleet was by now safely back in Constantinople and Philip would soon make his way home, sailing first to the capital of Byzantium where perhaps he saw those now redundant galleys moored up at the quayside. A tremendous opportunity had been missed.

In the final analysis, these seemingly providential events did little to change the long-term prognosis for Outremer. There would be a delay while Saladin was forced to consolidate his position inside the Muslim Middle East, but if anything, perhaps Montgisard did as much harm as good. For the Franks, though outnumbered, had won a great victory and some believed that this proved that Saladin was no match for a Western army.

It was understandable that the Franks for the time being gloried in the sweet scent of victory. Their king, though seriously handicapped by his ailments, had fought and led magnificently. And the Templars, the bearded warrior monks, had again proved their worth against a Muslim enemy. Certainly Saladin respected their fighting qualities and would mark down their prowess as something to be remembered in the future. For the moment, he contemplated the uncertainty of life and the transience of earthly success. Jerusalem was not to be his. Not for now at least.

FOUR

Dangerous Times

And I looked and beheld a pale horse: and his name that sat on him was Death, and Hell followed with him.

Revelation 6: 8

It is easy to perceive medieval Europe as a man's world. Our view of the period is coloured by stories of great kings, powerful, ambitious barons and mighty warriors. Women are seen as pawns in marriage bargains that brought together competing interests or helped to advance the fortunes of ambitious husbands. This perception may indeed be reinforced by considering the role of monarchy: no queen of England ruled in her own right until Mary and Elizabeth in the sixteenth century, though Matilda, daughter of Henry I, had tried to and chaos had resulted. Women appear as mere adjuncts to their spouses, existing mainly for decorative purposes and for the opportunities that their family name and fortune offered.

Recent decades have seen big steps forward in the area known as 'gender studies', whereby historians have attempted to redress the balance of the naive view of the role of women outlined above. It is now clear that medieval women could indeed be powerful individuals in their own right. A fine example of this, contemporary with the Hattin period, is Eleanor of Aquitaine, wife successively of Louis VII of France and Henry II of England. Her case is particularly appropriate in that she herself was a Crusader who accompanied her husband on the Second Crusade. And her son from her second marriage, Richard the Lionheart, of course holds a proud place in the history of the Crusades.

71

But Eleanor is by no means the only example of a woman who helped to shape the course of events in medieval history. Several played a critical part on the road to Hattin. Foremost among these was Agnes, the Queen Mother (her son was the leper king, Baldwin IV), her daughter, Sibylla, and Sibylla's half-sister, Isabella.

Agnes of Courtenay came from an important 'colonial' family. Her father and grandfather had both been Counts of Edessa until their city was lost to Zengi in 1144, to be followed by the rest of their territory in the years following. They had fought hard for Christendom, sometimes with success, sometimes not, but ultimately had fallen on hard times with the loss of their county to the resurgent armies of Islam. They suffered more than most other noble Outremer families during the first half of the twelfth century. The Courtenays represented something of a riches to rags story, and had a burning desire to restore their damaged fortunes. Such very human motivations should be borne in mind when considering the character of the woman who was to play a prominent, and far from happy, role at a particularly sensitive time in the kingdom's history.

Agnes's brother, Joscelin, was in effect a lord without a fiefdom. For many years, he was a companion of Reynald of Chatillon in captivity. But, in contrast to Reynald, he was a weak individual and, following his release in 1175, destined to play an inglorious part in events. Thanks to the influence of his sister, he would assume a prominent position in the government of the kingdom, a role for which his flawed temperament and judgement would ill suit him.

If Joscelin's influence was negative, that of Agnes was disastrous. To understand why, we need to consider briefly her chequered history and her frequent forays into the marriage market. She and her brother had arrived in Jerusalem in 1151, to all intents and purposes in internal exile now that the County of Edessa had ceased to exist and their family, once great, baronial vagrants. Agnes was a widow: her husband had died in battle in 1149. Her family's position improved significantly with her marriage to Amalric, Count of Jaffa and Ascalon, brother of King Baldwin III. The match appeared to offer the Courtenays hopes of a revival in the family fortunes; and so it proved, but not as completely as might have been hoped. Children followed: Baldwin and Sibylla. However, domestic bliss was to prove short-lived, for in 1162, Baldwin III died and Amalric, the nearest hereditary claimant to the throne, was duly elected. But before Amalric could become king, it was made a condition of his succession that he should first obtain a divorce.

There were several reasons for the barons' dissatisfaction with Agnes. The couple were related, a position that generated a good deal of adverse comment. They were third cousins, within the boundaries prohibited by the Church, as a result of which the Patriarch of Jerusalem had refused to confirm the legitimacy of the marriage when they wed. There were in addition a number of rumours concerning Agnes's alleged promiscuity.

These were two obvious reasons to doubt Agnes's suitability as Queen of Outremer. One wonders, given her later actions and interference, whether her strong personality further alienated support. Faced with a choice of a divorce or a kingdom, Amalric chose the latter. But he was concerned about the legitimacy of his children. He only accepted an annulment on condition that his children were accepted as legitimate, a compromise that was agreed to. Agnes found herself frustrated once more. First deprived of her family's homelands and then of a splendid match, it is easy to imagine just how bitter she might become.

Amalric remarried, and his new wife, Maria Comnena, from the ruling family of Byzantium, conceived a daughter, Isabella. However, no sons followed. This problem became critical when it became apparent that the young child Baldwin was suffering from leprosy. This was a potential disaster for the kingdom since Baldwin would never be able to marry and sire an heir himself.

This prompted a flurry of activity as a suitable husband for Sibylla was sought. Sibylla could not rule in her own right but her husband could govern through her until an heir was conceived from their union. The identification of a spouse therefore became a matter of paramount importance. In 1170, delegations were sent to France to suggest a match with Stephen of Champagne, who came from a family with a well-established and honourable Crusader history.

This invitation enticed Stephen to journey to Outremer to see for himself what his potential kingdom had to offer. He was not impressed with what he saw on his visit. Desultory negotiations did not last long before he terminated them altogether and made his way back to Europe, suffering the indignity of losing his luggage to bandits on the way back.

With his son a leper, and his daughter unmarried and consequently heirless, the domestic situation was a cause of constant worry for Amalric. Following his death in 1174, the clouds of imminent crisis thickened. Baldwin, too young to rule regardless of his illness, could not yet govern and the appointment of Raymond of Tripoli as regent was duly made.

Soon after, Baldwin's mother, Agnes, returned to court. She had played little part in the upbringing of her children since her divorce. Now, the death of her ex-husband gave her another opportunity to involve herself in affairs of state. As Baldwin was a sick young man, with no father to turn to and unsure who he could trust, it was inevitable that he would be heavily influenced by a strong personality such as his mother. And that influence would prove to be malign and dangerous.

In the years before her return to court, Agnes had continued with her disastrous marital track record. Her third husband Hugh of Ibelin had died within a few years of marriage while a fourth, Reynald of Sidon, had obtained a divorce on the rather predictable grounds that he also was too closely related to Agnes. When Agnes returned to court after Amalric's death, not only did she seek to manipulate her young son to her own advantage, she also came into direct conflict with Maria Comnena, his stepmother. The two women hated each other and when Maria remarried to Balian of Ibelin she placed herself firmly in the camp of the doves. This put her in direct opposition to Agnes, who sided with the hawks in the kingdom.

These domestic events were to have significant repercussions. But there was one other marriage, in 1175, that was also important. Reynald of Chatillon had returned from captivity to find that, since the death of his wife, he had lost much of his influence. It took only a few months for his position to improve. Miles of Plancy, who was murdered shortly after Raymond had become regent,[1] left a widow, Stephanie, who ruled the lands of Oultrejourdain. She blamed Raymond for her late husband's death and married Reynald of Chatillon, who was firmly in the camp of the hawks in direct opposition to Raymond of Tripoli.

With the return of Reynald and the resurgent influence of Agnes, a formidable array of hawks was beginning to congregate that would exert considerable pressure on the governing councils of Outremer. However, the year 1177, when the young king reached the age of 16 and so inherited the right to rule without a regent, appeared to offer the hope of improving fortunes for the kingdom. And it was once more in the delicate world of marriage politics that an opportunity presented itself.

It was surprising, given the state of King Baldwin's health, that greater efforts had not been made to find a suitable husband for Sibylla. But in 1175 negotiations had begun with the aim of marrying her to William Longsword, the eldest son of the Marquis of Montferrat. It was a good potential match. First of all, William had connections, being related both to the King of France, Louis VII (who had probably done much to bring the match about) and also to the German Emperor, the fierce Frederick Barbarossa, who would a few years later lead a Crusade of his own to the Holy Land with tragic personal results (he died en route).

Equally attractive was William's access to considerable wealth – his father was one of the richest men in the Italian peninsula. Although older than Sibylla, who was just a teenager, he was courteous and considerate and Sibylla therefore appeared happy enough with the match. William landed in Outremer late in 1176, and a few days after first setting foot in the country the couple wed. The match offered much to Outremer as well as Sibylla. In particular, William's connections to the most powerful men in the West promised a great deal in terms of support.

The year 1177 started well, as it became apparent that Sibylla was pregnant. At last, prospects seemed to have improved. If, as appeared likely, Baldwin did not live for long then Sibylla could rule alongside her husband as regent until the child that she bore – it was hoped a son – came of age and could rule in his own right. But it was a cruel delusion. William soon caught malaria, was unable to fight it off and died in June. Shortly afterwards, however, came news that Sibylla was safely delivered of a son, predictably named Baldwin. At least an heir had been provided to help secure the future.

That same year also saw the defeat of Saladin at Montgisard, and so for a while Outremer was offered respite from his predations. The next two years were characterised by occasional raids between Frank and Muslim rather than all-out warfare. One such raid took place in 1179 when King Baldwin sought to seize flocks of sheep passing close to Banyas. However, aware of what was happening Saladin had sent a trusted lieutenant, his nephew Faruk-Shah, to intervene.

Baldwin was lackadaisical and off-guard when he was attacked. Badly exposed in the forests around Banyas he only managed to survive because of the actions of an old and respected warrior, Humphrey of Toron. Humphrey bought Baldwin's life by sacrificing his own and died soon after the battle of the wounds that he had received in saving Baldwin's life. The Lords of Toron were an old-established colonial family. Humphrey had served his country at the highest levels, being its constable. His family were to play an important part in the future of the kingdom, too. His son, also Humphrey, had been the first husband of Stephanie, the lady of Oultrejourdain now married to Reynald of Chatillon. His grandson, yet another Humphrey (original names do not seem to have been a custom of the times), would in a few years' time play a crucial but inglorious role in the events that led the kingdom towards oblivion.

Humphrey's loss was deeply felt, as even the Muslims respected him. The victory buoyed up Saladin's spirits and he resolved to try to take advantage of it. A raid was launched through Galilee and into Lebanon. King Baldwin moved out to meet him. By his side rode Raymond of Tripoli and the Templars. This is significant. It shows that, at this stage, the kingdom was still unified, with future hawks and doves still prepared to cooperate with a shared view of the mutual interests of the kingdom. Irrevocable schism was still some time away in the future.

But Saladin was ready for the army of Jerusalem. Battle was joined on 10 June 1179 in a valley close by the Jordan. The Templars charged headlong into battle against their Muslim foe. Subtlety does not appear to have played a great part in Templar operations, and attack was often seen as the best means of defence. But, if the initial charge of Frankish heavy horse could be resisted and its impetus broken, then opponents had a good chance of turning the situation to their advantage as the Christian forces tended to quickly become uncoordinated.

This is exactly what happened. The Templars were forced back into the Franks packed behind them and mass confusion ensued. There is nothing more guaranteed to break morale than chaos in the heat of battle, and the initial reverse of the Templar cavalry soon transmogrified into a comprehensive rout of the whole army.

Baldwin and Raymond escaped to the safety of the nearby castle of Beaufort. Others were not so lucky. Many Christian troops were slaughtered and a number of prisoners taken. There were some prominent men numbered among the latter group. Baldwin of Ibelin was one, along with Hugh, Prince of Galilee. Hugh was ransomed soon afterwards by his rich mother, the Countess of Tripoli. However, Baldwin was considered to be much more valuable by Saladin and consequently he would only be released if a ransom three times greater than Hugh's were paid. In the end, Baldwin would be exchanged for 1,000 Muslim prisoners and a promise to pay the money at some point in the future.

Another important prisoner was the Grand Master of the Templars, Odo of St Amand. A deal was proposed to exchange him for an important Muslim captive. It has been rather uncharitably suggested that Odo was too proud to admit that anyone was as important as him,[2] but a more generous interpretation is that the Order's precepts discouraged the use of ransom of any sort being paid to release a Templar knight, even one as important as a Grand Master. So Odo went off to prison, where he did not live for very long, leaving an opening for an ambitious Templar knight by the name of Gerard of Ridfort to climb another rung up the Templar ladder.

Saladin may have been discouraged from pushing home his success by the timely arrival of another batch of French Crusaders. Instead he instead succeeded in taking the Templar castle at Jacob's Ford. The loss of this border castle was felt particularly keenly by the leaders of Outremer. Construction at the castle had only been started in 1178, in response to the increasing pressure being directed against Outremer from the direction of Damascus,[3] and its capture by Saladin must have badly dented the morale of the kingdom. It would also have been a grave personal blow for Baldwin, who had spent much time supervising the construction.

The castle was strategically important, as it dominated a shallow crossing of the River Jordan – an obvious point of attack should an army from Damascus ever decide to attack Jerusalem. But it was not only a point of defence, it could also be used as a springboard for an attack on Damascus. It was built on a massive scale and at huge expense. The sensitivity of the region, which was in one of the most volatile frontier areas between the two kingdoms, had led to Saladin previously offering to reimburse the enormous cost of construction if the Franks would only destroy it. When they refused, he felt that he had no option but to take the castle by force.

The action started on 24 August 1179. Baldwin was nearby with his army and so a quick resolution was vital from Saladin's perspective. The attack started with an arrow bombardment, which was in part a cover for his miners to start chipping away at the walls. Even as Baldwin's relief army was setting off, the mines did their work and the walls collapsed, leaving an immense breach for the Muslims to pour through and overwhelm the defence. The slaughter was great (a view confirmed by recent archaeological excavation) and among the booty taken were 1,000 suits of armour. As he reached the outer approaches to the castle, Baldwin saw that he was too late. Flames were already licking the sky. He withdrew, and Saladin took his time in dismantling the castle stone by stone.

Since Montsigard then, the situation of the Kingdom of Outremer had slowly deteriorated, though not yet to a catastrophic extent. Given this, it may initially appear surprising that Frankish approaches for a truce early in 1180 were responded to favourably by Saladin. But there had been a drought in the region and the harvest had been poor. In addition, Saladin did not yet rule the whole of Syria and he wished to subdue those who held out against him, particularly the crucial city of Aleppo, before overextending himself against Outremer. In this year Saladin forged an important alliance with the leading Turkish warlord in Asia Minor, Kilij Arslan II. The truce with the Franks was duly agreed in May.

In view of later accusations of treason against Raymond of Tripoli, it should be noted that his principality was initially excluded from the truce. At this stage, therefore, Raymond had excited the wrath of Saladin rather than his friendship. However, although an Egyptian fleet raided Tortosa soon afterwards, Tripoli was eventually also included in the truce. Saladin then shifted his attention to enemies within the Muslim world, leaving the Franks to their own devices for a time.

This is perhaps an appropriate time to consider the Franks' position. The recent past had seen what might be termed a series of unfortunate events: a resurgent Islamic Syria and an Egypt now largely combined under one dominant leader was one issue of concern, the decline of the Byzantine Empire and a consequent loss of protection another. Recent reverses in battle emphasised the shift in the balance of power in the region. External factors were therefore conspiring against the kingdom's chances of survival.

Internal factors were no less gloomy. Within the Kingdom of Jerusalem itself, King Baldwin's frail health and the uncertainties of the succession were a worry. Given the rise of Saladin, a strong monarch in Outremer was crucial to the viability of the Frankish state there. But not everything was negative. In recent campaigns the Franks had fought largely as a united entity. There were still reasonable relationships between, for example, Count Raymond and others of the high nobility. So, although Outremer was advancing towards a position of danger, its movement took the form of a slowly growing snowball rolling down a hill rather than an object plummeting over the edge of a cliff into oblivion.

There was still a possibility that the position might get better. Crucial to such a scenario were an improvement in the position of the monarchy and a semblance of unity among the Frankish leadership. However, rather than this, relationships within the ruling hierarchy of Outremer became more fractious and complicated. And, in particular, the stability of the monarchy was about to take a turn for the worse.

Pivotal to the future security of Outremer was Sibylla, or more precisely, her husband. Following the tragic death of William Longsword, negotiations began for her to be wed to Baldwin of Ibelin. As a representative of one of the longer-established settler families, such a match appeared to offer a good bargain for both sides. It would cement relationships between the monarchy and the nobility while putting the government of Outremer in the hands of a local man. However, before these discussions could meet with a satisfactory conclusion, fate intervened. Baldwin was captured in Saladin's campaign of 1179 and subsequently imprisoned.

Sibylla wrote reassuring letters to him, asserting that if he could negotiate his freedom she would happily take him as a husband. Saladin was initially unhelpful. He had no need for money, he said, and would benefit much more from keeping such a prestigious lord in one of his prisons. The *Chronique d'Ernoul* offers a strange story about what happened next. Against his better judgement, Saladin agreed to a ransom but one that was so large that it would be virtually impossible to pay.

Baldwin demurred at the price of freedom and, angered at his response, Saladin threatened to pull all the teeth from Baldwin's mouth until the ransom was agreed to. After two had been extracted, Baldwin begged for mercy and said that he would raise the ransom, whatever it cost. He wrote to his brother, Balian, and arranged for him to send as much money as he could and obtain pledges for the rest. Satisfied with this response, Saladin let Baldwin return to Outremer.[4]

Baldwin returned to the kingdom intent on finalising plans for his wedding. Sadly, the possible future queen's affections seemed to have cooled in his absence. It would be wrong, she said, to proceed with the wedding until the large outstanding debt was cleared. It was a question of honour, after all, which a queen of Outremer valued highly. There were practical concerns too: Baldwin might use her lands as a pledge to pay off the ransom, thereby weakening the kingdom. This could not be allowed to happen.

It was not the most romantic of responses but Baldwin reacted with uncharacteristic meekness. There was only one man rich enough to help, and he was far away in Constantinople. At the time, Manuel was still Emperor and there was a family connection since Balian of Ibelin was married to his great niece. Manuel loved a dramatic gesture, so when Baldwin told him of his plight, the Emperor felt honour-bound to help. He sat Baldwin on a chair in the middle of the room and then heaped a pile of gold coins over him that was so large that they covered him from head to foot. It was more than enough to pay off what was owed and Baldwin locked this treasure up in a safe place until a galley to take him back to Outremer was prepared.[5]

It was no doubt a self-satisfied Lord of Ibelin who cruised his way down the Mediterranean coastline back to Acre. He arrived in the port and paid off the enormous outstanding debt. Then he went to claim his prize, only to find that it was no longer available: someone had stepped into his shoes in his absence, a flamboyant knight from the West called Guy of Lusignan.

Instrumental in this decision was the meddlesome Queen Mother, Agnes of Courtenay. She was no friend of the Ibelins and had no desire to see their power strengthened. One of her former lovers was a Westerner, Amalric of Lusignan, who became constable on the death of Humphrey of Toron. It was said of Amalric that 'many times had he had his way with the queen's mother', as a classic double-entendre by the *Chronique* put it.[6] Amalric had a younger brother, Guy, still back home in France. Amalric told Agnes of Guy's good looks and charm, and suggested that he would make a perfect match for Sibylla. It was quickly arranged that Amalric would rush back to France to fetch Guy.

There was another key player in this decision, the King himself. As his condition worsened, and he lost the use of all his limbs and began to go blind, he increasingly felt that men were seeking to depose him. He was particularly concerned about Raymond of

Tripoli whom he believed sought the kingdom for himself. To counteract this, it was important to secure the continuity of the royal line by ensuring that Sibylla married as soon as possible.

Guy offered hope of an ongoing Western interest in Outremer. Crusading in the East was already declining in popularity, a situation that the general failure of the Second Crusade had done nothing to correct. The marriage would encourage future support from the West. And so it was concluded. Guy was every bit as charming and good-looking as described, and Sibylla was more than happy to offer herself to this dashing knight from the West. The arrangement with Baldwin was quickly brushed aside.

But whatever presentational qualities Guy may have had, they did not compensate for the disadvantages of the match. His character was crucially flawed in several respects. Although a man of war and a brave soldier, in the political sphere he was weak and easily led and as such vulnerable to manipulation from more powerful figures. This suited those such as Agnes and her clique, which included the hot-headed Reynald of Chatillon. It clearly did not suit the Ibelins, deprived of a great prize by the arrival of Guy and from this point on implacably at odds with the hardliners including Agnes and Reynald. Power politics reared its ugly head once more.

There were social reasons, too, for frowning on the match. Although Guy, who came from the Poitiers region, was a scion of a noble family, he was not of the highest rank. In those times, where birth and lineage were important social considerations, such issues were keenly felt. On the previous occasion when a prospective king had come from the West, it had been Fulk of Anjou: Anjou was one of the most prestigious dynasties in France from which the Angevin kings of England emanated. Put simply, Guy's family simply did not come up to the mark as far as the high nobility of the kingdom were concerned.[7]

But now of course it was not just the high nobility that mattered. There were other relatively recent arrivals from the West who had managed to put their stamp on Outremer life. Reynald of Chatillon was one, who had made his fame and fortune by the judicious use of marriage alliances. And then there was Gerard of Ridfort, who had sought to do the same, only to be checkmated by Raymond of Tripoli, and who had instead sought his path to glory through the ranks of the Templars. These newcomers had a very different view of the world from other members of the high nobility of the kingdom and were much more amenable to one of 'theirs', another Westerner, becoming king – particularly when he could be easily manipulated.

The reasons for this seemingly inappropriate match were the subject of much debate. William of Tyre believed that the King, ailing and no doubt in much mental and physical discomfort, was pushed into the match by the arrival of Bohemond of Antioch and Raymond of Tripoli in Jerusalem. Baldwin believed, according to William, that this presaged an attempt to take power from him, a fear no doubt heightened because he was 'afflicted by his illness worse than usual, and every day the signs of his leprosy were becoming more and more evident'.[8]

Afraid that his grip on power was about to be loosened, the King agreed to the marriage with Guy, even though far more appropriate matches could have been made. So intent was he that Sibylla should wed Guy that the wedding took place during Easter, even though it was customary not to hold such ceremonies during this holy period in this especially sacred place. Seeing the suspicion that their arrival had engendered, Raymond and Bohemond left the city shortly afterwards.[9]

There was unsavoury gossip surrounding the match. Such tittle-tattle should of course be treated with suspicion, but this does not mean that it should be discounted altogether. The gossip was committed to print by an English writer, Roger of Howden, according to whom, after the death of Sibylla's first husband, William Longsword, the King took his sister back into his household. Guy was a man of certain virtues. His family, for instance, had a reputation for military prowess: his brother, Geoffrey, had killed the Earl of Salisbury in battle in 1168. To kill a noble in conflict was a point of some honour and actions such as this helped to cement a family's martial reputation.

Guy was physically attractive and was also noted for his prowess as a warrior. According to Roger, Sibylla was swept off her feet by this dashing young lord, so much so that the two became lovers before they were married. When Baldwin discovered the assignation, he was furious. His anger was so great that he wished to have Guy stoned to death and was only dissuaded from doing so by the Templars and 'other wise men', whoever they might have been. He then relented and allowed the marriage to proceed. The story lacks credibility: it seems strange that Baldwin would so easily change position from wanting to stone Guy at one minute and accepting him as a brother-in-law at the next. But at least it demonstrates that such scurrilous rumours are not the exclusive preserve of modern society.[10]

In retrospect, the marriage marked a decisive moment in the kingdom's march to destruction. It was another crossroads decision, sending Outremer irrevocably on a path of recrimination and internal division when it could least be afforded. This was a road that would terminate in implosion and self-destruction. King Baldwin, weak both physically and also in terms of his ability to face up to his strong-willed mother, soon seems to have realised the dangerous turn events had taken. After Sibylla and Guy had married at Easter, he arranged for the betrothal of his half-sister, Isabella, to the younger Humphrey of Toron, grandson of the late lamented constable of the same name, in an attempt to redress the balance. But he also appointed Guy Count of Jaffa – which it may be remembered was one of the four great fiefdoms in the land – and Ascalon.

Humphrey was a cousin of Baldwin of Ibelin and as such this could be seen as a sop to the offended sensibilities of the family. But it was an ineffective one. Isabella, unlike Sibylla, currently had no real power, although of course that could change if her half-sister died heirless. And Isabella was nothing more than a child, 8 years old: her heirs were a long way into the future. Nor was Humphrey a great catch: he was as ineffectual and weak as Guy would be, but without any real power. No one, least of all the Ibelins, was fooled that this was anything other than an uninspiring consolation prize.

Where the balance of power now really lay in the kingdom became apparent soon after, in October 1180. The death of the incumbent Patriarch of Jerusalem left one of the most prestigious sees in Christendom vacant. The choice of a replacement fell on

Heraclius, the current Archbishop of Caesarea. It appeared an unlikely decision. Heraclius was poorly educated, though certainly not unskilled in the ways of the world, and, worse still, there were widespread rumours about his disrespect for the vows of chastity he had taken. Significantly, it was rumoured that Agnes was numbered among his many lovers and that it was her influence on the Chapter of Jerusalem, responsible for electing a leader, that proved decisive. Against these disadvantages, he had already had direct experience of the church in Jerusalem, being archdeacon there by the year 1169.

William of Tyre, who, as well as being an important chronicler was also the Archbishop of Tyre, rushed to the Holy City to intervene. He was a widely respected figure, being the former tutor of King Baldwin, but his influence counted for little against the ascendant powers of Agnes and her clique. Although the canons of the Holy Sepulchre agreed with William that it would be best to appoint an archbishop from overseas, they decided to present both William and Heraclius to the King to make the final decision. When he was asked to arbitrate between them, Agnes pressured him into accepting Heraclius.

This method of appointment was important in that it required the support of both ecclesiastics and the secular monarchy. The process, as we have just seen, involved the Augustinian canons of the Church of the Holy Sepulchre nominating two candidates to the King, who then decided between them. The fact that Heraclius had been nominated by the former group shows that he had supporters within the Church hierarchy, though the ultimate choice fell to Baldwin.

The power wielded by the patriarch inevitably allowed him to play a strong part in matters political as well as religious, an attribute that Heraclius was not slow to exploit. This was indeed a great prize. Even if the patriarch was not quite as powerful as might have been hoped by the ecclesiastics accompanying the First Crusade, he nevertheless held a very prominent position. The patriarch had his own quarter in the north-west of Jerusalem, where his palace was situated close by the Church of the Holy Sepulchre. He was responsible for the administration of Church law. All the archbishops of Outremer answered to him, that is, those at Tyre,

Caesarea, Nazareth and Petra. So too did the bishops of Lydda, Bethlehem and Hebron, who had no archbishop over them.

In addition to his reputation for a lack of learning, Heraclius was reputedly good-looking, a quality of somewhat doubtful use to a bishop but one that seems to have served him well at a personal level. Agnes was particularly attracted to him and it was said to be because of her influence that he had progressed through the Church hierarchy. He had a well-known mistress, a married woman called Pasque de Riveri. She was married to a draper from Nablus, and it was rumoured that she spent two weeks at a time living with Heraclius in Jerusalem.

Heraclius was at least prepared to look after both Pasque and her husband, making sure they were financially secure. In return for this, the husband was apparently content to lend his wife to the churchman as and when required. When the draper died some time after the affair commenced, Pasque gave up all pretence and moved in with Heraclius. She went about Jerusalem dressed in great finery and adorned with precious stones, so much so that she might be mistaken for a woman of great wealth by a stranger. But for the locals there was no such misidentification. As they passed her in the street they would say 'there goes the patriarchess!'[11] Before long there were rumours of a daughter being born to the couple.

Having lost the battle for Jerusalem, William of Tyre now faced a very uncertain future. He muttered that just as Jerusalem had been won by a Heraclius (the name of the seventh-century Byzantine Emperor who had captured the city from the Persians), so too would it be lost by one. This was effectively the end of William's career aspirations: Heraclius, every bit as disastrous an appointment as William predicted he would be, gained his revenge in the spring of 1181, excommunicating him. The chronicler journeyed to Rome in an attempt to overturn the decision, but died soon after. Conspiracy theorists put his demise down to poisoning but, murder or no, it was a shabby end for one who had led an illustrious life in the Church and done much for Outremer.

This deterioration in fortunes mirrored another downward turn in those of Byzantium. On 24 September 1180, the Emperor Manuel died. His reign had been one of much promise, not always fulfilled in reality. But on the whole he had been an effective ruler who had succeeded in slowing down the Empire's rate of decline. Myriocephalum had of course been a disaster and whether that terrible reverse had been a symptom of his diminishing powers or a cause of them is a moot point. But he had, notwithstanding his increasing (and legally justified) interference in the affairs of Outremer, as well as in Antioch, been a good friend to the kingdom, prepared to work with the late King Amalric in particular to advance their mutual interests.

There were some very tangible signs of the closer relations between Byzantium and Outremer in one of the most sensitive areas imaginable in the Holy Land, that of new churches. During Manuel's reign Orthodox monasteries had been dedicated to St Elias, near Bethlehem, St John the Baptist next to the Jordan and St Mary of Kalamon close to Jericho. Several churches were built in Jerusalem too.[12] All this evidenced stronger relationships between the two cultures that cannot have helped but increase the security of the Kingdom of Jerusalem. Now, with Saladin's star rising, the Byzantine Empire passed to the uncertain hands of an 11-year-old child. The timing was potentially disastrous.

The child emperor in Constantinople would not last for long. The Emperor's cousin, Andronicus Comnenus, was a larger than life adventurer. Possessed of impressive good looks (one writer described him as being 'already sixty-four years old but looked nearer forty') he was an experienced and successful campaigner, both on the battlefield and in the bedroom.[13]

Unfortunately, those he seduced were not unimportant servant-girls but close relations of some of the greatest men in the land. This attracted the wrath of some very important people. His greatest conquest, and probably his greatest love, was Queen Theodora, widow of Baldwin III of Jerusalem. Andronicus had for a time lived as an exile in Damascus, an outcast because of his indiscretions, but had managed to manoeuvre a return to Constantinople: he was, in short, a survivor. Sensing the weakness of Byzantium, Andronicus waited for an opportunity to strike. He did not have to stay his hand for long.

The rise of Saladin and the demise of Byzantium posed a danger that was recognised far and wide. The condition of Outremer in the face of these growing threats was noticeably becoming riskier, too. Concerns about the state of the kingdom reached well beyond its borders. In 1181, Pope Alexander III issued a proclamation, informing the Christian world that 'sinister rumours [are] reaching us from the region of Jerusalem'. He went on to refer to the fact that the kingdom had been 'devastated by the incursions of the infidel and deprived of the strength of men of valour and of the counsel of men of experience'.[14]

Given the change in the *realpolitik* of the region and the increasing frailty of King Baldwin, such concerns were understandable. The reaction was promising, though cynics would not have been overimpressed when Henry II of England vowed to set out: they had already heard such commitments too many times in the past. But Alexander's statement is interesting. It proves demonstrably that the loss of the kingdom, now just a few years away, cannot have come as a total shock to the West, which had been rather slow to react to the growing threat of Saladin.

Because of the rising powers of Saladin and the weakening of Byzantium, Outremer needed stability. The kingdom could not afford to involve itself in a war and the truce negotiated with Saladin bought valuable time. However, it was at this moment that Reynald of Chatillon began to rock the boat. As Lord of Oultrejourdain, his castle of Kerak stood astride Muslim trade routes between Damascus and Mecca. The sight of poorly defended but richly provisioned caravans passing nearby offered a bait that Reynald was unable to resist. There had been a long tradition of extracting tolls from caravans, even those transporting pilgrims for the *hajj*, who passed near Oultrejourdain, but Saladin's recent conquests had virtually put a stop to this.

An attack on a Muslim caravan en route to Mecca in the summer of 1181 resulted in complete success for Reynald however. Much boosted by this triumphant attack, the headstrong Frankish warlord even considered a move on Medina, which would have outraged Islam, but a counter-raid into Oultrejourdain at Saladin's behest distracted him. At one stage, though, even Mecca had come under threat.

Saladin was seriously alarmed at these manoeuvres into the Hijaz, particularly as Reynald seemed to have obtained the support of local tribesmen in his enterprises. And attacks against the holy cities of Mecca and Medina would challenge head on Saladin's assertions to be the protector of Islam. Having distracted Reynald for the time being, Saladin then sent an irate message to King Baldwin demanding compensation for these flagrant breaches of the truce. Baldwin was unable to force the issue. His protests to Reynald were in vain. It was clear that the King's command was increasingly ineffectual.

Although Reynald's actions were unwise in a politico-strategic sense, he was an outstanding warrior. His raiding took him hundreds of miles into the desert. This shows that he was well organised and disciplined. It also suggests that he had excellent scouting networks. The local Bedouin were quick to sense profit and realised that in Reynald they had a perfect ally: they could supply information and he could bring well-armed troops to the party, a potent combination indeed. Reynald was the perfect leader for this kind of activity. Cunning, ruthless, strong and with an eye for an opportunity, in a later era he might have made a living sailing the Seven Seas as a buccaneer.

This was a pivotal moment for Outremer. A strong king would have been able to bring Reynald to book, which would have sent a signal to Saladin as much as anyone. But Baldwin's inability to control Reynald demonstrated that the battle between the monarchy and the nobility for control of the kingdom was going the way of the latter. In effect, Reynald was acting regardless of the laws of Outremer.

Outremer could only survive if the kingdom was united and the only focal point around which it could rally was the king. But the demise of monarchical power left a vacuum which was filled not just by one man but a number of nobles, competing against each other for pre-eminence. The result was a cancerous malaise, as the competing interests of the high nobles began to eat away at the fabric of Outremer.

Saladin was enraged by Reynald's actions and took his revenge at the first opportunity. A party of Christian pilgrims, 1,500 strong, was forced by a storm to put into Damietta in Egypt. They were all put in chains. Saladin then sought to use them as a bargaining chip and offered to release them in exchange for the goods seized by Reynald in his raid. Reynald had no interest in the well-being of his fellow Christians when weighed against material gain, and refused to countenance the offer. Once more, Baldwin was incapable of forcing him into line.

Rebuffed anew, Saladin decided that it was time to teach the recalcitrant Franks a lesson. War was now the only possible course of action. Saladin gathered his forces and prepared to move on Outremer. Reynald was proving to be a thorn in the side of Saladin, a painful irritant that must be removed. The Kingdom of Outremer was about to find itself embroiled in a period of extended conflict that it was ill-equipped to cope with. It was the first time that Reynald's opportunism had caused Saladin to fight back with massive force, but it would not be the last.

FIVE

The Leper King

Therefore shall her plagues come in one day, death, and mourning, and famine . . .

Revelation 18: 8

On 11 May 1182, the bustling crowds of Cairo raised their voices in exhortation as the army of Saladin marched towards Outremer. The kettle drummers, perched precariously on horseback, beat out their driving rhythms, setting a steady, hypnotic pace, urging the soldiers of Allah on towards their appointment with the Infidel. Thousands upon thousands of tramping feet churned up the dust of the streets, creating suffocating clouds that enveloped those cheering on the army. In the distance, the great pyramids looked on impassively, monuments to would-be conquerors of civilisations and times long forgotten, totems of dead gods and ancient religions. In their shadow there now rode another ruler of ambition, determined to bring the world to its knees and impose the rule of Allah on his enemies.

Many among the crowd must surely have felt ambivalent. As faithful Muslims, they wished Jerusalem to be restored to Islamic rule. Yet, at the same time, they wished Saladin, the Sunni usurper, to fall to earth. That this was, however, a moment of solemn significance was apparent. One voice in the crowd spoke aloud an old poem. Its meaning must have resonated deep within the soul of Saladin as its import was that he would never again see Cairo. And so it was to be.

Some hundreds of miles away, Jerusalem prepared for the forthcoming storm. It is useful to consider something of the city itself at this stage in its history, to capture something of its colour and unique status. It has been estimated that there were about 30,000 inhabitants within the city, making it similar in the size of its population to contemporary Florence or London.[1]

That population was, however, extremely cosmopolitan. The city was taken by the Crusaders in 1099, and any Muslim and Jewish inhabitants who survived the ensuing massacres were ejected. This may have seemed a good idea in the fanatical euphoria that attended the moment – it appeared less so shortly afterwards, when most of the Crusaders, believing their mission accomplished, returned to their homes in the West and demographic disaster appeared imminent for the city, which soon began to resemble a ghost town.

During the course of the twelfth century, the problem had gradually been addressed. Only a few Muslims and Jews had been allowed to return, though some certainly had because they are mentioned in surviving documents from the time. However, there was a huge range of other nationalities present within the city's 4km-long walls. The contemporary writer, John of Würzburg, lists Greeks, Bulgarians, Latins, Germans, Hungarians, Scots, Navarrese, English, Flemish, Bretons, Franks, Georgians, Indians and Egyptians in the city. This was partly the result of a conscious effort by the ruling administrations to encourage people in, for example by the use of trade concessions to attract merchants. It also reflected positive repopulation policies, for example moving some of the residents of Transjordan to the north-eastern quarter of the city.

It is typically the stories of great men that have survived the passage of time and live on through the centuries. Such men were inevitably the wealthier element of society: kings, barons, patriarchs, other important clergymen or burgesses. This should not disguise the fact that the lot of these relatively fortunate individuals was not representative of the majority. For Jerusalem, like all cities, had its poor. It is significant that 20,000 people were unable to pay a small ransom for their release when Saladin took the city in 1187.

But Jerusalem was also the home of a king who lived in a recently constructed palace in the south-west corner of the city. We know little of this building as it does not survive and written accounts of it are scarce, but it was a large residence with gardens to the south. The kings of Jerusalem had initially lived in the Tower of David, Jerusalem's citadel, a huge building that glowered over the David's Gate, in the west of the city. It appeared impregnable and on the occasions when it was attacked directly, proved to be formidable. It served many purposes, for example as a place of refuge in times of danger (the Muslim and Jewish inhabitants of Jerusalem had used it as such when the Crusaders had taken the city) and an observation post. From its highest point, sentries could see an enemy coming from far away. When such an event happened, the populace were warned by a trumpet blast from the summit of the citadel.

There was also a huge transient population of pilgrims. The pilgrim trade has been described as the medieval equivalent of the tourist industry.[2] The analogy is in some ways appropriate, in that many of those journeying to the city certainly did so to see its sights, to visit the places that were sacred to Christians and tick them off a metaphorical list. But the resemblance should not be overplayed. No doubt, like Chaucer's pilgrims, there was a wide range of characters present in any itinerant company, but we should not doubt the spiritual motivations of many of those who made the journey, at great expense and no little risk to life and limb.

It would have been a strange city to many of them, with noises, smells and colours that seemed a world removed from their home countries. Jerusalem was a city of narrow streets, of bustling markets and noisy merchants. Within it was a wide range not only of nationalities but also Christian sects. The Latins were prominent. Known collectively as the Franks – a term applied locally to anyone who came from the West – they ruled the roost. But there were also Greeks and Syrian Christians, adherents of the Orthodox rite. And there were Monophysites, a sect that fundamentally disagreed with the Orthodox Church as to the nature of Christ. These included Copts, Georgians and Armenians.

All these sects had rights of sorts, though the Monophysites seemed to have the better of things vis-à-vis the Greeks. For the latter had traditionally provided the Patriarch of Jerusalem. But when the Crusaders arrived in 1099, the previous incumbent had conveniently died just a few weeks before. This meant that the Latins could install their own man with minimal opposition. Relations between Greeks and Latins therefore got off to a bad start, from which they never recovered.

The complex relationships between the different strands of Christendom within the city are exemplified by the access of rights granted them to the Church of the Holy Sepulchre. This was undoubtedly the holiest site in Christendom and understandably every Christian group wanted a share of it. Traditionally an Orthodox church, it was now indisputably a Catholic one, though the spectacular reconstruction of the twelfth century did incorporate Greek designs, and an Orthodox altar was allowed within the body of the church. The Jacobite sect, too, was allowed a chapel at the entrance, while the Armenians only had one in the courtyard. It was symbolic of the fact that, although many strands of Christendom were permitted, there was definitely a first and second class system in place.

The first patriarchs had tried to claim all of Outremer for themselves as a patriarchal fief, but the secular authorities opposed them. So kings were crowned and barons grew powerful while the patriarch, though influential in his own right, could only look on in frustration as his authority was kept in check. He had his own quarter, in the north-west, but it was but a pale reflection of what he aspired to.

At the heart of the city, metaphorically if not literally, were its great churches. The Church of the Holy Sepulchre, rebuilt in the middle of the twelfth century, was *primus inter pares*. This was the Christian Holy of Holies, a place unrivalled in Christendom, a church that inspired the construction of imitations across Europe. Its very history was a microcosm of the vicissitudes that had beset Christian Palestine for centuries. The first structure on the site had been erected by Constantine the Great in the fourth century, but this had been destroyed by the Persians in the seventh. When the Christians took the city under Heraclius a few years later it was rebuilt, though on a modest scale. Despite the Muslim capture of the city shortly after, it survived more or less intact until the eleventh century. Then, in 1009, the Fatimid Caliph al-Hakim, a man whose life (and death) was shrouded in mystery, ordered it to be dismantled. When he died soon after this a treaty between his successor and the Byzantines allowed the latter to fund reconstruction of the church. This was done on a scale significant enough to impress visiting pilgrims such as Abbot Daniel, a Russian pilgrim of the twelfth century who left a detailed description of the church, with its six entrances and galleries and sixteen columns. He also spoke of its mosaics of the holy prophets, so vivid that it seemed 'as if they were alive'. [3] The altar was crowned by a figure of Christ in mosaic.

The church was inadequate, however, for the increased volume of pilgrim traffic, so a new structure was designed, cleverly constructed so that pilgrims could move around it freely without interfering with the services that were held there regularly. It was laid out so that several Masses could be held at the same time. Everything seemed to be thought out with the efficient processing of pilgrim traffic in mind, a production line of prayer and worship.

The treatment of some of the more sacred parts of the site was strange to say the least. Abbot Daniel described how he was allowed into the aedicule, the tomb chamber of Christ that lay within the church. There was a dome over it, resplendent with a massive silver statue of Jesus. He told how the guardian of the tomb, impressed by Daniel's obvious devotion and emotion in this sacred spot, 'pushed back the slab that covers the part of the sacred Tomb on which Christ's head lay, and broke off a morsel of the sacred rock; this he gave me as a blessed memorial, begging me at the same time not to say anything about it at Jerusalem'.[4]

With guardians like this, it was little wonder that the authorities responsible for protecting the site became increasingly alarmed at the damage done to it. Steps were taken to prevent this from reaching disastrous levels. Within the church lay the Chapel of Calvary, beneath which the rock of Golgotha, site of the Crucifixion, stood. Here, pilgrims laid their cross, carried throughout their journey, as a symbolic conclusion to their pilgrimage. There is a tradition recorded by Theoderich, a contemporary writer, that the crosses were burned on Easter Eve, a symbolic assertion of the triumph of Christ over death.

The range of attractions available to the pilgrim was overwhelming. If, after visiting the tomb and Calvary, he was not yet sated he could also visit the Chapel of the Finding of the Cross. This was built on the site where Helena had discovered the remains of the Cross, along with the Crown of Thorns and the hammer and nails used in the Crucifixion. All in all, it was an incredible site for the Christian pilgrim and it is easy to see how so many of them felt a sense of intense spiritual euphoria when they visited the place.

There were a host of other churches, including that of John the Baptist, those of St Basil, St John the Evangelist, St Michael the Archangel, St Euthymius, St Catherine, St Nicholas, St Theodore, St Demetrius, St George, St George in the Market, St Anne, St Thecla, St Chariton and Sts Mary (Major and Minor). Other important churches stood just outside the city, such as that of the Holy Cross: it was said that this stood on the spot where the tree from which the Cross had been hewn had grown. In all, it has been estimated that there were about sixty churches in Jerusalem, a phenomenal number given its area of only 84 hectares.[5]

One should also not forget the magnificent Dome of the Rock, built on the site of Solomon's Temple and even, in the eyes of some contemporary visitors, actually believed to be the original edifice. It was clear that to many of the pilgrims the building was overwhelming, Abbot Daniel describing it as 'wonderfully and artistically decorated with mosaics, and its beauty is indescribable'.[6] It was originally gilded in brass but the Franks, perhaps thinking the structure outshone the Holy Sepulchre, had covered this in lead. Needless to say, the gilding was restored when the Muslims recovered the city in 1187. But the Franks, while they were in possession of it, installed a group of Augustinian canons and erected a gold cross on the roof.

One of the more intriguing aspects of the Christian conquest of Jerusalem was the way that the two most prominent Muslim sites, namely the Dome of the Rock and the Al-Aqsa Mosque, were treated. In the heat of victory, there must surely have been an urge among the more fanatical Crusaders to destroy them as sites associated with a religion to which the Christians were implacably opposed. But the Dome of the Rock survived, and so too did the al-Aqsa Mosque. Maybe wiser heads did not wish to outrage Islam so much that it united against the Christians, or maybe some wished to insult Islam by converting these sites into places of Christian worship. Certainly, the Franks were well aware of the significance of these holy sites to Muslims as would be shown when the defenders of Jerusalem in 1187 threatened to destroy them if they were not offered merciful terms of surrender.

Turning these sites into Christian places must have inflamed devout Muslims. Given the intense emotion present when Jerusalem was taken in 1099, it is difficult to avoid the conclusion that the Christianisation of these places was purposely done to hammer home the triumph over Islam. The use of these buildings in this manner marked a determined and deliberate attempt to completely Christianise Jerusalem, as is also evidenced by the expulsion of Jews and Muslims from within its walls when the city was first conquered. The Islamic world was well aware of the fact: when Saladin recaptured Jerusalem in 1187 one of his first acts would be to demolish the Augustinian monastery erected in the forecourt of the Dome of the Rock in his efforts to reclaim the city symbolically, as well as actually, for his own faith.

One of the most sacred relics in the city was housed within the hallowed environs of a small chapel dedicated for the purpose. The fragment of the True Cross that had been discovered shortly after the Crusaders took the city had iconic significance for its citizens. Just as the Jews of the Old Testament carried the Ark of the Covenant before them into battle so too did the Franks carry their holy relics when they went out to face the foe. On such occasions, the fragment was given into the protection of the Templar commander of Jerusalem along with a permanent escort of ten men.

As was customary for sacred relics at this period, this totem was placed in a magnificent reliquary, adorned with gold and pearls. The reliquary was described as having the form of a large cross. So precious was it that a permanent guardian was appointed to watch over it. It played a crucial role in the life of the city, and not just in times of war. For the religious significance of Jerusalem was marked by regular ceremonies throughout the year, some of which had the True Cross at their heart.

One of the greatest of these was that held every year on Palm Sunday. The patriarch and other religious notables from the city, along with the True Cross, would gather before sunrise at Bethany. In the meantime, the secular population would assemble at the Temple Mount carrying palm leaves. These were blessed and the throng would then move out of the city to meet the patriarch and his entourage.

The two groups would converge and re-enter the city through the Golden Gate, where Christ Himself had entered the city in triumph over a millennium before. They would then hold a service within the Holy Sepulchre. Important religious ceremonies were held at other times of the year too, Easter, Good Friday, Christmas and in particular on 15 July, which was the anniversary of the city's capture. On this date the citizens would process solemnly to the graves of the martyrs who had died in taking Jerusalem to remember their sacrifice.

This then was the world of Outremer, or more specifically Jerusalem, a world increasingly under threat of obliteration. To face up to this possibility, King Baldwin assembled his forces as well as he could. Urged on by his council, including the troublesome Reynald whose selfish intransigence had brought the invasion about, he took up position in Oultrejourdain in an attempt to block the Muslim army as it made its way towards his kingdom. Saladin, however, would choose the time and place of battle and would not be brought to a premature confrontation with the Frankish army. Instead, he moved out in a wide sweep and bypassed Baldwin's forces. He then made his way to Damascus, the centre of his power, and gathered his strength there. Only when he was ready, and not before, did he march to the south of the Sea of Galilee.

In advance of his projected attack, Faruk-Shah had already raided into Galilee. He had taken 1,000 Frankish prisoners and many cattle. The scale of the raid must have sent shock waves through the immediate region and buoyed the spirits of the Muslims greatly. It was a thoroughly auspicious start to the conflict, and it was a content Saladin who joined up with Faruk-Shah in Damascus. The two men then rode off at the head of the army and towards the arrayed ranks of the Franks.

Baldwin, aware that he had been outflanked, had moved up his forces to face the imminent threat. The two armies clashed in the shadow of the great fortress of Belvoir. The charge of the Muslim armies failed to break the Frankish lines but the counter-attack of the Western knights was equally unsuccessful. Both sides moved back, effectively recognising that the outcome for now was stalemate. But this was not the end of Saladin's plans. Soon after, in August, he struck at Beirut like a coiled cobra suddenly lashing out at its prey. However, even though Saladin had coordinated his attack with the movements of the Egyptian fleet, which suddenly appeared offshore, the walls of the city were strong and the defence resolute. The attackers, though determined, were beaten back and the battle was again indecisive.

Baldwin came to the rescue and, seeing that a force of Franks was coming up to face him, Saladin withdrew. These manoeuvres were an attempt by Saladin to probe for weaknesses in his enemy's defence. Although the Franks were outnumbered their forces were strong and their opposition formidable. They would not easily be defeated in battle but their position dictated that they fight with caution. The onus was on Saladin, as the aggressor and the man not in possession, to win. For now, it was enough for the Franks to avoid losing.

There was another reason for Saladin's apparently lacklustre attempts to overcome the Franks. A more tempting prospect had come into view elsewhere. Aleppo, focal point of power in northern Syria, had stubbornly refused to come under his thrall. The city was given to Imad ed-Din of Sinjar to hold but in the end it fell, not gloriously through conquest but through nothing more than apathy. Imad ed-Din, perhaps feeling that the rise of Saladin was inexorable, simply handed over the city in return for a much less notable fief elsewhere. There was no love lost for him and the citizens jeered him freely as he left to take up his new life elsewhere.

Rather than a sense of relief that the war had come to so little, it should have been with feelings of grave concern that the Franks learned of these developments. The grip of the vice had been turned another revolution tighter. Saladin now had complete control of Syria and in addition had possession of the considerable wealth of Egypt to finance future expeditions. The buffer that had been Byzantium was to all intents and purposes now little more than a stiff corpse, incapable of active intervention should a new Muslim threat arise.

For events in Constantinople had deteriorated markedly. The young emperor, Alexius II, was not yet of an age to rule and his mother, Mary of Antioch, ruled in his place as Regent. She was deeply unpopular: her Latin background did not endear her at all to her Byzantine subjects, neither did her strategy of advancing the interests of Latin merchants in Byzantium. The people mumbled under their breath at first, then began to agitate more openly. There were rumours of plots and conspiracies: at the heart of the most prominent was Andronicus Comnenus, popular, successful and, most of all, a member of the long-lived imperial dynasty.

By August 1182, Andronicus was ready to strike. The army and navy rushed to his cause. In advance of his arrival as he marched on the capital, the mob began to riot in Constantinople. The detestation of the Latin merchants felt by many of the population of the metropolis had been kept under cover while the Empress Regent held sway: now the lid was off the pot and emotions boiled over. None was safe, not even women and children, nor the sick in hospitals. A bitter hatred of all things Latin manifested itself, which was hardly encouraging for the future of the Latin Kingdom of Outremer. A cloud of death hung over the city as a dreadful massacre unfolded.

Andronicus did not so much take power as have it handed to him on a plate. The Empress was thrown into prison, where she was shortly after strangled. Andronicus acted as co-ruler with the young Alexius at first, but no one believed this would last and it can have come as no surprise when just a few months later the latter was strangled in his bedchamber. The boy emperor had been married to Agnes, a princess of France. Andronicus married her in indecent haste and is supposed to have immediately consummated the marriage: the fact that she was a 12-year-old child, over half a century younger than her seducer, apparently counting for nothing.[7]

For those who thought about such matters, this was a time of great danger. In Jerusalem, a policy of thoughtful action, designed to buy time and build up the kingdom's resources so that Saladin could be held off, was a prerequisite. But once more, such a strategy was not possible, not because of any unpredictable external action but because of the Franks' own folly. And not for the first time, nor the last, it was the heavy-handedness of Reynald that made a policy of watchful conciliation towards Saladin impossible.

While Saladin's attention had been diverted northwards towards Aleppo, the sensible action would have been a policy of retrenchment. But such passive reactions were not for Reynald. He saw the prospect of rich pickings to the south while Saladin was looking northwards. His Bedouin eyes and ears were everywhere as his spy network set to work.[8]

The Red Sea was at the time a Muslim lake, criss-crossed by trading ships journeying from India and Aden to Africa and back as well as by pilgrim ships making their way to Mecca. Reynald saw the chance to fill his treasure chests from what he regarded as soft targets. Galleys were built and tried out on the Dead Sea, adjacent to his territory of Oultrejourdain. Satisfied with the results, he then took them across country to the Gulf of Aqaba.

Cross-country transportation of ships was a tactic often employed by the Vikings, and the piracy that followed would have done them proud. Reynald took the port of Aqaba, though the island nearby held out against him and was subsequently blockaded. Then, with the help of local privateers, the pirate fleet set out. The African coast was totally unprepared for the assault that followed, and a rich but unarmed pilgrim caravan passing through the region was decimated. Buoyed up by their triumph, the fleet then pounced on Arabia itself, raiding the port areas of Mecca and Medina and sinking a pilgrim ship complete with its human cargo.

This was a spectacular raid but the sacrilegious nature of these actions outraged Muslim sensibilities. Nothing could have been more guaranteed to harden a brittle Muslim world against the Franks than the slaughtering of unarmed pilgrims in cold blood. A final conflict of sorts was quick to arrive. The Egyptian admiral Husam ed-Din Lu'lu was despatched post-haste with a fleet to stop the mayhem. When he arrived on the spot, Reynald had long gone with his ill-gotten gains, but much of the pirate fleet remained.

Lu'lu fell upon it like an avenging Fury. What remained of the Frankish armada was largely taken. Some of the captives were taken in chains to Mecca, where their ritual decapitation formed one of the highlights of the next *hajj* celebration. The rest were taken to Cairo, where their blood too would stain the dust vivid red. For Saladin the merciful, the offences against Islam that these men had perpetrated were unforgivable. But he knew that the greatest criminal, he who had organised and led the raid, had escaped his vengeance. As far as Saladin was concerned, the battle against the errant warlord was now a personal one.

This made another attack on Outremer inevitable. Saladin made his way from Damascus, backed up by a large force of soldiers eager to eject the Franks from the land they had seized nearly a century earlier. He crossed the Jordan, causing the local populace to fly in panic to relative safety behind the walls of Tiberias.

A crisis point had been reached. Baldwin was too ill to lead the army in person. Command instead devolved to Guy of Lusignan, the most probable next king of the kingdom should Baldwin die in the near future – which seemed increasingly likely. Guy was supported by several of the leading men of the kingdom, including Raymond of Tripoli and the Grand Master of the Hospital. Reynald of Chatillon also took part, along with Balian and Baldwin of Ibelin. Fortunately for the Franks, a large influx of Crusader pilgrims had just arrived from the West, led by the Duke of Brabant and Ralph of Mauleon. However, a party led by Humphrey of Toron was ambushed by the Muslims while en route to liaise with the main army and he was badly wounded.

The campaign that followed had striking resemblances to the Hattin campaign four years later, at least up to its end point. On this and the future occasion the Frankish army launched its response to

Saladin's attack from the town of Sephoria, well provisioned and watered but on the edge of an arid and difficult landscape, well suited to ambush. Almost as soon as they had left the relative security of Sephoria, the vanguard of the Franks' army was attacked by Muslim cavalry. Fortunately, on this occasion the timely intervention of the Ibelins fought off the Muslim attack.

As they advanced, Saladin's force hove into view, deployed across the path of the Franks. The two armies came face to face by the Pools of Goliath, which at least offered water to the Franks. Fierce debate divided the Franks, some of whom wished to attack, the others to remain on the defensive. Predictably enough, Reynald was the foremost exponent for the offensive while Raymond and the Ibelins cajoled Guy to stay where he was. The situation was not easy: Saladin's army had almost surrounded them and food was in short supply. It was difficult to bring up more supplies from Sephoria and only the unexpected discovery of fish in the Pools of Goliath, which must have seemed like a divine intervention of almost biblical proportions, helped to alleviate the situation.

It was here and now that the debates that so affected the outcome of the Hattin campaign were first played out. On the one hand stood the hawks, led by Reynald and pushing for action, and on the other those who wished to stare the Muslims out, led by Raymond and his Ibelin allies. In the middle, vacuous, vacillating, out of his depth, stood the supposed decision-maker, Guy of Lusignan. As contrary arguments came at him from both directions, Guy agonised over what to do. His indecision was made worse by attempts by Saladin to lure the Franks on to a position where his army could deal the deathblow to the blasphemous enemy.

In the end, it was the doves who won. The Franks stayed where they were and it was Saladin who moved. Seeing that the Franks were not going to obligingly walk into the noose that he had laid before them, and short of supplies himself, Saladin moved back. However, despite this apparently favourable outcome, many of the Franks were unhappy. The more aggressive elements of the army preferred confrontation, not containment, as their chosen military tactic. To them, a glorious opportunity to win a famous and perhaps decisive victory over Saladin had been missed. It was the Muslim leader who in their view had set the agenda in the campaign and who had been allowed to march scot-free back to Syria.

It was at this moment that the Hattin campaign was, with hindsight, lost. Guy of Lusignan had not made the right decision: in fact he had made no decision at all. He had merely given in to the views of the stronger party led by Raymond of Tripoli. He received little thanks from the hawks: to them, his actions had been cowardly and spineless, and he had shown himself to be a weak and uninspiring leader. As a result he had much to prove to them if he wished to earn their respect. Such doubts about his leadership ability would come home to roost with spectacular effect four and a half years later.

It has even been suggested that King Baldwin's subsequent fall-out with Guy reflects his displeasure at Guy's indecision.[9] In truth, Guy's actions contrast vividly with the King's victory at Montgisard a few years before. But that earlier battle had been fought in very different circumstances, where Saladin's proximity to a weakly defended Jerusalem meant that the Franks' attack was a desperate last gamble, a death or glory action because no other was possible. Guy's tactics, on the other hand, suited the situation in which he found himself, a defensive action when a defensive action was warranted. The criticism of Guy on this occasion was harsh and misplaced: it was damaging nonetheless.

But at least some time had been bought. The hawks in the Franks' camp had failed to appreciate the reality of the situation: for the Franks, surrounded as they were by a Muslim superstate that had far greater resources than them, ultimate victory was not possible – but neither was it necessary. The onus was on Saladin to win the decisive victory, since once he had done so then Outremer would collapse. The Franks' priority was to deprive him of the opportunity of a decisive engagement. As long as they did so, and Outremer survived, then that in itself was victory for the Franks and a blot on the record of Saladin, self-styled champion of Islam. Such a strategy lacked glory, but not effectiveness.

This reprieve, however, did not lead to much tangible improvement in the Frankish cause. On the contrary, deprived of a

Muslim enemy the Franks once more started to fight among themselves. Guy again showed his ineptitude, on this occasion in the political arena. King Baldwin, failing rapidly, wished to swap Jerusalem for the balmier climes of Tyre, in Guy's own patrimony; but Guy refused to comply.

It was an arrogant and stupid move on Guy's part. The prize of Jerusalem was no mean one, though Tyre was a wealthy city, and cooperation with the King – who would clearly soon be dead – was the sensible policy. But his intransigence backfired badly. It served merely to re-energise the flagging King. Baldwin summoned his barons together and told them that Guy was an unsuitable prospective king. When Baldwin died, his successor was to be Baldwin, his nephew, son of Sibylla from her first marriage.

The fact that a 6-year-old child seemed a better prospect to Baldwin than Guy of Lusignan is evidence enough for the flaws of the latter. So determined was Baldwin to be rid of Guy that he cajoled Sibylla to divorce him, thus depriving him of his claim to the crown. She did not comply and King Baldwin, too weak to move and even to sign his name to anything, was unable to persuade her to change her mind. Baldwin continued to take advice with a view to dissolving the marriage between Guy and Sibylla, but Guy got wind of the plan and fled before he could be interviewed, persuading Sibylla to come with him. He made his way to Ascalon, refusing the summons that the King sent him, stating that 'he would not go because he would be disinherited'.[10] Baldwin decided that if Guy would not come to him then he would go to Ascalon.

Guy showed uncharacteristic decisiveness in his response to this sharp deterioration in his fortunes. However, his announcement that he no longer owned any allegiance to the King was tantamount to a declaration of rebellion. Fortunately for the kingdom, his obvious personal weaknesses meant that all-out civil war was avoided, but it was a close-run thing. Guy shut himself up in Ascalon hoping that the storm he had called up would blow itself out. He had strong allies at court. The Patriarch Heraclius appealed to Baldwin to forgive Guy's foolish actions, as did the Grand Masters of both the

Temple and the Hospital. However, all this served to do was enrage Baldwin still further and he banished them all from his presence.

When the King moved on Ascalon, the gates were firmly shut against him. He strode up to the walls and demanded to be admitted. But the citizens who were watching on were deaf to his requests, waiting to see what the ultimate outcome of this stand-off would be. Seeing that his demands were not to be met, Baldwin left in a great temper. He then moved on Jaffa, Guy's other significant fiefdom in the country, where this time he was received more compliantly and admitted to the city.

The council subsequently held in Acre that supported the King in his decision to banish Guy included Raymond of Tripoli and the Ibelin brothers as well as Bohemond of Antioch. Reynald of Chatillon was not present. The factions were crystallising. The doves, led by Raymond, were for the time being in the ascendancy. But how long this situation would survive the King's imminent death was a moot point. The hawks, led by Reynald of Chatillon, were strong. And they saw a potential ally in this situation. The prospect of a King Guy, weak and easy to manipulate, was very much to their liking. If they could not rule in person, they could govern vicariously through an insipid puppet.

At this council, Heraclius and the Masters of both the Temple and the Hospital attempted to persuade Baldwin that he should change his mind and accept Guy back into the fold. However, the King was determined that his decision should stand. The council had ostensibly been called with a view to summoning military assistance from the West, but the arguments concerning Guy prevented the subject even from being discussed. Unsuccessful in their attempts to convince the King to retreat from his decision, the Grand Masters left the city forthwith.

Guy, seeing that the King's heart was set hard against him, launched a raid against some Bedouin flocks near the town of Daron. Daron was one of the furthest outposts of the kingdom on the road to Egypt, but it was also symbolically important, as it was part of the royal patrimony. The Bedouins were under safe conduct from the King. The raid was therefore a direct challenge to the

King's authority. It was very successful when measured by the prize carried back to Ascalon; but it also succeeded in making Baldwin angrier than ever.

It was in this troubled environment that the King decided to proceed with the proposed match between his sister, Isabella, and Humphrey of Toron. The match would cement relationships between the crown and one of the leading families of the nobility and should strengthen its position as a result. But it would transpire that the young Humphrey, a youth of 17, was another weak and easily manipulated young man, a pale reflection of some of his illustrious predecessors. What Isabella thought of the match we cannot know, though the 11-year-old girl would have had little say in the matter anyway, and before long the teenager would find herself involved unwittingly in power politics of the most dangerous kind.

Humphrey was the heir to Reynald of Chatillon's great castle at Kerak, and the battle-scarred lord prevailed on him to hold the wedding feast there. The marriage celebrations offered an opportunity, in the close-knit world of the Outremer nobility, for the increasingly intransigent factions to attempt to heal their differences before it was too late. Queen Maria Comnena, so despised by the hawkish Queen Agnes, was the mother of the bride, and the presence of so many prominent individuals from either side of the divide offered some promise that the post-nuptial feasting might lead to something far beyond polite conversation.

All was set for a sumptuous affair. Large quantities of food and wine were packed into the cellars of the grim fortress. Musicians practised their repertoire, jesters their repartee and minstrels their songs, some lively, some reflective. An air of unwonted joviality began to warm the cold stone walls, generated by the good humour of the burgeoning population of Kerak.

Most of the great names of the nobility were there to offer their congratulations and, far more importantly, to ensure that their interests were adequately protected in the undercurrent of political intrigue that was ebbing and flowing just below the surface. After all, with the guest list something of a who's who of the nobility, the great and the good of Outremer, this was a perfect chance to build new alliances and strengthen existing ones, to work on the waiverers who had not yet picked their side and to chip away at the position of the opposition. However, the celebrations were about to be significantly dampened by the arrival of thousands of uninvited, and most unwelcome, guests.

Weddings could be spectacular affairs in Outremer. A Muslim traveller, Ibn Jubayr, has left a sparkling account of one near Tyre. He tells how

> all the Christians, men and women, had assembled and were formed in two lines at the bride's door. Trumpets, flutes and all the musical instruments were played until she proudly emerged between two men who held her right and left as though they were her kindred. She was most elegantly garbed in a beautiful dress from which trailed, according to their traditional style, a long train of golden silk. On her head she wore a golden diadem covered by a net of woven gold, and on her breast was a like arrangement. Proud she was in her ornaments and dress, walking with little steps of half a span like a dove, or in the manner of a wisp of a cloud. God protect us from the seduction of the sight.[11]

Ibn Jubayr goes on to say that before her there was a great procession of the notables of the region, dressed in their most impressive finery. She was followed by all the women of her class, dressed in clothes of great beauty and bedecked with fantastic jewellery. Leading the procession were the musicians. The population turned out, amazed at the ostentation of it all, lining the route along which the entourage passed. Finally, the procession stopped at the groom's house where an all-day feast commenced. If Ibn Jubayr was impressed with this particular wedding, one wonders what he might have made of that of a princess.

However, Outremer was a frontier land and that posed its own risks. Although the Franks had brought with them their settlers, the bulk of the population was still composed of those who were indigenous to the region.[12] Within Outremer's borders the general rule was one of peaceful coexistence between the Franks and the local population. Mosques stood close by Christian churches, Muslims and Christians rubbed shoulders as they traded in the bazaars of Jerusalem and the other great cities of Outremer, Muslim merchants grew rich from their activities along with their Frankish competitors. A downside though was that the nature of this coexistence made it easy for Saladin's spies to roam unmolested through the streets and pick up the gossip about affairs of state.

The peasantry, the 'villeins', would have felt no loyalty to their Frankish overlords: they were in effect little better than slaves. The records of Outremer provide evidence of arrangements between neighbouring landlords to return runaway villeins to their rightful owners. Such people could be traded away like any other commodity. An early grant from Pons of Tripoli (at the beginning of the twelfth century) expressly allows such transactions to take place, stating that 'I allow all my men who hold land from me, that if they wish, they may give one villein to the Hospital'.[13] It would not take much to encourage people such as these to act as spies. They might not have access to the corridors of power in Jerusalem, but preparations would have been needed at Kerak and it would have been quite easy to pick up useful pieces of gossip.

It was therefore inevitable that Saladin should find out about the wedding. As well as the lords of the realm, the excursion to Kerak would have involved hundreds of servants who no doubt muttered grumpily about the inconvenience of it all as they drank from their flagons of ale or their rough-hewn cups of watered-down wine. A trip through the desert, the need to cram themselves into overcrowded quarters beneath the fierce glare of the Palestinian sun, were not particularly attractive propositions. Tipsy servants talk freely, disaffected ones even more so, and soon after preparations for the wedding were made Saladin's spy network must have been buzzing with talk of it.

For Saladin, such news seemed like manna from heaven. Kerak was in an extremely exposed position, far away from the relatively secure coastline of Outremer. It was very close to Muslim lands from where Saladin could attack with very little warning. In addition, within its walls there would be the great majority of Outremer's aristocracy. In one fell stroke, Saladin could crush the ruling elite of the kingdom.

To make it even more attractive, the capture of Kerak would also satisfy a very personal drive for revenge against the infidel Reynald. It would not only leave Reynald in Saladin's hands (a situation in which he could not expect to live for long), it would also humiliate him – a perfect combination. Kerak was not so much a castle as an irresistible bait dangling seductively just before Saladin; the wedding offered him an opportunity that simply could not be missed.

It would not be easy though. Kerak was immensely strong. It had been built in its current form in 1142 by the splendidly named Pagan the Butler. Hewn out of solid volcanic rock, its construction offered no pretence at refinement. William of Tyre described how it stood on a very high mountain surrounded by deep valleys, on the site of an earlier fortress that had been allowed to fall into ruins. He tells how, 'outside the fortress, on the site of an earlier city, was now a settlement whose inhabitants had put their homes there as a fairly safe position: east of them lay the castle [it was actually to the south], the best of protection, while on the other sides the mountain was surrounded by deep valleys'.[14]

Saladin pounced on 20 November 1183. Levies from Egypt joined forces from Syria in prosecuting the siege. Saladin's arrival was announced by the sight of hundreds of peasants driving their livestock and carrying what few possessions they could to Kerak, cramming its already overcrowded walls. The garrison was caught off guard. The town around the castle quickly fell to the Muslims while members of the nobility frantically rushed over the bridge that led into the castle. The doors could only be closed against the Muslims because of the heroic actions of a latter-day Horatio who gallantly held the bridge against overwhelming odds while the timbers that supported it were hacked away from beneath him.

The two parties now settled down for a siege. Saladin's mangonels hurled huge boulders against the castle, crashing into the walls, sending sparks flying and splintering into primitive shrapnel that showered down lethally on the Frankish soldiers lining the machicolations. The mangonel was essentially an anti-personnel weapon, which threw smaller rocks than the larger petraries. The prime purpose of the weapon can perhaps be best gauged from one suggested source of the word 'mangone', which is that it derives from the Arabic word *al-majanech*, which can loosely be translated as 'crusher'.[15] In response to this deadly assault, the Franks' archers tried their best to pick off Muslim warriors who strayed within range and out of cover.

But as far as the wedding guests were concerned, nothing should be allowed to disturb their celebrations. So the dancing continued, the food and wine was consumed, the strains of the minstrel songs resonated around the hall and the incongruous sound of laughter proceeded unabated while, within earshot of the great feast, brave men breathed their last, crushed beneath the weight of boulders or their bodies pierced by the barbed arrows of the enemy. It was a scene that could have come straight from the pen of Edgar Allan Poe.

To add to the strange nature of this most unusual wedding feast, bizarre notions of chivalry also came into play. Humphrey's mother (and Reynald's wife), Stephanie of Milly, sent out food from the wedding feast for Saladin's personal consumption. Moved by this chivalrous gesture to respond in kind, Saladin asked that the Franks should tell him in which tower the newly weds would be sleeping: he promised to ensure that his mangonels projected their missiles far away from the spot so that their blissful repose would not be disturbed.

The truth is that neither gesture cost much. The loss of a few items of food would hardly decide whether the castle fell or not, while there were plenty of other areas to act as targets for the Muslim missiles. Saladin could afford to indulge himself in largely meaningless gesturing, since it helped to foster the image of a caring, merciful leader. His actions were a gift to his propagandists. They did not mean, however, that Saladin was in any way not in earnest in his attempts to seize the castle, and it is also very unlikely that the bridegroom's stepfather could expect any mercy if he fell into Saladin's hands.

While those of the local population who were able rushed inside the castle to seek protection, a few intrepid riders dug their spurs into the sides of their steeds and rode hell for leather towards Jerusalem. The Muslim army was large and it was crucial that reinforcements should be rushed up to Kerak as quickly as possible. Indeed, there was a small hope that this serious situation could yet be turned to the advantage of the Franks. By trapping Saladin between the substantial castle walls and the relieving army, the situation might yet be reversed.

Baldwin was shocked when he heard the news. Although by now seriously incapacitated he threw his energies into organising an army to go out and drive the enemy away. Too ill to lead it effectively, he nevertheless insisted on being carried at the head of the relieving force in his litter. Command of the army was delegated to Count Raymond (the fact that he was not at the wedding, incidentally, hinting strongly at the antagonism between him and Reynald). The army marched post-haste towards Kerak. When he heard of its coming, Saladin decamped as quickly as possible, hurrying back to Damascus. It was a marvellous release and, overcome at the gallantry of their terminally ill but valiant King, those inside the castle carried Baldwin inside the walls in triumph.

But this turn of events did little to end the internecine quarrelling of the leading lights of Outremer. Stephanie de Milly insisted that the young bride should have nothing to do with her mother in the future and the bitter squabbles of the Frankish nobility broke out once more. Relationships between the mother and her young daughter accordingly deteriorated. At any event, the marriage of Isabella into what has been called the 'court party' removed another potentially important personality from out of the clutches of their rivals.

It appeared once more that Outremer had seen victory, or at least survival, snatched from the jaws of defeat. Although Baldwin was ill, there was no doubting his commitment or his bravery. However, his condition inevitably affected his ability to govern effectively. The ability of more powerful personalities to sometimes dominate him – particularly for example his mother – naturally enough had negative results at times.

The tragedy was that his gallant spirit and determination suggested that, if he were well, then Baldwin could have made an outstanding king. But that was not to be. The disease that ailed him was degenerative and the prognosis for survival not encouraging. But for all his faults he exercised control after a fashion over the more rebellious elements of the nobility. His prompt and decisive response to Guy's insubordination, for example, showed that he could still exert a strong influence when the occasion required and his health was up to it.

Whatever his actions, there was no disguising the debilitation brought about by his disease. He was badly scarred by the illness, and his deformities became more apparent as the leprosy became more advanced. It attacked his mobility, eating away at his legs and arms so that he could no longer ride and had to be carried around in a litter. He also began to lose his sight, and an Arab writer noted that, by 1184, he took care to avoid all public appearances as far as possible. In an age very different from our own, where disease was associated with the judgement of God, the effect on morale within the kingdom and beyond must have been great. For leprosy was seen to be the mark of a sinner. And given the alleged promiscuity of his mother, the disease was also seen as a punishment for lust; in fact, it was sometimes believed to be a sexually transmitted disease.[16]

It is a wonder perhaps that Baldwin ever became king in the first place. Given his illness, it would have been easy for the barons of the realm to reject his claims. However, it has been suggested that the disease did not become apparent until he came of age, by which stage it was too late to depose him. Another theory has it that his leprosy might have been kept a secret until its advance made it impossible to hide any longer.[17] It is difficult to reconcile this interpretation, however, with the famous description by William of Tyre who tells how he first noticed that the then heir was a leper when he observed that he was impervious to any pain when his playmates pinched him as a boy. Once the nature of his illness became obvious, there were attempts to depose him, some genuine, some existing only in the imagination of the young king who, understandably enough, at times developed a paranoia that plots were being hatched with the aim of forcing him to give up his throne.

In one example, he was so convinced that Raymond of Tripoli was planning to depose him that in 1182 he forbade his entry to the kingdom. By this later stage though, the King realised that he could not possibly survive much longer. He even offered to abdicate but only on condition that the King of either England or France should take his place.

In these great events that were unfolding, it is easy to forget the human tragedy of the young king. His illness was terrible and his suffering great. One variety of leprosy, which given his symptoms Baldwin may well have had, is lepramatous leprosy, a form of the disease that attacks the nerves in the hands and feet and causes great sores. Not only was the disease excruciatingly painful and debilitating, it was also extremely humiliating, since the King's body literally began to fall apart:

> In the face the bone in the nose disappears, the front teeth may fall out and palate and larynx may become affected, thus affecting speech. The hands become paralysed and claw-like and fingers and toes may be lost, thereby giving a 'clubbed' appearance. It is a nasty disease which led to a slow death.[18]

In Christendom, some deeply embarrassing ceremonies took place to deal with leprosy. To all intents and purposes, those suffering from the illness were literally declared dead to the world. In France, during the ceremony held to identify lepers, victims were required to stand in open graves. Adopting the Sarum rite employed at Salisbury, in England, the leper was led to the church and made to kneel under two trestles and a black cloth, like a dead man. Following a Mass, the leper was led outside and soil thrown over his feet. The words 'be thou dead to the world, but alive again under God' were then recited. The leper would then be taken off to a hospital to live out the rest of his life.

From then on, lepers led a life regulated by rules designed to exclude them from society. They were not allowed to touch children. They could not make a will or plead in court. They must avoid churches and crowds. They must only eat or drink with other lepers.

All this applied to 'normal' lepers. They clearly cannot have applied to a King who must of necessity mix with his people, particularly the decision-makers in the realm. But it must have made life very complicated and the King's dreadful disease must have been a terrible burden not just for him but also for his people.

Given his illness, there was no getting away from the fact that Baldwin was living on borrowed time, and that this was running out. The effective deposition of Guy meant that the line of succession was far from secure. The kingdom was entering a period of uncertainty and insecurity at a time when it could least afford it. Flawed though his reign was, given the nature and effects of his illness, Baldwin provided the mortar that held his kingdom together. If he were to die soon, then the entire superstructure of the kingdom could be rocked as if by a violent earthquake. If that were to happen, then the whole edifice might come crashing to the ground, creating shockwaves that could reverberate around the world of Christendom.

SIX

Coup d'État

Be watchful, and strengthen the things that remain, that are ready to die: for I have not found thy works perfect before God.

Revelation 3: 2

The tragic life of King Baldwin was playing itself out to a sad close. However ill, he was determined to do his duty to the last. That meant, above all, that the succession must be resolved and, in particular, Guy must never be allowed to become king. His recent rebellion offered conclusive proof that his appointment would be a disaster. Incapable of keeping the powerful barons of Outremer in check Guy's weakness would make him little more than a pawn. At a time when Outremer needed a king with strength, capable of offering the kingdom leadership and building unity within its borders against the common threat offered by Saladin, his accession to the throne could prove a disaster of the first magnitude.

And so it was that Baldwin drew up his will with the very specific objective of avoiding just such an eventuality. In making a number of stipulations, he was probably helped by the absence of the Grand Masters of the Orders and the Patriarch Heraclius who were leading a delegation to Europe. The seriousness of the Islamic threat had clearly been recognised, since their objective was to draw on support in Europe to reinforce the Holy Land, in terms of both manpower and money. The power of Jerusalem as a symbol to inspire the hearts of men was still strong. A contemporary song encouraged potential Crusaders with the words 'If the Holy Cross freed you, then free the Holy Cross with the sword'.[1]

117

Some useful results accrued from the mission. Large sums of money were offered, especially from King Henry II of England. Henry had always been interested in Crusading and had been raising taxes to contribute to one as far back as 1172; only distractions closer to home stopped him from ever participating. He had originally planned to set out in 1172 and then again in 1176. It was understandable that he was attracted to the concept of Crusading: he had family connections with Outremer and an Angevin had been King of Jerusalem. But his prevarication demonstrates him to have been a reluctant Crusader, interested in the prestige it brought but unwilling to commit himself to the journey and the campaign to follow.

Nevertheless, to many Henry still appeared to offer the best hope of salvation. Heraclius made his way to the King, accompanied by a letter from the Pope urging Henry to support a Crusade. The Patriarch also carried with him the keys to the Tower of David, the foremost bastion of Jerusalem, and those to the Holy Sepulchre. These were offered to Henry, along with the banner of the Holy Cross, at Reading on 29 January 1185. But his barons would not let him leave England for the Crusade, and for his own part he himself discouraged his youngest son, John, who had seemed interested, from setting out either.

Heraclius' mission was in the end far from an unqualified success. He attracted adverse comment from men who distrusted the 'patriarch with the fancy clothes', adorned as he was with the purifying incense of sweet perfumes. One Western writer, Ralf Niger, was so shocked at the impression made that he talked of ostentation 'such as befuddles the brain'.[2] A small point perhaps, but one that hints at the large cultural gap between East and West. Money was raised though: according to some accounts some £20,000 was probably carried to Outremer in 1186.[3]

Neither did Heraclius seem to make much of an impression on the King, who appeared to have held him in low regard. According to Gerald of Wales, who as Henry's chaplain would have had access to such intimate conversations, the King muttered in private that 'these clerks can incite us boldly to arms and danger since they themselves will receive no blows in the struggle, nor will they undertake any burdens which they can avoid'.[4]

Tangible signs of Heraclius' mission may be seen even now. The Temple Church in London, built in the style of the Church of the Holy Sepulchre in Jerusalem, still bears a text over the door referring to its symbolic opening by Heraclius. The stone that is placed there now is a replacement of the original, erected during Wren's restoration in the seventeenth century. It states, translated from Latin, that 'on the 10th of February in the year of our Lord 1185, this church was consecrated in honour of the blessed Mary by the Lord Heraclius, by the grace of God Patriarch of the Church of the Holy Resurrection, who to those yearly visiting it, granted an indulgence of 60 days off the penance placed on them'.

However, few men promised to make their way out to Outremer to fight for the cause. The money would come in useful but, as it transpired, in a way that few in the West would have anticipated and even fewer would welcome.

There was certainly some cynicism in the West about the motives of the mission. Henry II is said to have confided to Gerald of Wales that 'if the patriarch or anyone else comes to us, they are seeking their own advantage, not ours'.[5] Neither was the timing of the mission helpful, for Outremer was then formally at peace. When a party of Englishmen arrived in Outremer in 1186, after the mission, it was to find a country where warfare was absent with the result that many fulfilled their vows at the Holy Sepulchre and then returned home again.[6] In fact, the major signs of war were not on the far side of the Mediterranean but, rather, too near to home. Henry's sons were engaged in a bitter succession dispute with their father and it hardly seemed sensible for him to turn his back on England and his domains in France when matters there were so uncertain.

But the absence of such men as Heraclius from Outremer served another purpose. It enabled Baldwin to draw up his will without opposition from many of the hawks who were so far away. Although the terms of the will stated that Baldwin's young nephew should succeed, it confirmed that Raymond of Tripoli was to be regent until the boy was old enough to rule in his own right; and as it would be some years before the young Baldwin came of age, it effectively handed control of Outremer to its leading dove – a result that few of the hawks would have accepted if they had been present.

King Baldwin was failing fast. By the time that he had drawn up his will he was confined to his bed, never to rise again. He gave the fiefdom of Beirut to Raymond in return for his acceptance of the regency. However, Raymond refused the offer made that the wardship of the King's nephew should pass to him. Ominously, the young child was not strong and there were concerns that he would not long outlive his uncle. In such circumstances, Raymond did not wish to assume responsibility for him. Should he die, then there would be many who would quickly accuse him of murder. Raymond did not wish to be such a hostage to fortune.

The frailty of the young Baldwin also meant that further thought had to be given to the situation should he die in the near future. The King stated in his will that, should this happen, then the kings of England and France should arbitrate on the succession between the princesses Sibylla and Isabella. This recognised something of the strangeness and uniqueness of the Kingdom of Outremer. As a new kingdom with its roots back in the West, Outremer still looked to Western Europe for help in times of trouble. A few decades previously, similar succession problems had resulted in the authorities of the kingdom arranging for a French baron, Fulk of Anjou, to be their king, and other initiatives along these lines were launched at various times in Outremer's history.

Raymond of Tripoli appeared to do particularly well out of the will. If the young king died, then he was to remain regent until 1195 when the arrangement concerning the kings of England and France should be activated. The arrangement offered the prospect of power to Raymond for a very long time, a decade in which the Count would benefit from the advantageous position he had been granted.

The wardship of the young Baldwin was settled on Joscelin of Courtenay, who was soon after building bridges with Raymond. This appeared to be good news. It suggested that the succession could be used as a way of reunifying the kingdom. However, this new-found friendship proved to be cosmetic and, when a crisis point was reached, Joscelin would abuse his position and do more than most to send the kingdom down a road that led to disaster.

Despite Joscelin's untrustworthiness there was some political sense in the move. As Seneschal of the kingdom, he held one of the foremost positions in the land. The seneschal was effectively the king's chief civil servant, his main responsibility being control of the treasury. He also had highly visible ceremonial duties to perform such as carrying the king's sceptre at his coronation. In short, the seneschal was a crucially important person. The role was in fact far too important to be entrusted to someone like Joscelin.

Soon after the terms of the will were drawn up, the delegation from the West returned. They all swore to uphold its terms, including Heraclius and Roger de Moulins, Grand Master of the Hospitallers. As far as the Templars were concerned, there had been dangerous developments recently: while on the mission to the West, their Grand Master, Arnold of Toroga, had died, and in a stormy electoral session, Gerard of Ridfort was confirmed as successor. Significantly, he, too, took the oath to support the terms of Baldwin's will.

Arnold's death at Verona on 30 September 1184 was a seminal moment in the history of Outremer, for it brought Gerard of Ridfort to the fore and with it a fundamental change in Templar strategy. Despite occasional aberrations, such as that at Ascalon a few decades earlier, the Templars were essentially a conservative organisation, even militarily. Arnold was an experienced commander, who had learned his trade as Master of the Order in Spain and Provence. He was therefore an outsider as far as Outremer was concerned, which may have been no bad thing as it meant that he could assume a degree of political neutrality.

One of the strengths of the Orders, especially the Templars and the Hospitallers, was that they could attract recruits from the West and did not rely on local knights to fill their ranks. This enabled them to tap into a large reservoir of manpower. Joining the Orders was an attractive proposition, particularly for younger sons of the Western knightly caste. The Orders offered a mix of military activity and a spiritually based way of life. It was an honourable calling and there was a steady stream of recruits. This meant that even after heavy losses in battle, replacements could be called up from overseas. It also enabled Westerners to aspire to a high position with great influence in Outremer. Gerard was one such man.

The recent campaign, when Guy had led the army defensively, fits well with the prudent approach that a tried and tested man like Arnold could be expected to support. Gerard, on the other hand, was anything but prudent, and his subsequent record, one of largely unmitigated disaster, shows him to be a hothead. As Marshal of the Templar army when Guy went on the defensive against Saladin, he was influential, and we can be confident that he was at the forefront of those who berated Guy for his timidity. Now, as Grand Master, he could dictate Templar policy, both in the corridors of power and on the field of battle.[7]

Baldwin's reign had promised little and in many ways had delivered more than expected. He had led his army in battle when well enough, and he had managed to maintain a truce with Saladin for much of the times, even given the best efforts of Reynald of Chatillon to destroy his plans. But the efforts involved in doing so had exhausted his frail body, and the end was near.

Realising that it was time to prepare himself to die, Baldwin, who was just 24 years of age, summoned his barons to his deathbed. He reminded them of their oath to support Raymond as regent while his nephew was not yet old enough to govern. He even ensured that his young nephew went through a coronation ceremony before he died. The child was so small that he was carried into the Holy Sepulchre in the arms of 'a big, tall man', Balian of Ibelin.[8]

Such a ceremony was unique in the history of the kingdom and showed how dangerous the situation regarding his succession was. Despite his reservations about Raymond of Tripoli, Baldwin clearly believed that his rule of the kingdom would be more beneficial than Guy's would have been. He feared that, on his death, the latter would try to seize power. It was therefore critical that the legitimacy of his nephew and heir should be established for all to see, making it much more difficult for Guy to launch a coup.

This was especially important as the King now found it difficult to trust anybody. His distrust of Guy was clear, but only a couple of years earlier he had been openly distrustful of Raymond of Tripoli. Even now, the royal castles were to be placed in the hands of the Military Orders rather than the regent until his successor came of age; this was possibly a decision based on military realities, but it was a snub to Raymond nevertheless. There are several possible explanations for this lack of trust. One is that this stance reflected the understandable paranoia of a young man who knows he is dying, and who for years has been suffering the most awful agonies and humiliations as a result of his terrible illness. This interpretation sees the King suffering a moral and psychological collapse as a result of his physical decline.

But a less simplistic interpretation suggests that the King was right to be distrustful of all parties. Guy had shown himself to be incapable of uniting the kingdom, while Raymond had appeared opportunistic. Baldwin had been trying to maintain a balance, and continued to do so even as the shadow of death fell over him. This more charitable interpretation of Baldwin's actions appears the more plausible, but the flaw of the dying King's policy was that it would not outlive him. It was his hand that kept the scales balanced: once that was removed then power would oscillate between one extreme and the other until one side triumphed definitively – or until another external power intervened.

Shortly after, the King died, leaving a kingdom in fear of its own shadow, let alone Saladin's. As the end approached, all the important men of the kingdom were summoned to his side. The day after he died, in March 1185, his funeral was held. A great procession made its way through the streets of Jerusalem and 'they buried him in the church of the Sepulchre where the other kings had been buried since the time of Godfrey of Bouillon. He was buried between the hill of Mount Calvary where Jesus Christ had been put on the cross and the Sepulchre where he was laid.'[9] So, the leper king was laid to rest alongside all the other kings of Jerusalem. His presence did honour to them all.

Even the Muslims respected Baldwin, one of them, the Arab historian al-Imad, noting that 'this leper child made his authority respected'.[10] The King's performance had been exceptional. The situation facing him had been overwhelmingly difficult: his death left the kingdom in a parlous state with two rival factions implacably opposed one to the other. Given the horrific disease that blighted his all too short life, he had achieved far more than anyone had the right to expect.

His was not the only important death during this period. Although the exact date of her demise is uncertain, it is known that by February of that year Agnes of Courtenay, his mother, also passed away.[11] At first, despite the fears of Outremer, the succession went to plan. The young Baldwin V assumed the throne and, more importantly in the short term, Raymond took up the post of regent. He was faced by significant problems. The crops had failed and there was a renewed prospect of famine. There was, though, a significant new arrival from the West in the form of William, the old Marquis of Montferrat. He settled down in Outremer and his son, Conrad, also set out to join him.

Conrad was a larger than life figure, an intriguer and adventurer. While en route to Outremer, he stopped off in Constantinople. The city, once the proud 'eye of the world', was a cesspit of plotting and duplicity as one emperor after another vied for possession of the throne. Recent years had seen a drastic downturn in fortunes, which was disastrous for many, not least the inhabitants of Outremer who had once relied heavily on the invisible hand of the Byzantine Emperor for protection. Conrad sniffed an opportunity in Constantinople and decided to stop there. He would not make it to Outremer – not yet, anyway. But his significance to the Frankish enclave was far from over.

Raymond considered that the onset of famine made a truce imperative and a request for one was duly made to Saladin. Times were desperate: one account said that 'in the first year after the death of King Baldwin the Leper it did not rain at all in the Kingdom of Jerusalem with the result that in Jerusalem there was no water and hardly anything to drink'.[12]

The Muslim ruler was happy to oblige. He had problems of his own. Egypt was still quarrelsome and there were rumours of disquiet from the important city of Mosul. He was not yet ready to take on Outremer, not at least until his back was well and truly covered should he launch an expedition against the Christian territories and he therefore agreed to the suggestion of a truce. Trade between the Muslim hinterland and Outremer started anew and ironically it was often Muslim corn that filled the bellies of the Christian inhabitants of Outremer after the truce was signed. In the aftermath of the truce, supplies from the Muslim world flowed into Jerusalem, saving the city from the imminent threat of starvation.

Neither was this the only truce of the year. Saladin had been courting the Byzantine Empire for a while. He realised that the Kingdom of Jerusalem would be badly isolated if he could secure the neutrality of the Empire. In 1185, his plans came to fruition. Distracted by internal problems and much weaker than they had been during the reign of Manuel, the Byzantines accepted Saladin's approaches. The truce bought the Sultan much needed time to strengthen his position inside Islam before attacking Outremer.

The reason for Saladin's willingness to agree to these truces soon became apparent. In April 1185, he gathered together his army and moved towards Mosul. The city's emir, Izz ed-Din, frantically sought out allies to come to his aid but, intimidated by the growing power of Saladin, few volunteered. Before long, Saladin had positioned his army in a tight and suffocating grip around the city of Mosul. Izz ed-Din sent out his mother to plead for mercy, but Saladin had not marched this far just to meekly move away again. The walls though were strong and the defence resilient. A long siege seemed inevitable.

There was one enemy stronger than any other in the East: nature itself. The fierce heat and the choking dust combined with the unavoidable depredations of siege warfare to start to strike down Saladin's armies in their droves. To counteract the growing threat of disease, Saladin took his armies to the cooler highlands further north. Soon after, he himself was taken ill and struggled to the castle of his friend Kukburi at Harran. Barely able to stand, his condition deteriorated. It seemed to all that the great lord, hope of the Islamic world, was dying.

The fading Saladin summoned his council. He insisted that they should comply with the terms of his will and protect the line of succession he had outlined. It was a wise move: Saladin knew that the Islamic world he had created had only survived because of his own personal qualities and those of Nur ed-Din before him. Once he was no more, then he feared, with good reason, that the superstate he had created would quickly fragment. So he made his peace with Allah and prepared for the death of a devout Muslim.

But his time had not yet come. Against all odds, his health began to pick up. He grew stronger once more and by January 1186 the crisis point had passed. He probably never recovered completely: only a few extra years had been granted him. But what years they would be! Years of unimagined triumph, years that would cement the place of this extraordinary man in the pantheon of Muslim heroes. How the Franks must have wished that the reprieve had not been granted!

In the meantime, there had been more upheaval in Constantinople. Andronicus had shown himself to be a cruel despot. He had eliminated much of the corruption that had blighted the Byzantine administrative hierarchy before his coup, but only so that he could secure absolute power for himself. When a Norman army from Sicily – traditionally the greatest opponent of Byzantium – marched on the Empire, panic gripped its people. Rumours of plots took hold. Soldiers were sent to arrest one of those at the centre of the conspiracy theories, Isaac Angelus, the usurper's cousin.

An indecisive, unimpressive individual by nature, Isaac now acted completely out of character. When he resisted arrest, many rushed to his support. He was proclaimed Emperor in the great church of St Sophia. Andronicus looked for help, but found none. Seeing that the game was up, he tried to flee but was captured soon afterwards. Brought back to answer for his actions to the new Emperor, his right hand was hacked off and he was thrown into a dungeon. Deprived of food and water, he was then blinded, the traditional mark of disgrace for deposed emperors.

His subsequent end was truly awful. He was paraded on a camel through the streets in front of the mob, which had first brought him to power and then grabbed it back. Then, in the words of Nicetas Chionates:

> they beat him, stoned him, goaded him with spikes, pelted him
> with filth. A woman of the streets poured a bucket of boiling
> water on his head. . . . Then, dragging him from the camel, they
> hung him up by his feet. At last, after much agony, he died,
> carrying his remaining hand to his mouth: which he did, in the
> opinion of some, that he might suck the blood that flowed from
> one of his wounds.[13]

These events accelerated the implosion of Byzantium and made any help for Outremer an even more remote possibility. And such help was needed more than ever given Saladin's tightening grip on power. His recovery to relative good health had secured success in the campaign against Mosul. Izz ed-Din had sent envoys to his camp to sue for peace. The terms were surprisingly lenient in the circumstances. In return for his submission to Saladin, Izz ed-Din was allowed to keep his city. However, lands to the south were put in the hands of men known to be loyal to Saladin, who could keep an eye on him.

Saladin then took himself off to the important city of Homs, where his son-in-law, Nasr ed-Din, was ruler, well satisfied with the seizure of Mosul. One practical by-product of his success was the addition of some 6,000 men from the city to his army.[14] But Nasr ed-Din had been implicated in a plot against Saladin. No one was therefore shocked when he was found dead in his bed soon after. As honourable a man as Saladin might have been by the mores of his times, he could, when occasion demanded, be ruthless.

There was no doubt that the death of Saladin would have brought welcome respite to Outremer. But it was not to be. Saladin grew stronger and so, commensurately, did the threat to the Kingdom of Jerusalem. And, as Saladin improved, so did the young boy king of Outremer weaken. Never robust, Baldwin V was not destined to see adulthood. Still only 8 years old, in August 1186 he died at Acre.

This was a grave blow to the kingdom, though not for immediately obvious reasons. The young king had never ruled in his own right and would not have done so for some years hence. His death at this stage meant little tangible difference to the day-to-day government of the realm. The real impact was subtler than this: it removed some of the case for Raymond to continue as regent, not legally, as Baldwin IV's will had stated that he wished Raymond to continue as regent in such an eventuality, but in a more practical sense.

It was debatable for one thing whether Baldwin IV had any right to stipulate such conditions in his will. The kingdom, although it generally followed hereditary principles in practice, was legally not the king's property. It was theoretically awarded by election and therefore the high nobility of the kingdom had considerable influence over who would be king. Raymond of Tripoli encountered a number of enemies included in their ranks, men who resented his influence and who had a more aggressive attitude towards their Muslim neighbours. These included Reynald of Chatillon and Guy of Lusignan, the latter particularly powerful as the husband of Queen Sibylla. The presence of Gerard of Ridfort, the new Templar Grand Master in their camp, strengthened their position and weakened Raymond's. In the light of this, Raymond's actions in the next few days were extraordinarily naive.

Raymond was present at the King's deathbed, as was the landless lord, Joscelin of Courtenay, brother of Sibylla, son of Agnes of Courtenay, a man firmly in the camp of the hawks and not renowned for his scruples. Raymond's guard should have been up, but when Joscelin politely suggested that the Templars should accompany Baldwin's body to Jerusalem while Raymond went to Tiberias and waited for the barons of the kingdom to join him there, the latter meekly complied. Raymond was married to Eschiva of Bures, Princess of Galilee, where Tiberias was the major city and the seat of Raymond's headquarters. But it was a long way, in terms of political, if not geographical, distance, from Jerusalem.

Jerusalem was the seat of power and the boy king's funeral cortège would give a ready-made excuse for the leading men of the kingdom to assemble there. The resultant congregation of the hawkish party would be unlikely just to offer up devout and sincere prayers for Baldwin's soul while they were together. The occasion was ripe for a plot and, just when Raymond needed to be there to keep an eye on things, he was miles away.

Raymond's decision would prove to be a mistake of staggering proportions. In trusting in Joscelin, he made an error of judgement from which he would never recover. As Raymond rode blithely towards Tiberias, Joscelin sent messengers to Jerusalem, barely believing his luck. While Baldwin's body was sent to the Holy City in the safe hands of the Templars, Joscelin burst into action.

First of all, he sent his troops to occupy Tyre and Beirut (the latter granted to Raymond in Baldwin IV's will). He himself secured the port of Acre, which, as one of the few safe harbours along the coast, gave control over seaborne entry and exit to the kingdom: if Jerusalem was the symbolic heart of the kingdom, then the port of Acre was its key. In the meantime Joscelin's messengers alerted Reynald of Chatillon of the situation and also Sibylla and Guy in Ascalon.

The hawks descended on Jerusalem for the funeral, circling as if aware that a rich prize was not very far away. Raymond in the meantime had discovered that a major plot was afoot, one which could well intervene in the plan of succession outlined by Baldwin IV. He rode to the castle of his ally, Baldwin of Ibelin, at Nablus and summoned his supporters to join him there. The dignity of the late King's funeral was threatened with interruption from an unseemly civil war, which was unfortunate, since this ceremony was to be of profound significance, though this would only become clear in retrospect. For Baldwin V, a child faced with a difficult and uncertain future had he lived, was destined to be the last Frankish King of Jerusalem to be buried in the Church of the Holy Sepulchre.

Among those present at the funeral was William of Montferrat, the young king's grandfather, the Patriarch and the Masters of the Templars and the Hospitallers. Sibylla sought the advice of the Orders as to what to do next. According to one chronicler they told her 'not to worry for they would crown her in spite of all the men in the land – the patriarch out of love for her mother [after all, the two were allegedly lovers] and the master of the Temple out of hatred for the Count of Tripoli'.[15] They then summoned Reynald to join them, which he did – some accounts say that he was at Acre at the time, others that he was at his base of Kerak.

In the meantime, a powerful ensemble surrounded Raymond at Nablus. As well as Balian, there was his wife, the dowager Queen Maria Comnena (though in theory her remarriage removed that august title from her). Crucial too were Maria's daughter, Isabella, and her husband, Humphrey of Toron. Other important members of the nobility such as Reynald of Sidon and Walter of Caesarea were there with their retinues. Sibylla's advisers suggested that she should summon Raymond and the barons with him to come to her coronation. Instead, those at Nablus despatched two Cistercian monks to Jerusalem to remind the rival party assembled there of the terms of Baldwin IV's will and advising them against hasty action.

But the party in Jerusalem held a number of trump cards. First of all, they held Jerusalem and other major cities such as Tyre, Ascalon and Acre, so that the capital and the major seaports of the Outremer coastline were in their possession. Moreover, they included powerful people in their number. Reynald of Chatillon was there, and the Patriarch Heraclius offered his support. But the linchpins were Sibylla and Guy, since in them the chance of constitutional power rested. They had many supporters, not because of any merits they may have had but because others saw the opportunity to govern through them. A fuse had been lit and an explosion was inching ever closer.

There were also some who sided with Sibylla because she represented the rightful heir. Her legitimacy had been confirmed many years before when King Amalric had insisted on her rights being recognised before he would divorce his wife Agnes. Although the throne was not a hereditary possession, the principle was still important. And, as the oldest child of a previous King of Jerusalem, her claim was, in hereditary terms, superior to anyone else's.

Sensing that this was their moment, the hawks in Jerusalem sprang into action. Hardly was the late king cold in his grave when arrangements for a coronation were made. There is no reason to believe that this was because men like Reynald and Gerard de Ridfort were inspired by the qualities of Sibylla and her rather unpopular husband; but, rather, that they believed they would be subject to more freedom and less censure should they be crowned. Ambitious men of all eras have never taken kindly to strong authorities but have, on the contrary, sought wherever possible to advance the claims of weaker mortals who can easily be ignored once they have achieved a nominal degree of power.

But the hawks also sensed that Raymond would not take this rejection of the late King's will lying down. For it was he who stood to lose more than anyone as a result of the coup. As regent, he would have had a good opportunity to be seduced by the allure of power and prestige. He was de facto ruler while this had been the case, a position that had no doubt aroused the jealousy of many an ambitious individual in the ranks of the nobility. As it was expected he would resist Sibylla's succession, the hawks could take no chances and therefore manned the walls of the city, making sure that the gates were kept shut and closely watched. Nablus was only 12 miles away and there were fears that the barons there would attempt to seize power in Jerusalem.

The support of Heraclius was crucial. The sanction of the Church on any decision was critical in God's city. It was the Patriarch who would preside over the coronation ceremony, who would anoint the new ruler and pour on the holy oil. It was to him that the coronation oath would be taken. In this religious age, divine approval, given vicariously through God's clerical representatives, was of paramount importance.

Some forty years before, the greatest figure in twelfth-century Christendom, St Bernard of Clairvaux, had written to the then Patriarch, William of Tours, in terms that seem to verge on envy:

> The Lord has chosen many people, and of them he has made some leaders, so that they might have the dignity of the priesthood. But you, as a certain intimate favour, he has placed in the house of His child David . . . You alone, I say, have been chosen out by the

Lord to be His own bishop, to enter his tabernacle each day, and to adore Him in the very place whereon His feet have stood . . .[16]

The distance between the Pope in Rome and the Patriarch in Jerusalem gave the latter a considerable amount of latitude. The discretion this gave him was a powerful weapon. Despite this, his position vis-à-vis the monarchy could be an ambiguous one. The King of Jerusalem often interfered in the appointment of clerics far more than he would have been allowed to in the West[17] – a negative impact on the patriarchate of the distance from Rome: in Jerusalem the Patriarch could not be protected as promptly or fully from secular authority as he could in Europe.

The disintegration of monarchical authority in Outremer had presented the perfect opportunity for Heraclius to change the balance of power in favour of the Church, which at this stage was represented by him personally. If he supported the ultimate victor in this *coup d'état* then that fortunate individual would be forever in his debt. It was too good a chance to miss, and Heraclius threw in his lot with Sibylla's party with enthusiasm.

In the meantime, the barons at Nablus wished to find out what was happening in Jerusalem. They therefore dressed one of their sergeants up as a monk, but, when he attempted to enter through the main gates, he was stopped and turned away. Still determined to enter, he persuaded an abbot of one of the Christian groups in the city (the Jacobites) to let him in through a postern gate. Once inside, he made his way surreptitiously to the Church of the Holy Sepulchre and hid himself away nearby to await developments.

The ceremony took place soon afterwards. The Knights of the Hospital boycotted the event, a minor inconvenience in the scheme of things though indicative of the divisions within the kingdom now opening up like major fault-lines in an earthquake. Gerard of Ridfort and Reynald of Chatillon, those two arch-schemers, appropriately enough led the soon-to-be-crowned queen to her appointment with destiny. In the hallowed environs of the church that reputedly stood on the place of Christ Crucified, an act of subterfuge and deceit was about to be acted out.

But it was still important that the proper rituals were complied with. Symbolic acts at such times were important: failure to observe them could subsequently fuel concerns about the legitimacy of the coronation. Even now, as the ceremony was about to begin, there was an unseemly dispute. The royal insignia were kept locked up in a chest to which there were three keys. One of them was held by the Patriarch of Jerusalem, the other two by the Masters of the Temple and the Hospital respectively. Heraclius gladly provided his, as did Gerard de Ridfort. Roger de Moulins, the Master of the Hospital, was however more stubborn. He clearly did not agree with the proposals for the succession and stubbornly refused to hand over his key.

Perhaps this reflected something of the relative moderation of the Hospitallers, who were renowned for their temperance towards Muslims. A contemporary account wrote of the Hospital in Jerusalem that:

> knowing that the Lord, who calls us all to salvation, does not want anyone to perish, mercifully admits men of the Pagan faith [Muslims] and Jews . . . because the Lord prayed for those afflicting him, saying: 'Father, forgive them for they know not what they do'. In this blessed house is powerfully fulfilled the heavenly doctrine: 'Love your enemies and do good to those who hate you': and elsewhere: 'Friends should be loved in God and enemies on account of God'.[18]

It is hard to imagine anyone writing this of Gerard de Ridfort.

However, the others browbeat de Moulins until, in disgust, he threw his key out of the window. This was an act of cowardice. It suggested not that de Moulins was fiercely opposed to the succession but rather that he lacked the will to resist it. Effectively, his actions meant that he washed his hands of the whole business. All of this in the same city where eleven and a half centuries before Pontius Pilate had adopted a similar approach, with even more far-reaching consequences. His actions served no practical purpose. The dusty courtyard was quickly scoured and the key was recovered. The insignia were duly taken out, ready for use. The ceremony could continue.

Even Heraclius felt ill at ease. Gerard and Reynald, having picked up the key of the Master of the Hospitallers and recovered the insignia, had brought two crowns back with them and placed them with all the dignity they could muster on the altar. Heraclius lifted one of them and placed it gently on the head of Sibylla, who now became Queen of Jerusalem. But he would not crown Guy, instead asking Sibylla to choose who should be king. She called her husband forward, saying that she knew of no better choice for the role.

She solemnly placed the crown on his head. At her side, symbolically placing the crown on Guy's head with her, was Gerard of Ridfort, a man who clearly saw himself as a kingmaker. Guy, the adventurer from the West, rose to his feet a king. Cries of acclamation went up and the royal procession made its way with great solemnity out through the sacred portals. Their new subjects shouted their welcomes, but not loudly enough to drown out the comments of Gerard of Ridfort. The Master blustered that now, at last, the insult paid him by Raymond of Tripoli many years before had been avenged or, as he is alleged to have said, 'this crown is well worth the marriage of Botron'.[19] For him at least it was not a case of what was best for Outremer, rather one of what was worst for Raymond.

Gerard has been castigated by many historians over the years. One called him 'an adventurer, and furthermore he was mean, incompetent and arrogant'.[20] The Master cannot have been completely devoid of talent: any man who could rise to his position within just a few years of joining the Order must have had some qualities, even if they were machiavellian in nature. But his casual attitude to the future of the Kingdom of Jerusalem, dictated by petty desires for vengeance rather than any interest in what was best for the kingdom, speaks volumes for his deficiencies and his unsuitability to hold this crucial position at this critical period in the kingdom's history.

If this account of the coronation is true – and its writer was probably Ernoul, squire to Balian of Ibelin, who was of course on the other side in this particular argument and therefore hardly objective – then it appears that Gerard's prominence in the coronation ceremony suggested that Guy owed him a great deal in return. Assuming that the account were indeed accurate, then it makes a great deal of sense in terms of the pivotal moment of the Hattin campaign less than a year later.

The chroniclers could not agree on the details of the ceremony and the events leading up to it. Raymond of Howden, an English commentator, asserted that the leading men of the kingdom insisted that Sibylla should divorce Guy before ascending to the throne. Their reasons were that although his skill in arms was accepted, he was simply not of high enough stock to be married to the Queen of Jerusalem. Sibylla, seeing that she could not become queen unless she agreed, went along with the plan on condition that she was allowed to choose her next husband.

They concurred and the coronation then went ahead. At the climax of the ceremony the Queen was invited to nominate a king. She stepped forward and spoke out in loud tones that:

> I, Sibylla, choose for myself as King Guy of Lusignan, the man who has been my husband. For I know that he is a worthy man and in every way of upright character: with the help of God he will rule his people well. I know that while he lives that I cannot, before anyone else, have anyone else, for as the Scripture says 'Whom God has joined, let no man put asunder'.[21]

Many of those present were reputedly outraged, but were forced to accept the decision. The story, though providing a dash of colour, does not ring true. Surely the leading men of the kingdom would have had some idea in advance of what Sibylla's intentions were? And it is not mentioned in other sources at all. But a more convincing account can be found in the writings of Guy of Bazoches. He simply says that the queen was told to divorce Guy before the coronation and bluntly refused to comply. The nobles therefore reluctantly agreed to Guy becoming their king.[22] Taking the stories together, there are enough similarities to suggest that even some of the more hawkish elements of Outremer society believed that Guy was an unsuitable king and should not be crowned, but that their objections were unsuccessful.

Raymond's spy in Jerusalem now slipped out of the city and made his way post-haste to Nablus. Raymond resolved to gather his forces together and waited for the right moment to strike back. Crucial to his plans was the presence in the town of the realistic alternative to Guy and Sibylla, Humphrey and Isabella. He had strong support from Baldwin of Ibelin who avowed that he had no intention of staying in a nation where such things could happen. But Raymond did not need exiles, he needed men to fight by his side. He therefore asserted that they must all stay together and do their utmost to overturn the accession.

The major stumbling block to Raymond's plans to retaliate was the defection soon after of Humphrey and Isabella. Humphrey, a weak young man who appeared to desire nothing more than a quiet life, slipped away soon afterwards, making a midnight escape to Jerusalem. This was checkmate for Raymond. He had lost his major bargaining chip and his plans to fight back were terminally affected by this unforeseen turn of events.

Humphrey arrived in Jerusalem and presented himself to the new Queen. Cold towards him at first, she soon accepted his submission and then led him to Guy. Humphrey argued that he had taken no active part in Raymond's plans, and so was duly forgiven. He then did homage to the King and was accepted into the camp of the hawks. His actions appear to have knocked the stuffing out of Raymond, who meekly relieved the barons gathered around him from the vows they had taken to support him. Most of them duly left his side and went to make obeisance to the new rulers in Jerusalem. Joscelin in particular benefited from his treachery by receiving the lands of Toron in return, along with an agreement that his daughter should be married to a brother of King Guy.

Realising that he did not have sufficient support to dispute the succession, Raymond's reaction was to withdraw from all involvement in the affairs of Outremer. Soon after, Guy asked him to account for the money that he had had control of while regent, a request that Raymond took umbrage at, giving him the excuse to withdraw from court life. His wife's ownership of Galilee meant that he could do this while still being close to the kingdom and, if necessary, being able to intervene in affairs there should the occasion demand. The position of the principality was of crucial significance, effectively being a buffer between Muslim Syria and Frankish Outremer.

Baldwin of Ibelin reaffirmed his vow to leave Outremer as he could not live under the rule of men like Guy. His brother Balian did not follow suit, deciding that however difficult it might be, he would stay in the kingdom and try to accommodate himself to the new regime. It must have seemed hopeless to Raymond to carry on with active resistance when men such as Balian, fiercely opposed to the hawks, felt that there was no point in continuing with the struggle.

Although it was not obvious at the time, Balian would play a crucial role in the future government of the kingdom. Raymond could never bring himself to submit to the dictates of the new regime, but Balian's less inflexible attitude meant that he could act as a bridge between Raymond and the hawks, allowing some form of dialogue to be maintained, albeit one that was typically strained and often downright antagonistic. But the two camps were at least still talking after a fashion.

A fascinating cameo took place shortly after in Acre. It was here that King Guy, no doubt glorying in his new position, first held court. The situation of this meeting was significant: Jerusalem may have been the symbolic head of the kingdom, but Acre, with its bustling markets and deep-water harbour which acted as the major conduit of goods in and out of the country, was its rapidly beating commercial heart.

The nobility of the kingdom presented themselves here. It was a good opportunity for Guy to assert his authority publicly so that no one should be in doubt as to who was ruling the country now. Among those in attendance was Baldwin of Ibelin, a man who would show himself to be possessed of both courage and a flair for the dramatic. When it came to the moment that the nobles were to pay homage to Guy, Reynald of Chatillon called Baldwin forward. Boldly, Baldwin strode towards the throne. Without hesitation he stated to the King that he had a son, Thomas, to whom he had given his lands at Ramleh. When Thomas was old enough he could decide for himself whether or not he wished to offer his homage for it. As far as he was concerned, he had no intention of making his obeisance to anyone in this court. He would, as stated previously, rather leave. He would be gone within three days.

Then Baldwin took himself off from court, leaving Thomas in the hands of Balian. Baldwin had been offered lands in Antioch where Prince Bohemond was sympathetic towards Raymond and was pleased to offer land to men of experience and reputation like Baldwin. Outremer's loss would be Antioch's gain. Bohemond's actions offer an interesting insight into the state of the kingdom at this stage. Antioch considered itself a separate entity from the Kingdom of Jerusalem and reserved the right to act autonomously. Experience in the very near future would demonstrate that this attitude might be of considerable benefit as far as the principality's prospects for survival were concerned.

Guy could not afford to let Raymond off the hook though. He was a focal point for opposition to the new regime and therefore must be made an example of. He was consequently deprived of Beirut, which had been given to him as part of the terms of his regency, and was commanded once again to account for the public monies that had been given to him while he had been in that position.

Guy's peremptory summons, with its implication that Raymond had not been entirely honest in his use of the kingdom's money, would have been regarded as an insult of the first order. Raymond sulked in the town of Tiberias and brooded over his next actions. Now it was his turn to think of revenge. He had been outmanoeuvred at every turn during recent events and as a result his position had been systematically demolished. He had enjoyed the trappings of power for several years; now they had been torn from his grasp.

The outcome of the succession dispute must have embittered Raymond and left him with an unquenchable desire for vengeance against those he saw as his enemies. For him, the foe was not Muslim: he was in Jerusalem, in the varied guises of the King, the Master of the Templars, Reynald of Chatillon. Raymond saw enemies all around him. So the Lord of Galilee pondered on the future and sat patiently, looking for his opportunity to strike back at those who had deprived him of his prize. He would not have long to wait.

SEVEN

The Tempest Looms

*And the nations were angry and thy wrath is come, and the time of
the dead, that they should be judged . . .*

Revelation 11: 18

The major threat to the truce still in place with Saladin was the
temper of Reynald of Chatillon. His headquarters at Kerak stood
close by some of the major roads north and south, a conduit for
Muslim traffic between the northern part of Saladin's empire in Syria
and its western extremity in Egypt. The caravans that passed by,
laden with spices and other valuable merchandise, continued to
present tempting bait for Reynald. Only a strong guard on the
caravans would dissuade him from swooping down on the merchants
and travellers who passed ominously close to his killing ground.

The truce had been negotiated because it was in the best interests
of both Outremer and Saladin. The hardships brought about by the
recent poor harvests meant that both power blocs needed a
breathing space. But higher political considerations such as these
meant little to ambitious barons like Reynald. The leper king had
found it almost impossible to keep him in check and there was little
real possibility that the new king, Guy, would have any more
success. On the contrary, King Guy owed his position to the support
of men such as the Lord of Kerak. Given the weaknesses in his
character, it was always unlikely that he would prove any more
fortunate than the gallant Baldwin in his efforts to keep Reynald on
the leash.

And so it proved. Towards the close of 1186, a great caravan
moved out from Cairo. It was protected by a small guard of Egyptian

141

troops, ostensibly because of the danger posed to it by Bedouin raiders. These men of the desert were indeed the scourge of the unwary traveller, of whatever religious persuasion. Saladin had found this out for himself when his dejected men fled after the disastrous reverse at Montgisard a few years earlier when the Muslims had managed to snatch defeat from the jaws of victory. But on this occasion, a much more dangerous predator was on the prowl.

The caravan may have felt safe in the knowledge that a truce had been signed, but they reckoned without the avarice of Reynald. One of Reynald's spies got wind of the caravan and the considerable value of the goods that it carried. When the caravan was off guard, Reynald leapt on it, slaying the troops charged with its protection and overwhelming it easily. Those who survived were taken back to the grim walls of Kerak. Reynald made a fortune from the raid – the caravan was one of the biggest for many a year. But he also brought down the wrath of Saladin on the Kingdom of Jerusalem. Saladin's interest was particularly keen because his younger sister was a member of the caravan and had been taken along with the booty.[1]

The Muslim ruler was prudent in his response, acting in a reasoned and methodical manner that put Reynald to shame. This might well have been a calculated stratagem: by his measured actions, Saladin could show himself to be a man of honour and discretion, encouraging support from among the Muslims who, after all, had only relatively recently been united under his rule. His first step was to write to Reynald, asking for reparations – a request to which he can surely not have anticipated a positive response.

When Reynald's reaction was predictably unhelpful, Saladin then wrote to Guy, making the same reasonable request. Guy agreed that the truce had been breached and undertook to broach the subject of reparations with Reynald. But he was powerless to enforce a resolution to the dispute. Payback time for Guy had arrived already. Reynald returned a perfunctory message to the King's demands to placate Saladin, saying that he was free to do as he wished within his lands. He was effectively arguing for autonomy for Oultrejourdain, as if it were a separate principality with the same status as Antioch or Tripoli. Guy's word counted for nothing. War was now inevitable.

By the beginning of March 1187, Saladin had begun to raise his army. In that month, he sent letters to neighbouring countries asking for them to provide troops for a forthcoming *jihad*. Just a few days after he did so, his brother al-Adil led his forces out of Egypt towards Syria. Lu'lu, his favoured admiral, headed with his galleys north up the Nile to Alexandria. Meanwhile, Taqi al-Din moved with his forces to Aleppo, close to the frontier with Antioch. A ring of steel was tightening around Outremer. In the meantime, thousands of pilgrims were making their way towards Mecca, and Saladin broke off his planning for a short time to concentrate on protecting them. He launched a raid against Kerak while a number of his party lay waste to the surrounding countryside.

As Saladin began to garner his forces, the true extent of Outremer's divisions became apparent. Bohemond of Antioch, nominally an independent principality, hastened to seek a separate truce with Saladin. The Muslim ruler was quick to accept. His major argument was with Jerusalem. It suited his purpose not to have to contend with the army of Antioch as well as that of the Kingdom of Jerusalem. It would give him the chance to pick off the Franks one by one.

Much more controversial though were the actions of Raymond of Tripoli. He had of course suffered the most from recent developments in the kingdom and it would be understandable if a sense of bitterness had gripped him, as well as a possibly genuine feeling of foreboding about the future. He also sought to come to terms with Saladin. That he might do this as Lord of Tripoli, again nominally autonomous, was one thing, but the fact that he also sought to include his wife's lands in Galilee in the deal was of doubtful legality. It could indeed be construed as treason. Galilee was part of Outremer and, by entering into a truce to protect it, Raymond was effectively showing defiance towards his king. It was an act of unspoken rebellion that even Guy could not ignore.

Therefore, as Saladin began to gather up a huge force, Outremer, rather than uniting against the threat, instead sought to destroy itself. Gerard of Ridfort was vociferous in calling for action against his old foe, Raymond. Guy responded to his injunctions and led his army to

Nazareth, where Christ Himself had grown up – a most inauspicious setting for what threatened to be a very unholy war. Guy had nothing less than the subjugation of Galilee in mind. He could not countenance such an open affront to his authority and therefore determined to crush Raymond underfoot before facing Saladin.

It was said that Raymond was so alarmed by this threat that he sent word to Saladin, seeking his help. According to the same source, Saladin responded by sending knights, sergeants and crossbowmen.[2] The Muslim leader brought up his troops to Banyas, just 5 miles from Tiberias, to give Raymond very tangible proof of his support.

What threatened to be a disaster was averted by the timely arrival in Guy's camp of Balian of Ibelin. He was about to demonstrate his usefulness as an intermediary, very necessary in the light of the strained internal relations then in evidence. When Balian reached Nazareth he enquired what the King's intentions were. When Guy stated that he planned to besiege and subdue Tiberias, Balian bluntly asked him to think again. Reminding the King that he had already lost the best knight in Outremer (his brother, Baldwin – family pride may have in part inspired this assertion), he remonstrated with Guy, advising him to ensure that he did not also lose the last vestige of support he may have had from Raymond.

Raymond, however, would not consider rapprochement with the King unless Beirut were returned to him, a price that the King felt to be excessive; but he did, however, grant permission for Balian to journey to Raymond to see if he could negotiate further. It was important that a cross-section of the Franks' leadership should accompany Balian if there were to be any real prospect for success. So it was agreed that both Gerard of Ridfort, the Grand Master of the Temple, and Roger de Moulins, his counterpart in the Hospital, would also form part of the delegation along with Josias, the Archbishop of Tyre. Reynald of Sidon was also in the party.

It was, however, a small delegation accompanied by just ten Hospitaller knights as an escort. The relative smallness of the retinue suggests that the Franks did not yet believe that Saladin, or his supporters, had entered Outremer. It was a grave mistake, explicable

1. A Crusader prays, perhaps seeking God's blessing for the campaign ahead.
(© The British Library/Heritage-Images)

2. Crusaders march around the walls of Jerusalem in a religious procession during the First Crusade. *(Mary Evans Picture Library)*

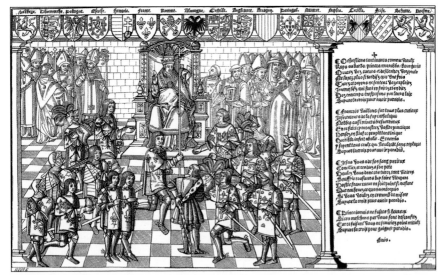

3. The Crusade was a sacred undertaking, summoned by the Church and offering great spiritual rewards. Here, Pope Urban II calls the First Crusade at Clermont. *(The Print Collector/Heritage Images)*

4. Crusader and Muslim armies face each other at Antioch. *(Mary Evans Picture Library)*

JERVSALEM. C.D.

1. Porte de Jaffa.
2. Le Chateau.
3. Couvent d Cordeliers.
4. l'Eglise du st sépulcre.
5. la maison de Zébédée.
6. la Porte ferrée.
7. la maison de St Marc.
8. la maison de St Thomas.
9. l'Eglise de St Jacques.
10 la maison d'Anne pontife
11. la porte de David.
12. la maison de Caïphe.

13. le St Cenacle
14. où les Juifs voulurent ravir le corps de N. Dame
15. où St Pierre pleura son péché.
16. la fontaine de Siloé.
17. la fontaine de N. Dame.
18. Porte Sterquiline.
19. l'Eglise de la Présent. N. D.
20. la place du Temple.
21. Temple de Salomon
22. la porte dorée.
23. la porte St Etienne.
24. l'Eglise St Anne.

25. la probatique Piscine
26. le pretoire de Pilate.
27. la maison d'Herode.
28. l'Arc de Pilate
29. le Chap. de la pasmoison de notre Dame.
30. Simon Cyrénée.
31. Maison du mauvais riche.
32. maison du Pharisien.
33. la maison de Véronique
34. Porte Judiciaire.
35. Porte d'Ephraim.
36. Place du marché.

5. A contemporary Islamic map of Jerusalem. *(Mary Evans Picture Library)*

6. The Holy Sepulchre, most sacred church in all Christendom. *(Mary Evans Picture Library)*

7. A Templar in contemporary armour – an engraving of a tomb in the Temple Church in London. *(Mary Evans Picture Library)*

8. A knight receives a standard from a bishop before setting out on a Crusade. *(Mary Evans Picture Library)*

9. The 'Third Force' in the Middle East: the Byzantine church of St Sophia in Constantinople. *(Mary Evans/Explorer/E.S. Collection)*

10. The council of Acre discusses the disastrous campaign against Damascus during the Second Crusade. *(Art Media-Library at Lyon/Heritage-Images)*

11. The romantic image of Templars sharing all their worldly goods is captured in this modern statue of two of them sharing a horse: in practice some contemporaries castigated them for their pride and greed. *(Author's Collection)*

12. The Temple Church in London, modelled on the Church of the Holy Sepulchre in Jerusalem. *(Author's Collection)*

13. The interior of the Temple Church in London, dedicated by Patriarch Heraclius on his visit to the West to gain support for Outremer. *(Mary Evans Picture Library)*

14. Saladin, the man who reconquered Jerusalem for Islam. *(Mary Evans Picture Library)*

Neantmoit les twis chuallieis
Siffus nommes se tindient sur
leur place les trente tome tout
acomplis et oultre puis sen retour
nerent tout par loisir chascun en
son lieu. Quant ilz furent venue

a pure qui leur furent bonne chie
re ce fut bien raison car moult
vaillamment se stoient portes et
grandement auoient garde lhon
neur du royaume de france come
bien y pure auoit iouste. IIII.

15. A Crusader fleet embarks for its journey to the East. *(© The British Library/Heritage-Images)*

The Coronation Procession of Richard I., 3rd. September, 1189. (Royal. M.S. 15 G. IV.)

16. The coronation of Richard I, who attempted to rescue Outremer after Hattin. *(Mary Evans Picture Library)*

17. Siege warfare during the time of the Crusades – confrontation at Jerusalem. *(Mary Evans Picture Library)*

18. The Hospitaller super-fortress at Krak, one of the few places to remain in Crusader hands in the immediate aftermath of Hattin. *(Mary Evans Picture Library)*

19. Saladin lays siege to Jerusalem: a fifteenth-century image from a history of the Crusades. *(© The British Library/Heritage-Images)*

20. Saladin and Richard I clash: a well-known image from thirteenth-century tiles from Chertsey Abbey. *(© The British Museum/Heritage-Images)*

21. Siege warfare during the Crusades: the armies of Philip of France and Richard of England around Acre. *(Mary Evans/Edwin Wallace)*

22. The survivor: a romantic image from a later age might glamorise defeat to a large extent but nevertheless eloquently captures the spirit of desolation that subsumed Outremer after the disasters at Cresson and Hattin. *(Mary Evans Picture Library)*

23. A Crusader camp during the time of the Third Crusade. *(Mary Evans Picture Library)*

24. In the end, attempts to rescue Outremer only bought it more time: the end came with the fall of Acre in 1291. *(Mary Evans Picture Library)*

only by a lack of scouting and an unacceptable degree of complacency in the ranks of the army's leaders. To have so many powerful men travelling with such a small escort was foolish in the extreme.

It was 29 April 1187 when the force left on its journey to meet Raymond. There was a tragic inevitability about the events of the next couple of days, though the apparent coincidence may not have been wholly accidental. It is quite likely that Saladin's spies knew of the delegation and sought to intercept it. But at any event, the position of Raymond was about to become shrouded in more controversy than ever before.

The very next day, 30 April, a Muslim delegation presented itself at Raymond's court in Tiberias. It had been sent by command of al-Afdal, the son of Saladin, from his base at Banyas. The delegation was treated with courtesy and respect, as befitted the state of truce existing between Raymond and Saladin at that time. Its mission though was a cause of concern for Raymond. Al-Afdal wished to send a reconnaissance expedition into Galilee during the course of the next day. It was a request that forced Raymond, if not actually to cross the Rubicon, at least to draw dangerously near its banks. Raymond's agreement would further enflame the hawks in the Frankish camp, many of whom already regarded him as guilty of treason.

This was a defining moment and one that would probably have caused Raymond to think long and hard. But he felt he had no option but to agree, so he acquiesced. However, he was not unaware of the danger that the raiding party might present. He accordingly sent out warning messages to his vassals, telling them to steer well clear of the raiding party. He granted permission to al-Afdal on condition that no houses or property were seized or damage done. He also insisted that the Muslims should not enter Galilee before daybreak on the next morning and that they must leave by sundown, conditions which they agreed to comply with.

With portentous timing, it was now that Raymond heard that a delegation was en route from Guy to meet him. If they continued with their journey, they could be riding headlong into a trap. Aware of the danger, Raymond frantically despatched riders to their camp to give them due warning. Its import was clear. There was likely to be a large Muslim force in the region on the morrow, and the delegation should proceed with extreme caution.

The delegation had spent the night of 29 April at Nablus. In another tragic turn of events, Balian – who could have used his wisdom to counterbalance some of the more hot-headed Franks – had some business to transact, so he advised the party to proceed the next day without him and he would catch them up the day after. At this stage, the delegation was unaware that a large reconnaissance party would be in the region in less than 48 hours.

It was not until the next evening that Raymond's warnings reached the leaders of the delegation – still without Balian – at the castle of La Feve. When he heard of it, Gerard of Ridfort insisted that the Franks should fight fire with fire. Although Roger de Moulins desisted, Gerard would not be swayed and summoned up the forces of as many local Templars as he could find. The Marshal of the Temple, James of Mailly, was only 5 miles away with about eighty knights and he quickly rode his cavalry into camp. Another forty secular knights, members of the royal garrison, joined the next day at Nazareth.

The small, hastily-assembled army looked for the Muslims. They were not difficult to find. They had stopped to water themselves and their horses at the nearby Springs of Cresson. There were by some accounts about 7,000 of them and if this were true it was clear that they hugely outnumbered the Franks – eighty Templars, the ten Hospitallers in the escort and the forty royal knights: there were also Frankish infantry but they would play no part in the fight. The Muslim forces were led by Gökböri and included forces from Damascus and Aleppo. Considerations of numerical inequality would have counted for nothing with Gerard. God was on his side surely, and in any event, the greater the odds, the greater the glory of victory. Roger de Moulins, still recommending retreat though, was seconded by James of Mailly.

Faced with their opposition, Gerard resorted to the tactics of the bully. He accused those counselling caution of cowardice. He was particularly scornful of James of Mailly, accusing him of being afraid of losing his blond-haired head to the enemy. James replied that he was no coward, as he would prove shortly. He was not so sure though about Gerard. The tension between these two senior Templars was palpable.

The Franks had surprise on their side, but little else. Even if the Muslims had spotted the small army, they would never have believed that they would be foolish enough to attack. But the battle that followed was short and fierce. At the end of the brief engagement, the Master of the Hospital lay dead on the field. So too did James of Mailly, gallantly redeeming his promise of brave action. He had at least died a martyr's death. Before long, legends were growing up around him. Within five years, the following account, of uncertain provenance, was current:

> He was not afraid to die for Christ. At long last, crushed rather than conquered by spears, stones and lances, he sank to the ground and joyfully passed to heaven with the martyr's crown, triumphant. It was indeed a gentle death with no place for sorrow, when one man's sword had constructed such a great crown for himself by the crowd laid all around him.[3]

This account even added the strange detail that one of his assailants was so impressed by the Marshal's gallant defiance that he cut off his genitals in the hope that such a personal totem from a valiant warrior like this would help him to sire a worthy heir in the future.

By James's side fell all except three of the Templar knights, who rode away wounded. Predictably enough, one of them was Gerard, the architect of this disaster. The secular knights were taken prisoner, as were a number of villagers from Nazareth who had foolishly made their way to the battlefield to help themselves to what they felt sure would be easy pickings from the Muslim dead. Instead, they themselves became the easy pickings and were taken away to a life of slavery. However, the squires with the decimated force did at least manage to escape with the baggage before they could be taken.

The survival of the forty secular knights, implied by the account of William of Tyre's continuator, Ernoul, contrasts with the death of all of the Templars and Hospitallers save for the three who managed to escape. Those killed were all decapitated. The savage treatment of the Orders' knights confirms a particular hatred towards them on the part of the Muslim enemy, warranted by their reputation for being fierce warriors. It was a brutal forerunner to the treatment meted out to the knights of the Orders captured at Hattin a short while later.

Increasingly, the battle is the subject of debate. Some historians now argue that the Muslim numbers were probably closer to 700 rather than 7,000. If this is the case, then the view that Gerard's actions were reckless to the point of being suicidal is unsustainable: rather, this looks more like a closely matched battle where Gerard was less rash in launching an attack.

One must not overdo the excuses even then: Gerard was hardly a successful commander and the fact that his small army was slaughtered hardly speaks well of his military prowess. But Muslim chronicles speak of a battle that, though short, was indeed keenly fought. They say that it took place in a forested area, where the heavy cavalry of Gerard's forces could not be deployed to their best effect.[4]

From what we can glean of the battle from surviving Muslim sources, it appears that the initial charge of the Franks took the enemy unawares. Sadly it also meant that their cavalry and infantry were separated, seriously impeding the effectiveness of the attack. Although this initial assault met with limited success, it was not decisive. The Muslims were able to regroup and lead a counter-attack. This resulted in the Franks' cavalry being surrounded and overrun. There was no doubting the end result: a resounding Muslim victory, a crushing blow to Frankish morale and a major fillip to that of their enemies, along with a serious loss of manpower among the Orders.

There was one sub-plot, however, which is worthy of particular note and that is the difference of opinion as to tactics between Gerard of Ridfort and James of Mailly, perhaps representing a clash in views between the aggressive and impulsive Master and a representative of the old school, preferring a more cautious approach. This suggests that all was not well within the Order itself, hardly an auspicious omen with a major campaign looming.

While these events were taking place, Balian had been further delayed at the city of Sebastea, where the bishop persuaded him to stop awhile and hear Mass. After he had done so, he rode off to La Feve as quickly as he could. When he arrived at the camp and found it empty, Balian was filled with great foreboding. The only people there were two sick Templar knights. No one else was in sight. In an agony of suspense, he waited and waited for news, but none came. After several awful hours, he could wait no longer and set out. He had not gone far along the road to Nazareth when a solitary Templar approached him.

Balian enquired as to the news. With laconic simplicity the knight responded 'it's bad'.[5] With a growing sense of horror, Balian listened to his account, of the destruction of virtually the entire Templar force, of the death of Roger de Moulins, of the capture of the royal knights. He was overwhelmed by the immensity of the defeat, and particularly by the knowledge that if he had not stopped off at Sebastea he would easily have arrived in time for the battle and might even have stopped it. He would certainly have tried to.

There was one particular feature of the battle and its aftermath that suggested grave repercussions for the Franks' army if a larger-scale defeat were inflicted in the future. It is notable that when Balian of Ibelin visited the castles in the area searching for their garrisons he found them deserted. Every available man had been taken to participate in Gerard's impromptu attack. All Balian found were two sick knights, too ill to fight. Imagine if all the garrisons across the kingdom had been called out to fight and a great battle had been fought and lost. Who then would defend the Holy Places of Christendom?[6]

The shock of this battle at Cresson was great for Balian, but must have been even worse for Raymond. The reconnaissance party kept its part of the bargain and left his lands before sundown. As they passed Tiberias on their way into Galilee, he had ensured that the gates of the city were shut so that no one could go out to intervene.

When the Count next saw them, twilight was approaching. The Muslims were riding towards Tiberias, dust clouds rising as they were silhouetted against the dying sun. It was not until they were close to the walls that he saw to his horror the heads of their victims impaled on their lances.

In their wake were Christian civilians, bound as prisoners, being dragged away into slavery. A feeling of dread came over him, a sick sensation in the pit of his stomach. Raymond knew at that moment that he could no longer sit on the fence. And, despite his antipathy towards so many of the hawks, in the final analysis, he would have to swallow his pride and cast his lot in with the Franks. He was, for the moment, more than anything relieved that Balian had survived and sent fifty of his knights to escort him in to safety.

Shortly after the disaster, Gerard of Ridfort wrote to the Pope in an attempt to stress the urgency of the reverse. He emphasised the seriousness of the situation in Outremer, which was ironic given his part in causing the problem. As the Pope's subsequent missive to the English clergy, which drew on Gerard's information, put it, 'the illustrious king of the people of Jerusalem, and that noble man, the count of Tripoli, have a grave enmity for one another, and they are thought likely to come into armed conflict unless the hand of the Lord restrains them'. The letter played on the disparity of the forces at Cresson. As the missive states, 'although they had only 110 knights with them, inflamed with Christian zeal they fought against 6,000 enemy'.[7]

Gerard claimed that he had suffered serious losses of horses and arms as well as men as a result of the defeat. The Pope, Urban III, in turn emphasised to the English clergy the onus on them to persuade the 'princes, barons and other faithful men' to respond with positive assistance. We get hints at some of the underlying problems previously experienced with eliciting actions rather than promises from the West in phrases such as 'have such care over these things that something definite is done about it' and a comment in the preamble to the main body of the letter that 'there are few Christians on this side of the seas who aid that land'. Now Gerard was pleading for both horses and men and something ought to be done to meet these requests.[8]

Sadly for Urban, it was all too late. The letter was dated 3 September 1187. Nearly two months before, a far greater catastrophe had befallen Outremer on the field of Hattin, which Urban knew nothing about when he wrote these words.

Raymond's decision to commit to Outremer's cause was the one positive outcome of the disaster at Cresson. There were some important negatives to set against it though, the worst of which was the loss of men. Eighty Templars represented nearly one-quarter of the Order's fighting men in Outremer. These were men who were desperately needed for the major battle yet to come. The death of Roger de Moulins was also a blow, as his moderating influence in the councils of the kingdom was crucial in the current climate. A loss, too, was that emphasised by Gerard, that of horses and arms. Horses were expensive commodities in the medieval world and the level of losses that the Grand Master implies in his appeals for replacements demonstrates that their numbers could not be easily replenished.

There were, of course, effects on morale too, negative in the extreme for the Franks, positive for the Muslims who were cock-a-hoop after their triumph. The battle represented all that was best and worst about the fighting prowess of the men of Outremer – brave but foolhardy, as so often in the past. The reverse did, however, give the Franks an opportunity to learn a painful lesson. They did not have a God-given right to victory, neither were they superior to the enemy.

But the Templars would still be led into battle in the future by Gerard of Ridfort, one of the few survivors of the disaster, and he was not a man to be taught a lesson easily. Perhaps the worst outcome of Cresson was the survival of the Grand Master, who was to play a crucial role in leading the kingdom itself to the bitterest of defeats. But to one writer, the impact of the battle was clear: 'it was the beginning of the loss of the kingdom'.[9]

On the morrow of this terrible defeat, a party was despatched to the battlefield to carry out the sorry task of retrieving the headless bodies and burying them with Christian dignity. All the packhorses that could be found in Nazareth were sent to the field of death, to return to the town soon after with their gruesome load. Balian and what was left of the delegation journeyed on to Tiberias. Reynald of Sidon joined them there. Raymond was beside himself, with grief for the loss of so many Christian warriors and with anger at the foolishness of Gerard whom he held responsible for the slaughter. In all probability, guilt weighed heavily on him too. He asked Balian what he should do. The reply was to suggest that the Count should expel all Muslims from the city and throw in his lot with the King.

In the aftermath of the battle, Raymond rode post-haste to Guy. In an act that must have been extremely painful at a personal level, he paid homage to the new king. The meeting was not in the least acrimonious. Guy, for all his faults, realised that the kingdom needed Raymond and his knights in the army and its councils. When Raymond knelt down before him, Guy lifted him to his feet, embraced and kissed him. This was at least a positive symbolic attempt at reconciliation.

For the time being, the situation appeared to improve. Discussions were held at Nablus. Guy even apologised for the way in which he had been awarded the crown. Raymond seemed prepared to forgive and forget but tempered this with a healthy dose of cynicism about the King's advisers' abilities to act in the level-headed manner that Guy wanted to adopt. Then they journeyed to Jerusalem where great crowds turned out in the streets to welcome their apparent reconciliation. The men took their leave of each other and Guy requested (one assumes that in his new-found conciliatoriness ordering Raymond to do anything was out of the question) that the Count should meet him with his men at the springs of Sephoria, near Nazareth.

Raymond then wrote formally to Saladin, cancelling the truce between them. Saladin did not bear a grudge towards those he respected and was not embittered by this volte-face on Raymond's part. In some ways it perhaps made things easier. It would be hard to dispossess the Count of Tripoli if he were an ally, much easier if he stood as an enemy.

In any event, Saladin had other things on his mind. He had gathered together a huge army, his call to arms being particularly emotive as his objective was to be a holy one, nothing less than the recovery of Jerusalem itself. No longer would the Infidel defile its sacred places: the al-Aqsa Mosque, home of the Templars, would be returned to its former glories and the Dome of the Rock, built on the spot where Mohammed ascended into Heaven, would once again be returned to the use of the True Believer.

Saladin had recently escorted a caravan on its way to Mecca. He then returned to find his ranks swelled by men from Mosul and Aleppo, eager to strike a blow for Islam that would resound down the ages. Never again would Saladin have a greater chance than this and he knew it. Never again would an army this big be under his command. It could not stay long in the field. The rank and file would have lands that needed to be tended and if battle were not joined quickly they would start to desert.

He increased the pressure by joining with al-Adil's Egyptian forces to ravage Oultrejourdain, perhaps to try to tempt Reynald out from his lair. Showing understandable but unwonted caution, Reynald stayed where he was. As a result, he held on to Kerak and Montreal, though most of Oultrejourdain came under Muslim control. But the triumph of Cresson meant that the focus of the campaign inevitably shifted further north. Saladin sent out new messages telling his forces to concentrate in Syria. He arrived there and joined al-Afdal on 27 May. Then he waited for others to join him.

On Friday, 26 June he set out towards his Promised Land. For five days he moved slowly as his spies gathered all the information they could about the enemy. Even at the time, men who witnessed his vast host wrote of it in apocalyptic terms, the historian al-Imad saying that 'the day on which it was reviewed made men think of the Last Judgement', for Armageddon was not an exclusively Christian concept.[10] On 1 July, his massive army crossed the Jordan. The very waters that had once been used to baptise Christ were now churned up by the hooves of Muslim cavalry and the eager feet of thousands upon thousands of infantrymen determined to reconquer Jerusalem.

At their head rode Salah ed-Din Yusuf, an ambitious man undoubtedly, but also a devout Muslim who believed in the divine justice of his mission. To him had been given the opportunity of everlasting glory, a chance to be remembered as the man who recovered the Holy City for Islam. If he were to triumph, it would be the crowning moment of his career and his life. Never again would he have such a prospect. For him, and for the sake of his place in posterity, it truly was a case of now or never.

EIGHT

Eve of Battle

For the great day of his wrath is come: and who shall be able to stand?

Revelation 6: 17

Hindsight may make us believe that the outcome of the campaign was inevitable when Saladin took his momentous decision to cross the Jordan in 1187. The sequence of events from that moment on played into his hand at every turn. But the reality is that the catastrophe that was about to hit Outremer could have been avoided if greater wisdom had been displayed by those responsible for leading the largest army that had ever been raised in Outremer's history. Saladin had a plan of action and it was a good one, but it required that the Franks should act in a certain way for it to succeed; and it was as if the leaders of Outremer went out of their way to ensure Saladin's triumph.

The situation was made more serious still because the garrisons responsible for protecting the towns and castles of Outremer were denuded of virtually all their men in their efforts to raise an army. Therefore, defeat would mean not only the loss of a battle and indeed a war but almost certainly of a kingdom also. Everything was to be gambled on one flamboyant throw of the dice.

Even Bohemond of Antioch, though strictly speaking neutral, sent a contingent of troops to swell the ranks of Outremer's army. This was led by Baldwin of Ibelin, still clearly concerned about the well-being of the kingdom that had caused him so much grief in recent times. By the end of June there were 1,200 knights, a number of light cavalry and perhaps up to 10,000 infantrymen in the camp.[1]

155

Most of the key men of the kingdom were with this huge host and many of the knights: those who owed feudal duties in return for their benefits in Outremer were generally required to serve between the ages of 15 and 60. There was one notable absentee though. The Patriarch Heraclius had been asked to come with the relic of the True Cross but had failed to complete the journey, accompanying the precious relic so far and then placing it into the hands of the Bishop of Acre to carry into battle.

Guy raised as large an army as he could by offering good pay to would-be combatants. For many of the soldiers the campaign was not a spiritually motivated exercise, but was essentially a business transaction. To help subsidise the army, Guy used money sent by Henry II of England to the Templars. Henry was infamous in his day for his unsavoury part in the murder of the Archbishop of Canterbury, Thomas Beckett. The murder of the Archbishop on holy ground in his own cathedral scandalised both England and Europe. For his very unfortunate exhibition of the famous Angevin temper which led to the undignified slaying of the recalcitrant cleric, Henry was forced to walk virtually naked through the streets, being flagellated for his sin, and required publicly to beg forgiveness.

But in order to restore his reputation further, Henry stated that he would go on a Crusade to earn forgiveness. Many errant kings and nobles made such gestures, but, as we have seen, Henry did not in fact set out. However, to demonstrate his good intentions, he sent large sums of money to both the Temple and the Hospital to help in their efforts as warriors of Christ – one of the positive outcomes of Heraclius' mission to England.

There was a certain irony to this. There had been many in the West who believed that little good would come of any expedition to Outremer. God, it seemed, had abandoned the kingdom. Voices urging the kings of Western Europe to desist in any plans to journey eastwards were particularly vocal after the failures of the Second Crusade. One of the loudest of these had been the now deceased martyr and Archbishop of Canterbury, Beckett himself. While in exile in 1169, he had counselled Henry II that the King's involvement in a Crusade would be profitless particularly after 'the most wretched outcome' of the failed Second Crusade, calling such doomed enterprises 'grievous to the Church'.[2] Now, seventeen years after his murder, the money that his martyrdom had helped to raise was funding an expedition in Outremer – the very thing that he had wished to avoid.

The Templars' money would prove useful in raising an army: that given to the Hospital would have a much less martial application, as we shall see. The need for funds was pressing. Outremer was reliant in part on the employment of mercenaries to raise an army. As a result of Henry's donations, some of the soldiers hired with the money would soon be marching into battle against Saladin beneath the banner of the King of England, perhaps around 4,000 of them. There were also a few English soldiers involved, the most prominent of them being Roger of Mowbray and Hugh Beauchamp. The arid Palestinian landscape, baked brick hard by the omnipotent sun, must have seemed a long way from the damp greenery of England.

Guy ordered his great army to assemble at Acre. There was no doubt that the threat was a massive one. Foremost among the troops were the men of the Temple and the Hospital, desperate to avenge their brothers slain at Cresson. But there were also a large number of secular knights, Turcopoles (light cavalry) and foot soldiers both from the Orders and from other sources within the kingdom. One commentator assesses the size of the army at 1,200 knights and 30,000 foot soldiers.[3] Medieval historians are notoriously unreliable at their attempts to give an accurate assessment of numbers, but it was clearly a large force.

The King had a number of key officials who helped him raise the army. The *Marechal* (marshal) was responsible for recruitment but operated within certain conventions. Knights could not fight on foot or in places where they could not be taken by their horses. Some knights were required to offer service if they owned fiefs (though the duty no longer applied if their land was lost). Soldiers were also drawn from other areas: the towns of Outremer, the Church and the Orders of course. If an emergency was particularly extreme a general summons, the *arrière ban*, could call up all able-bodied men.

There were two other important officials of the realm to consider. One was the *seneschal*, responsible for looking after the fortifications of the realm except for the king's own palace. In battle, he usually led the king's division. The *connetable* (constable) commanded the army when the king was not in the field. He played a key role in organising the army on the eve of battle, making sure that the knights and their squires were ready for action.

The army marched into battle behind great banners. A Muslim chronicler, Baha al-Din, stated that the Kingdom of Jerusalem marched into battle behind a particularly impressive standard, 'on a staff as tall as a minaret and set up on a cart drawn by mules. It had a white background with red spots. The top of the staff was surmounted by a cross.'[4] The standard served as a rallying point in battle, in much the same way as the eagles of the Roman legions in antiquity.

The religious status of the expedition that was setting out was reinforced by the standard of the Cross. There were undoubtedly men in the army, some of them Western pilgrims, who were motivated by the quasi-spiritual nature of the venture, having been inspired to make their journey by the self-sacrifice it necessitated. These pilgrims had risen to the challenge thrown down by preachers and poets in their home countries, wherever that might be, men such as the anonymous twelfth-century writer who penned the following tender verse:

you who love with a true love, awaken! Do not sleep! The lark draws day towards us and tells us in its speech that the day of peace has come which God in his great sweetness will give to those who will take the cross for love of him and will suffer pain night and day through their deeds. Then he will see who truly loves him.[5]

Peace through pain was a maxim in tune with the times, as was love through sacrifice. But although visiting pilgrims could be utilised as supplementary warriors, there were never enough men to go round. This is why the kingdom increasingly relied on mercenaries to provide an army. Some were employed on what virtually amounted to rolling contracts, which were renewed monthly and came with stringent punishments for desertion: a knight could forfeit his horse – an expensive commodity indeed – while a humble footsoldier would suffer the considerably more painful experience of having their hands pierced with a red hot iron.

Weapons too posed a problem. The Latins in Outremer never developed much of an arms industry of their own and were forced to rely on imports from the West, especially from Italy. The Italian merchant fleets formed a crucial role in keeping the Frankish states provisioned in arms as well as many other commodities. The Franks also recycled weapons captured from their enemies in the region. At this stage in history, chainmail was still a crucial part of a Frank's armour. Horses, too, would be armoured in mail caparisons.

The infantry used a variety of weapons. As well as pikes, javelins, bows and crossbows they would also use maces and axes, of which a particularly brutal example was the Danish, double-headed axe. The cavalry on the other hand would use a lance and a sword. They also commonly carried a mace as well as daggers and a shield. Cavalry sergeants would typically be slightly less well armoured, for example lacking the mail mittens worn by the knights. In terms of numbers, records from the reign of Baldwin IV suggest that the army numbered about 675 knights and 5,025 sergeants. Including contingents from Antioch and Tripoli, the army could field 1,000 knights.[6]

There were no Muslims fighting on the Frankish side but there were Turcopoles, light, indigenous cavalry, sometimes even converted Muslim prisoners of war. No Jews were employed either, as they were believed to be sympathetic towards Muslims. In the north, Armenians were often engaged as infantry in the army of Antioch, while Lebanese Maronites were sometimes used as archers, though not normally integrated with the forces of Outremer.

The king was nominally in command of the army. In theory he could summon his knights to serve for one year at a time, much longer than the forty days that was the norm in England for example, but this was an empty regulation since the length of service was in practice normally negotiated at the High Court. And the king's authority was not quite as absolute as he might have hoped. The increasing power of the high nobles meant that their voices gained in power in the councils of the realm. In the absence of a strong king this could be disastrous, as the Hattin campaign would vividly demonstrate.

The kingdom did not have a professional army; by contrast, at least some of the Muslim army included soldiers employed on a virtually permanent basis. The closest the kingdom came to a professional army were the Orders, but they were completely independent of the monarchy and owed the king no allegiance whatsoever. This made his reliance on their services something of a double-edged sword. It meant that he could not dictate battle tactics or wider military strategy and instead had to rely on their cooperation. This could not be taken for granted, particularly when the Templars and Hospitallers did not always see eye to eye.

But it is important to recognise that the essential motivation of the Orders was unambiguously spiritual. When a Templar took his vows to God and St Mary, it was for life. He could never desert the Order, though he could be transferred to another stricter Order if permitted to do so, or he might move to the Order of St Lazarus if he contracted leprosy. He could, however, be expelled if his behaviour was inappropriate: this not only meant sinful acts but also carelessness, such as the loss of weapons or horses.

The knights of the Orders fought for God and their Order. They were typically not learned men. A simple Templar treatise published in the twelfth century on the Book of Judges in the Old Testament spoke of the battle to win the Holy Land, which was an appropriate motif for the Military Orders. To some theologians, the world was still in an eschatological phase and the conquest of Jerusalem was a crucial step towards the Last Judgement. The Last Days of the world would be marked by a battle against the Antichrist, whom some saw as Mohammed.[7] Some may even have seen the forthcoming battle as Armageddon itself.

The religious imperative that underlay the decision to become a Templar, or indeed a member of another religious Military Order, was emphasised by the Orders' peacetime attire. Members wore the clothes of a monk with the soft head-cap, which was the sign of many religious men at this time. In wartime, the knights wore a padded jerkin, a *haubergeon*, under their armour. On top of this they wore a long-sleeved chainmail hauberk, as well as chainmail hand coverings and a *coif* of similar manufacture for their head, over which a helmet would be worn. Chainmail leg coverings completed the ensemble. Over their hauberks, the Templars wore a white surcoat to keep the sun off their metal armour: otherwise, they would bake beneath the ferocity of its rays. The surcoat was often decorated with a red cross, the symbol adopted by the Order that showed that they had given up the compensations of worldly life in return for the longer-lasting rewards of a higher body.

Shields would be triangular or kite-shaped in design. A long broadsword would be carried as well as a lance, made of wood, preferably ash and very long, typically about 13ft in all.[8] Maces were carried too, as well as an array of daggers. Some of the Templars carried crossbows, a ferocious weapon with immense stopping power, though there were sometimes concerns expressed about the length of time it could take to load one. But it could be more easily used by a relatively untrained warrior than could the longbow. However, the difficulties involved in loading meant that these weapons would probably only be employed either when the knight was dismounted or when he was involved in a siege.

Sergeants (the name more literally translated means 'servants', which gives a clue as to the often auxiliary role of these men) wore less complete armour. They probably still put on a padded jerkin beneath their suit but the mail that they wore did not cover their arms and that which protected their legs did not cover their feet, so that they could move more easily when they were walking. Nor did they wear a full head covering, but rather a kettle helmet that gave them less protection.

Discipline was crucial to success in battle and, although it was not always present, the Orders in particular could operate in a well-regulated manner. More difficult though was to get the various other elements of the army to coordinate their actions, these being a hotchpotch of what were effectively professional knights and a pot-pourri of feudal levies, who were not. We cannot assume, either, that all mercenaries were in any sense professional soldiers. Although they fought for money, many of them only did so when the opportunity presented itself and spent the rest of their time in civilian careers.

The heavy cavalry were the shock troops of the army, but it is misguided to ignore the importance of other troops. The infantry were critical and performed a key role in protecting the flanks of the cavalry on the march. In battle, they would be drawn up in front of the cavalry, again as a shield against the enemy, and when the time came for the charge the cavalry would make their way out from in between them. Their key role was not looking after the knights – their armour would protect them at long range – but rather their much more vulnerable horses.

The horses were the Achilles heel of the army, for without them the knights were virtually useless. This was appreciated by the Muslims: at one stage Saladin hired 300 bandits specifically in an attempt to steal horses from the Franks.[9] But there were inherent problems in the horses themselves. When the Western warriors first invaded Palestine, their horses were not highly regarded by the Muslims. One writer, Ibn Battuta, listed ten breeds of horse and placed the Frankish horse at the bottom. Known as the *Afrendji*, the Frankish horse was disdained by Muslim horsemen. It lacked stamina and endurance, meaning that if the charge of the Franks' cavalry could be repelled or, more likely, avoided, then the stallions would tire quickly, giving the advantage to the enemy.

The importance of horses to the army of Outremer can be gauged from the fact that over 100 Templar rules applied to them, a number exceeded only by the rules on praying.[10] The army contained several different types of horse, warhorses, Turcopole horses, palfreys, mules and pack horses for example. The warhorses would not generally be ridden during campaign; only when battle was imminent would they be mounted. At other times, even a humble mule would do for transport.

The Western horses were also very susceptible to local diseases, lacking the necessary resistance to fight them off. Attrition was heavy and, although reinforcements were requisitioned from the West, they were never enough to make up the numbers. The cavalry were therefore forced to rely to some extent on local horses, taken in battle or raids, which of course was ironically of benefit if those taken were better than those of Western *Afrendji* stock.[11]

The horses were the forgotten heroes of the Crusades. At the heart of the fiercest of battles, they often suffered appalling injuries from arrows, spears, sword cuts or from the many other weapons used. They were exposed to the elements, particularly the ferocious sun, a problem that was exacerbated by the difficulties in obtaining water. Yet they could show incredible bravery. Muslim records speak of a horse being pierced by the thrust of a spear, which left a hole that was so large that a man could fit his fist in it. In a horrific detail from another account, a horse continued to carry its rider even when it had been cut open and its entrails were spilling out, kept in place only by a tourniquet.[12]

It is important to note that the heavy troops of the Orders composed both knights and sergeants-at-arms. There may superficially have been differences – the former had more elaborate armour for example and also had three or four horses to the sergeants' one – but in practice they performed largely the same function in battle and carried similar weapons, although the latter could if the occasion demanded act as infantry.[13]

There was no doubting the impact of the knights on any foolish enough to get in their way. Usama ibn Munqidh noted the effect on one unfortunate victim of a twelfth-century Frankish knight, while at the same time emphasising the superiority of the medical skills available in the Islamic world to those in operation in the West:

> The Frank struck him with a sword on his face and cut through his eyebrow, eyelid, cheek, nose and upper lip so that the whole side of his face hung down to his chest . . . He arrived in Shayzar in that condition. There his face was stitched together and his cut was treated until he was healed and returned to his former condition, except that his eye was lost for good.[14]

Although there were good reasons for the interaction between cavalry and infantry, reliance on the latter made the Franks much more unwieldy than their Muslim foe. The infantry essentially fought in a defensive capacity. It was the heavy cavalry that was more likely to win battles, but to do so required coordination and an unlikely degree of cooperation from the enemy, who were required to meekly stand there and let themselves be steam-rollered by the charge.

In practice, Muslim foes soon learned their lesson and, when the Franks launched a charge, they were often met by the enemy opening their ranks to let the cavalry waste their momentum, or, alternatively, the Muslims feigned retreat. The Franks in contrast did not learn so quickly. Feigned retreat was often the prelude to an ambush, which some Frankish knights seemed extraordinarily slow to understand.

Writing of events just a few years after Hattin during the Third Crusade, the author of the *Itinerarium Regis Ricardi*, an account which was largely favourable to Richard the Lionheart and which was, in contrast, far from enamoured with Raymond of Tripoli, wrote of the tactics of Muslim cavalry thus:

> The Turks, unlike our men, are not weighed down with armour [he talks here of the light cavalry: the Muslims did have heavy cavalry which was as well armoured as the Franks] so they are able to advance more rapidly, and often inflict serious damage on our forces. They are almost unarmed, as they carry only a bow, a spiked club, a sword, a reed lance tipped with iron and a loose-slung knife. When forcibly driven off they flee on very swift horses, the fastest in the world, like swallows for speed. Also they have this trick of halting their flight when they see that their pursuers have given up the chase. An irritating fly, if you drive it off, will leave you, but when you desist, it returns.[15]

Saladin had clearly predicated his plan around his ability to lure the Franks into a well-prepared trap. He meant to lead them on into the hills where their much-feared cavalry would to a large extent be neutralised. A pre-requisite for this was to find a way in which the Franks could be made to leave their defensive positions, where recent campaigns had shown them to be strong, and force them onto the offensive. It is amazing that, with their experience of Muslim battle tactics, the Frankish leadership contained a number of people who failed to realise that they were being led into an ambush on an enormous scale.

Saladin planned to provoke a response by launching an attack on Galilee. A great army had been assembled at Tel Ashtarah, about 15 miles to the east of Lake Tiberias, at the end of May 1187. On 24 June, a review of the troops was held. It must have been an uplifting sight for the Sultan, with perhaps 45,000 men at his disposal.[16] This was a great host of soldiers, mounted and infantry, rich and poor, motivated by lust for plunder, by excitement, by prospects of glory and particularly by religious euphoria. A day of reckoning was imminent, a chance to right the wrongs visited on Al-Quts all those years ago, to repay insults which many felt had been ongoing every day that the infidel Franks held the Holy City.

They marched west on 26 June, making camp on the first night at Khisfin in the Golan Heights, still at that stage safely in Muslim territory. On the next day, small raiding parties traversed the Jordan and began probing across Galilee. The invasion had begun. But these were just the preliminaries. On around 30 June, at about the same time that King Guy moved his army from Acre to Sephoria, Saladin crossed the Jordan too, this time at the head of a mighty army intent on nothing less than the destruction of Outremer. The next day, Saladin moved right up to Sephoria itself, hoping to lure away the army of Outremer, but they would not yet fall for such a blatant trap. Caution at this stage was still the order of the day.

Saladin's next stop was Tiberias, Raymond's capital. Raymond was with the army at Acre and the town was the responsibility of his wife, Eschiva. It would be hard for the Franks to resist the urge to rush to the Countess's rescue. If they were rash enough to do so, then Saladin would be waiting for them.

Saladin's great siege engines were therefore rolled clumsily into position outside the town walls. The garrison had been denuded of troops, most of whom were now with the army. The town fell easily enough, but a number of the citizens retired to its citadel, a much more difficult stronghold to take. Before a siege could be tightly laid – or perhaps because Saladin wished it to be so and did not prevent him from making his escape – a messenger was despatched by the Countess to her husband telling him what was happening and asking for aid. Saladin surrounded the citadel with half of his troops while the remainder were deployed 5 miles to the west of Lake Tiberias, where they would wait for the expected counter-attack to be launched.

Some commentators have suggested that Saladin was taking something of a chance in his strategy, arguing that he could be caught between the counter-attacking army of King Guy and the garrison of Tiberias. Yet the risk, if it existed, cannot have been great. The garrison was short of men and in no position to cause much difficulty to Saladin's force. In reality, the risks were nearly all with the Franks, who would be forced to march across a landscape bleached bone dry by the sun in the middle of summer against positions that Saladin had carefully marked out as being ideal places from which to launch an ambush.

Raymond had already foreseen the possibility of an ambush. Before the great assembly had gathered at Acre, he had met the King at Jerusalem and asked for his permission to ride to Tiberias and prepare the defences there: permission was duly granted. When he arrived, he stocked up the place with provisions and weapons and told his wife that, should Saladin send a force against the town and it was too great to be beaten back, then she and the main officers should take a boat and sail out onto the Sea of Galilee for protection (if he cared that much about his wife, one is tempted to wonder why he did not take her away with him to safety). Then, in a phrase that his later actions contradicted, he said 'he would soon come to their aid'.[17] When the time came, it was the Count who was arguing vehemently that the Franks should do no such thing.

Meanwhile, at Acre a council was called to discuss what steps should be taken to resist the Saracens. It was Count Raymond who took the initiative. He pointed out that it was the middle of summer, and the combination of the extreme heat and a shortage of water would put the army at a terrible disadvantage should they attack. They should therefore stay on the defensive. This would leave Saladin with all the problems. He would have to find supplies for his enormous army and, when he began to run short, then his army would disintegrate.

Though not exactly glorious, it was sound advice and many of the knights in the camp were inclined to support it. After all, the strategy was very similar to the one successfully adopted when Saladin had last invaded. But it was not an approach that met with the approval of either Reynald or Gerard. Embittered by their differences of opinion with Raymond, they virtually accused him of being in league with Saladin. In a phrase that equated the Count with a duplicitous scoundrel, they said that his advice was 'mingled with the hair of the wolf'.[18] It was the first accusation of treachery to blight the campaign but it was far from being the last. It also graphically demonstrated that any reconciliation between Guy and Raymond was certainly not supported by the hawks with the army.

At any event, King Guy agreed with the views of Gerard and Reynald and gave orders that the army was to march out forthwith. The great host moved cumbersomely over to Sephoria. This was a spot where the king's army often assembled prior to a campaign in Galilee or on the frontiers of Damascus.[19] To pass beyond here was to pass the point of no return. Here there was water and pasture for the army and the horses. It was also a good defensive position. If the army were to stay put, then Saladin would be forced to attack. The armies were not hopelessly mismatched in terms of their size and Saladin would have needed a large numerical advantage to feel confident of victory should he go on the offensive.

Camp was accordingly set up at Sephoria. The *gonfanier* of the Templars called on the knights of his Order to make camp, in the centre of which a chapel tent was erected, and next to this the marshal pitched his pavilion. The brothers built up their encampment around this central point. The chapel tent was crucial. Its purpose was not just spiritual: if the camp were attacked during the night then this was the place where the brethren would gather to get their orders. Elsewhere, the profane soldiery found a place to sleep for the night, the wealthier in their pavilions, the mundane rank and file with much less glamorous surroundings.

The army settled down for the night. Cooks in mess tents dished out victuals to the army. It was not yet certain what tomorrow would bring, but all this was about to change. According to some accounts, it was now that messengers from Eschiva arrived (others say that the army was still at Acre when this happened). They told the King and his nobles of the parlous position that the Countess was currently in. The size of Saladin's army meant that it was only a matter of time before Tiberias fell unless a relieving force were sent at once.

This unsettling missive had a seminal effect on the mood of the camp. Many men felt that it would be wrong to leave the Countess on her own. Her sons, reportedly with tears in their eyes, begged that the army should rush to the aid of their mother. Raymond, however, sensing that the mood of the argument was turning against him, pleaded with even greater passion that the army should stay put. No one had better reason than he for going to the aid of his wife. But to do so would be playing straight into Saladin's hands. He possibly thought to himself that, even if Tiberias were to fall, his wife would be well treated by Saladin and could soon be ransomed.

There were good reasons for listening to Raymond. This was after all his land, his country, and he knew its terrain better than most. He knew that, after Sephoria, watering places were few and far between. The country through which the army must march if it went to the aid of Tiberias was not quite desert but, at the height of the Palestinian summer, was little better. There were simply too few places in which the men could refill their water pouches and those that did exist could not provide supplies for this many men. On the other hand, Saladin was close to water and could thus keep his men supplied. Again, the advantage if the Franks were to attack must lie with Saladin, who not only had supplies to hand but could also decide where and when to launch his counter-offensive against the soldiers of Christ.

That the town would fall unless help came quickly seemed inevitable. With its back against the lake, it was surrounded on all other sides by the Muslim host. As one Islamic writer, Ibn Athir, put it, 'The Sultan's army surrounded Lake Tiberias like the ocean, and great plains vanished beneath their spreading tents.'[20]

But Raymond doubted the ability of Saladin to hold Tiberias. His army was bound to disintegrate if a quick triumph was not forthcoming. Men would hurry back home to garner the crops or raise taxes; ironic, since these would be paid to Saladin, who could not have his cake and eat it. The best he could do was destroy the walls and make the town indefensible. And if he did so, then the walls could be rebuilt. It would be unfortunate if his wife were taken, but Raymond believed she would soon be freed. If not a glamorous solution, it does at least suggest that the Count had the kingdom's best interests at heart.

Raymond's proposals were not that the Franks should stay where they were but that they should instead move back towards Acre. Should they be beaten in battle, they could shelter behind the substantial walls of the city and live to fight another day. Many disagreed with this advice and were especially uncomfortable at the thought of leaving the Countess and her female attendants to their fate. Such a move was hardly in keeping with the then evolving traditions of chivalry. But it may have been perfectly good military sense for all that.

It seems that the debate was indecisive because in the evening the King ordered that it should be resumed. Raymond reiterated his arguments. He referred specifically to the great size of Saladin's army and the relative smallness of Guy's, which would not in his view be strong enough to defeat the Muslims. Raymond's entreaties had the desired effect. The army resolved to stay on the defensive. The conversation was heated, but Raymond this time appeared to have won the day. It was late, well on towards midnight, when the council broke up, having made the decision to stay at Sephoria.

King Guy retired to his pavilion. In the background, however, was a menacing figure. Gerard of Ridfort was no friend of Raymond, neither was he in awe of Saladin. To him, the proceedings of the evening smacked of unnecessary caution, cowardice even. Making his way into the tent, he launched a blistering verbal assault on the conclusions drawn as a result of the evening's deliberations.

Although eyewitnesses to the discussions were in short supply, the chroniclers' accounts of the conversations suggest that Gerard made great play on the dishonour that abandoning Eschiva would cause to fall on the army. Not only was she a noble woman in every sense of the word, she was also a vassal whom the King had pledged to defend from her enemies. Further, it would heap shame on the forces of Christendom were no positive action to be taken to defeat Saladin. It showed a lack of belief in the support of the Almighty and in his power to give the victory to the righteous, just as he had to the great men of Old Testament history, like Joshua and Gideon, when the odds were stacked against them.

When considering the effect of Gerard's bombast on Guy, it is important to remember the position of the King. Although his leadership of the army in a defensive campaign a few years before had been successful, there had been a number of the more hawkish members of Outremer society who had criticised him for it. Further, Guy was newly a king, eager to prove himself in his first major campaign since his coronation. He was also in hock to men such as Gerard and Reynald. And, to cap it all, he was weak and easily bullied. The combination of Guy's insecure political position and flawed character was to prove a devastating combination when faced with the bluster and aggression of the Grand Master of the Templars.

There was also the link between Guy's coronation and Gerard's support to consider. It was the Master as well as the Queen who had placed the crown on his head during the service. The implication at the time was clear: 'you are king because I say so'. Now it was time to remember that debt and to start to repay it.

The effect of Gerard's onslaught was electrifying. Within an hour of deciding that the army should stay at Sephoria, the King had completely changed his mind. At the break of day, the army would set out to confront Saladin in open battle. It was a momentous decision with momentous consequences. Guy retired to try to get a few hours fitful repose before leading the army of God into battle. However disturbed his sleep might have been, the horrors of this particular night would pale into significance compared to those of the one that was to follow.

As is often the case, contemporary chroniclers writing of these matters like to refer to a miracle to show divine approval or otherwise of an enterprise. Ernoul, Balian of Ibelin's squire and a man well acquainted with horses, had apparently noticed something strange. During the day, the heat had been suffocating. Despite this, when the horses reached Sephoria, where there were plentiful water supplies, they had shown no desire to drink. Instead, they stood with sad and sorrowing faces, refusing to take on liquid, with the result that on the morrow they would collapse under the blaze of the ferocious sun. Even the horses it seems did not trust the King to make the right decision.

NINE

The Road to Armageddon

*And he called them together into a place called in the Hebrew
tongue Armageddon.*

Revelation 16: 16

News of the change in plans swept through the camp like a bush
fire. The shouts of sergeants resonated through the pre-dawn
air, startling men from sleep. Given the fact that the change in orders
occurred at midnight, it is likely that it was around four in the
morning when the camp stirred itself into life.[1]

The infantrymen shook themselves, gingerly arising from their
rock-hard earthen mattress, while cavalrymen urged their squires to
ensure that their horses were made ready. There would surely have
been a mix of emotions present, with some exhilarated at the chance
to close with the enemy, to slay the Infidel and to deprive him of his
earthly possessions, and others feeling the cold hand of fear on their
shoulders. Battles were dangerous, men were killed and it might be
their turn today.

Those who knew the country through which they were to
progress would have shivered in apprehension of what lay ahead.
They were about to march through an arid, sun-dried region with
limited water, where there were many valleys and dried-up wadis, or
riverbeds, to impede smooth progress. There would be few hiding
places from the assaults of the sun. The plateau stood about 1,000ft
above sea level: Tiberias, their destination, nearly 700ft below, a
drop of nearly 2,000ft in total.

The route decided upon would take the army to Tiberias via Casal
Robert to the south, from where they would swing north-east to join

the main road to Touraan. There was a small spring here and the chance of revictualling. Then they could push on to Tiberias via one of two roads: the main one passed directly through Saladin's main army, which was camped at Cafarsset right across its path, or a less substantial track that ran via two adjacent hills known as the Horns of Hattin.

Everywhere in the camp the sound of prayer could be heard. This was a religious campaign, as evidenced by the presence of the fragment of the True Cross, and there were many priests in the retinue who were much needed now. They were perhaps the busiest people in the camp. Men confessed their sins to them, asked for forgiveness and prayed that, if they were to die, it might be in a state of grace so that God would accept them into His kingdom as martyrs. No empty ritual this but deeply felt prayers from men who might be facing their last day in this world. It was important that they died well, fully shriven (that is, properly confessed), so that their passage into Heaven might be eased.

And what of the men who were to lead the army? What were their emotions? To Raymond, the news of the change in plans must have been a profound shock. He had gone to his tent the night before convinced that the kingdom was in good shape, that a defensive campaign was to be fought with an excellent chance of success. Now he learned that an attack was to be made after all, one fraught with danger. An experienced warrior, he knew that this was the very battle that Saladin sought, that Saladin's prayers had been answered. All the advantages were with Saladin, and Raymond knew it.

And surely less altruistic thoughts entered his mind, too. The Lord of Tripoli and Tiberias was a proud man, one who was used to having his council followed. For years, he had been regent or chief adviser to the king. But recent times had seen his star plummet from the sky, a meteor that had once flamed brightly now burning itself out. Raymond knew that Gerard was responsible. Perhaps he reflected ruefully on the vendetta that had scarred the political landscape for too long now. But we can also assume that, not only did Raymond detest Gerard on a personal level, he also genuinely believed his influence to be a disaster for Outremer. Just how disastrous would become clear within the day.

The reverse was true for Gerard of course. In terms of tactics, no one could accuse the Master of being inconsistent. His urge to go on the offensive had created the disaster at Cresson a month before and his advice now had been exactly the same as then. Attack seemed to be the only maxim that he knew. His blunt and inflexible approach to warfare would never change. It would eventually cost him his life. But too late, far too late.

For other hawks, like Reynald, there would also have been contentment that a decisive confrontation was to be sought. For such men there was an inner certainty that the battle would be won and the enemies of Christ swept from the field. This sort of self-confidence is hard to understand in the cynical world of today, but it was a genuine state of mind then, not inspired solely by arrogance but also by a confidence in the support of a greater being who would surely give His people victory, whatever the strength of the enemy.

The most confused man of all though must have been the King. He had allowed himself to be talked into this change of heart, and in his vacillation we may sense not only weakness but also uncertainty. The responsibility accorded to him was indeed immense, for on the outcome of this expedition rested not only the success of the campaign but the survival of an entire way of life. In this situation, every decision would come under a microscope, every action would be subject to criticism. Herein lies the key to Guy's actions: he was a man who not only wanted to please everyone but really did not know what to do for the best.

Here also was someone whose personality was Lilliputian compared to the giants who surrounded him. Gerard and Reynald, not to mention Raymond, towered over him, dominating his decision-making to such an extent that the final resolution of crucial conversations was not his at all, but theirs. Raymond believed that Guy was patently not up to the task he had assumed. In this, if in nothing else, he was right.

For Saladin, the news of the decision to relieve Tiberias must have seemed like a gift from Allah. He would have had his spies inside the

Franks' camp, who would have managed to smuggle word of the change of plans to their compatriots without. At any event, he would have positioned his scouts to keep watch over the camp and as soon as the Franks started marching along the dusty road to Tiberias he would have known all about it.

The composition of his army was very different from that of the forces of Outremer. It was composed substantially of three different ethnic groupings, each with their own style of weapons and tactics. The largest group was made up of Turks, who were renowned for their skill as cavalry archers. The Turks' forces were in fact almost exclusively cavalry, as befitted a people who were largely nomadic. They had thousands of horses in their herds and, when they needed one, they would ride up with a lasso on a long stick and catch one round the neck.

Next came the Kurds, who fought principally as cavalry and archers, though they do not seem to have employed the same mounted archer tactics of the Turks. There were Arabs too. They were famed for the magnificence of their horses and usually fought with spear and sword. The Bedouin were widely mistrusted. Their nomadic ways sat uncomfortably with the many city dwellers in the Islamic forces.

Although the Muslim army was mainly a professional one, on a number of occasions religious volunteers, *muttawiyah*, took part, and they would play a significant role in the events of the Hattin campaign. They were zealous and enthusiastic but they were also difficult to control. If discipline was not imposed upon them, they could be more of a hindrance than a help. However, if they could be kept under control then they had a valuable role to play, particularly with regard to the harassment of enemy stragglers.

The army was divided into various groups. The smallest company, the *jarida*, consisted of about seventy men. The *tulb*, with up to 200 men, was the next unit. It had its own flag and also a trumpeter: the combination of the two provided some possibility of keeping tactical discipline and also instilling some *esprit de corps*. There were small bands of cavalry too, the *sariya* of about twenty men, which specialised in ambush techniques. They would be much in evidence during the events of early July 1187.

As far as the recruitment of troops was concerned, there were superficial similarities to the Western feudal system. Fiefs, or *iqta*, were allocated: in return the landholder (the *muqta*) maintained a number of troops which he was required to provide when war broke out. They were also required to collect taxes from the land that they held, which they would pay to the Sultan. An important distinguishing characteristic was that these lands could be repossessed at any time, in contrast to those held by Western knights.

The Mamelukes also played a crucial role. They were normally responsible for providing the Sultan's bodyguard, but also provided infantrymen, archers, crossbowmen or soldiers who fought with shield and spear. All professional soldiers received wages while they were fighting on campaign.

One area where the Muslim army hugely outperformed the Franks' forces was in that of its support services. There was a government postal service, the *barid*, which ensured good communication through the use of either carrier pigeons or couriers. The distribution of weapons was also much more efficient. These would be carried with the baggage train and issued on the eve of battle. There were some obvious advantages and disadvantages to this. The system enabled the troops to travel light and make good speed; but if intelligence were faulty, as in the Montgisard campaign a decade earlier, the army could be caught by surprise and suffer as a result.

A host of non-combatants accompanied the army, such as blacksmiths and engineers to look after any siege weapons, servants to look after the horses, mules and pack animals, all of which enabled the army to move. There were physicians as well, far more skilled than those available to Western armies, and of course holy men: this was an army that fought for its religious beliefs every bit as much as their Christian counterparts.

The army would have had a cosmopolitan look to it. The Turks wore their hair long, often plaited, while the Arabs were mostly shaven-headed. Nearly all wore beards and moustaches. Some of the men wore tall yellow caps called *kalawtas*, while others donned a stiff headpiece with a raised front fringed with fur. The wide variety of racial origins present within the army emphasised several things, in particular that this was not a war of nations but one of cultures and religions.

This was the unifying factor for both sides in the campaign. Saladin had been able to raise this army partly because he was evidently the foremost Muslim leader in the region, but this was not enough to guarantee loyalty, as many examples of desertion on the battlefield evidenced over the centuries. There were some men there, of course, who were mercenaries, who fought for the money and the possibility of a speedy profit. But, more than in most other campaigns, it was religious fervour that cemented the Muslim force together.

Saladin was fulfilling the ambitions of many in leading a campaign against the Latins. The increasing concentration on *jihad* during the twelfth century had been fuelled by the growing radicalisation of Muslim society. Saladin had been frequently criticised for failing to deal with the Franks because he was too involved in fighting other Muslims in his bid to increase his grip on power. His propagandists had had a field day writing out letters across the Muslim world, extolling Saladin's efforts to deal with Outremer in the name of the faith.[2]

Religious motivation was very helpful to Saladin's cause in some ways. It was a more reliable adhesive force than mere earthly ambition. But it was not without its dangers. Perhaps the foremost of these was the potential durability of such impulses. It was easy to be euphoric and spiritually inspired in the cool confines of the mosque and *medrasa*, the Islamic schools that specialised in theological teaching. It was much more difficult, though, to take men who were not by nature soldiers, such as the *muttawiyah*, away from their home environment, their families and their crops on an arduous campaign in difficult terrain. The longer the campaign went on, the greater the pressure on these volunteers and the harder it would be to keep the army in the field.

Arming all these troops posed its own challenges. Iron was in short supply and the capture of some mines from the Franks near Beirut gave the Muslims a welcome boost. Other supplies came from

Anatolia but a significant amount came from as far away as India. There were a number of weapons available: in addition to swords, spears and bows there were axes, javelins and lassoos. Swords could be curved, as typically portrayed in many modern presentations of medieval Muslims at war, but could also be straight. In general, it was the Turkish cavalry who were likely to carry curved swords.

Another ferocious and highly regarded weapon used by the cavalry was the mace, which could be anything up to a metre long. Some were made entirely of iron, others just had iron heads. There was no doubting that the effect of such a powerful weapon crashing down on an opponent's skull would have been lethal. Daggers were also carried, though used more as a last resort, particularly if the cavalryman had been unhorsed.

As far as tactics were concerned, Saladin made great use of horse archers backed up with auxiliary cavalry. These would sweep in and out of the enemy ranks with a flexibility and speed of reaction far surpassing that of the Franks' cavalry. The latter could be awesome, however, should the enemy stand up and try to hold its ground against a frontal assault. This was precisely why Saladin's cavalry opted not to do so at Hattin. Instead, they could move deftly to one side, allowing the momentum of the Franks' heavy horse to break harmlessly through their segmented ranks, after which they would quickly regroup and attack the enemy from the side and rear. Apart from the Turkish horse archers, most cavalry would be armed with a spear, sometimes two, one in each hand. Should these be shattered in battle then they could resort to their swords instead.

The horse archers had two main tactics. One was to fire using 'arrow showers', whereby the bowmen would shoot upwards so that their missiles could then fall to the ground with maximum velocity. The targets adopted in this approach were only general – the arrows would be aimed to fall in a particular 'killing zone' rather than at individuals. The other tactic commonly used would see the archers move much closer to the enemy so that arrows could be fired at short range, which would enable the archers to pierce all but the most solid armour. Then, before the enemy could fight back, they would move quickly out of range again.

This type of archery was an art form. It required a great deal of training for an archer to learn his trade and regular practice to keep his skills at a suitably high level. He would often carry other weapons too, which would have to be accommodated while shooting his arrows. For example, if he carried a sword it would dangle on a loop from his right wrist while he shot. He would be expected to be able to hit a yard-wide target from a distance of 75 yards. Such skills were made more difficult by his need to be able to do this at speed from horseback, though he might also fire from a stationary pose. It was not a question of luck but of carefully honed skill, as the instructions of al Tarsusi, a twelfth-century expert who wrote a manual for Saladin, demonstrate:

> When shooting at a horseman who is armoured or otherwise untouchable, shoot at his horse to dismount him. When shooting at a horseman who is not moving, aim at his saddle-bow and thus hit the man if [the arrow flies] too high and the horse if too low. If his back is turned, aim at the spot between his shoulders. If he charges with a sword shoot at him, but not from too far off for if you miss he might hit you with his sword. Never shoot blindly![3]

Saladin therefore had a range of tactical options available. Like the Latin knights, his soldiers' armour was virtually impenetrable when attacked from long range, and in addition he had his own heavy cavalry arm with which to launch a massive frontal attack at the army of Outremer. But horses were as expensive in the Muslim world as they were for Western knights. There was a huge difference in cost between a basic packhorse and a top quality cavalry charger, the former costing the equivalent of three camels, the latter 200.[4]

Many of these cavalrymen carried lances, which were often carried two-handed. A thrust with the lance could penetrate two layers of chainmail and come out the other side. Swords were carried too. There was not much subtlety in their use: the weapon was for cutting and hacking, not for thrusting. The power generated from one could be immense though, severing hands from arms, arms from shoulders, heads from necks.

180

But it was still the mounted archers who were Saladin's greatest weapon. Like a swarm of angry hornets, they could launch stinging attacks on their foe and then move out of harm's way before the much less mobile Christian heavy cavalry could react. Like an agitated elephant, the Franks would try to swat the troublesome pests away, only to find that their enemy was too nimble and agile for them. They would retreat as quickly as they had attacked and then look for the next weak link at which to direct their attentions.

The archers could cause significant damage. At long range they could injure both men and horses, though the knights with their heavy armour would have some protection against them. But the closer the archers came, the more difficult for the Franks, since the stopping power of an archer's arrow was considerable against all but the heaviest armour.

We read of knights looking like hedgehogs, with arrows sticking out of their armour in profusion while they themselves remained uninjured. But only the privileged few, the knights of the realm or the Orders, could afford armour of this quality; for the rest the damage inflicted by the archers must have been considerable. In any case, such accounts probably refer to attempts by Muslim archers to disable horses at long range: at close range even the best armour would be threatened by arrows.

It is not just weapons or men that win battles. The Islamic forces were far more adept than the Franks in maximising the advantages offered by the terrain. If there was one area where the Muslim army tactically outperformed the army of Outremer on a consistent basis it was here. The great Shirkuh had won battles by the use of a defensive position built on sand, which slowed the momentum of the Frankish forces almost to walking point. The Turks had slaughtered the armies that attempted to reinforce the Franks after their capture of Jerusalem in 1099 largely because they utilised their knowledge of the country that they had conquered to launch a series of devastating ambushes. Muslim tactics were generally more subtle than those of their Christian enemy, particularly in the exploitation of terrain. And this was about to be proved with spectacular effect.

For Saladin, 3 July 1187 was a momentous day. His place in posterity would be assured, or otherwise, as a result of the outcome of the battle that was clearly imminent. He had done everything he could to ensure a successful conclusion. His army was huge, it was well provisioned and it was motivated by religious fervour: a potent cocktail indeed. From this point on, his fate was in the hands not only of himself – for clear thinking and quick responses to changes in fortune would surely be needed – but also of a far greater authority. Just as the army of Outremer fought for their God, so did he for his. His *jihad* was as inspired by spirituality as much as any Crusade.

The Franks had not gone far, just past Nazareth, when the chroniclers tell us of a strange event that took place.[5] The army came across an old Saracen woman riding a donkey. Some of the local men recognised her as coming from Nazareth. They demanded to know what she was doing and when her answers did not seem satisfactory they began to torture her. Under this duress, she apparently confessed that she was a witch who had cast an evil spell over the Christian army. She said that she had circled round the host the previous night and enchanted them so that they would all be lost.

Then some of them asked the woman if it were possible to escape the effects of this dreadful spell. Her reply was that this could only be done if the Franks returned to their camp. Believing that this was a ruse to save Saladin, they sentenced her to die there and then. They collected brushwood and dried grass, built a pyre and threw her upon it. But either they did not tie her well enough or her powers were strong, for she kept leaping out of the fire. So one of their number came forward with a great Danish axe and cleaved her skull in two. Her corpse was thrown onto the fire and was consumed.

The sun was every bit as fierce as Raymond had dreaded. It was a scorching day, and the men were in for a hot and sweaty march. The road ahead would take them through rough country and would tax them to the limit. There would be few, if any, opportunities to replenish supplies of water en route. And to make matters worse, the Muslims were ready for them. The army had not gone far when it came under persistent attack from irregular cavalry, sweeping down from the hills, loosing their arrows into the massed ranks of the Christian army and riding away again as quickly as they had appeared. They were like biting ants, irritating but not deadly. But, here and there, a straggler would be picked off or a foot soldier would fall – though the heavily armed Frankish horsemen were largely impervious to these long-range arrows, even if their mounts were not.

The horses of the knights were protected, as normal, by a screen of infantry. These were needed to keep the Muslim horse archers at a distance, the only way of doing so being to deploy the lightly armoured mounted Turcopoles or archers on foot. Well proven though this tactic was, it slowed the army down, as the horsemen had to walk at a leisurely pace to enable the screen to keep up with them. The Muslim cavalry darted in and out of the ranks of their Christian enemy, loosing their arrows and then retreating swiftly to pick up a new supply. Although the Franks' infantry fought resolutely, they could not prevent many of the horse archers from getting close enough to start striking down horses in significant numbers.

Count Raymond, whose land this conflict was in, was given the honour of leading the vanguard, as was his right. King Guy was in the centre and Reynald of Chatillon, the knights of the Orders and Balian of Ibelin were at the rear. The army did its best to stay in order but the attacks of the Muslim cavalry, allied to the much deadlier work of the searing sun, began to take their toll. As men dehydrated in their heavy clothing, they began to slacken, allowing themselves to be picked off by the enemy, or they collapsed from exhaustion. Slowly at first, the triumphant procession that marked the progress of the army of Outremer began to transform into a death march.

It was a Friday, the Muslim holy day, and if the Christian army was increasingly demoralised, their enemy was anything but. Imad ad-Din wrote of the attacks in euphoric terms:

As the day of 3 July dawned our archers emerged, setting alight the people of hell-fire with a blaze of arrows. There was a creaking of bows and a plucking of strings on that day. And the army poured down on the Franks their scorching rays. As the heat flared up the forces of evil began to fade. A searing thirst descended; the air burned as passions turned to fear. Those dogs, their tongues lolling, plagued by a havoc of their own making, turned their minds to thoughts of water only to be met by the flames of hell and to be overcome by the fire of the midday sun.[6]

It was the rearguard that came under the greatest pressure. Using a familiar tactic, the nimble Muslim horsemen attacked the rear of the Franks' column, which did its best to stay in formation while progressing cumbersomely towards its ultimate destination. The intensity of the Muslim attack increased and the fighting at the rear grew fiercer. The pressure began to tell. As the day, and the march, wore on, the Templars and the men of Balian of Ibelin grew increasingly concerned as they found it more difficult to fight off the enemy.

The Templars were required to maintain strict order. Such discipline was indeed the foundation on which their military strength was built. At the start of the march they would have been placed in squadrons, *eschielles*. According to Rule 102 of their Order, 'when they are established in squadrons, no brother should go from one squadron to another'.[7] Charging without permission was a serious breach of rules. Any who broke rank could be humiliatingly stripped of his white mantle after the battle and forced to eat from the floor with the dogs for a while. Therefore, they kept tight order as far as was possible under this persistent assault.

Between morning and midday the advance came under heavy attack from skirmishers, which caused the Franks to suffer significant losses. By ten in the morning, they had covered about 8 miles.[8] The Muslim attacks would have been launched in a way that ensured that fresh cavalry were always charging into the fray, giving those previously engaged a chance to get their breath back. Bodies of horsemen could also keep watch, waiting to attack should the Franks' patience become exhausted, causing them to break their line of march as they launched a counter-attack. This was a long-established tactic, referred to in the contemporary military manuals of al-Tarsusi:

When it is the enemy's habit to charge en bloc and to rely on the shock impact of their detachments, as do the Franks and those neighbours who resemble them, this array is very effective because if one group of enemy attacks it can be taken in the flank and surrounded.[9]

There were springs of water not too far away, but the strength of the Muslim forces blocking the route meant that there was no option but to carry on straight ahead. As soon as Saladin heard of the Franks' decision to leave Sephoria, he called most of his men back from Tiberias, leaving only a small force to keep watch on the citadel. By noon, Guy's army had completed only half the journey from Sephoria to Tiberias, and the shortage of water was already causing serious problems. The intensity of the Muslim attacks was now so great that the march had slowed down to a crawl. The King sought the council of Raymond.

Raymond believed that the only hope of survival was to fight through to water. According to one version of events, he advised the King to push on to Hattin, where there were supplies of water, where the army could restore its strength and complete the march to Tiberias, fully rested, on the next morning. Quite what they would do when they arrived at Tiberias was anybody's guess. The limitations of the Frankish leaders' strategic thinking was beginning to show through: it appeared that the only objective was to bring Saladin to a decisive confrontation, on ground of his own choosing when he had access to water and the Franks did not. It was madness.

The decision to push on to Hattin was a major modification to the plan. It meant that the option of reaching Lake Tiberias was already being abandoned as unachievable. To add to the frustration, the lake itself, with its life-giving waters, could be seen in the distance, though it was still about 8 miles away. But it was not yet a hopeless situation, as the springs at Hattin were only 3 miles ahead. The changed destination did mean abandoning the prospect of attacking the Muslim forces head on though, and this was an important psychological change in tactics: the campaign was already turning from one of offensive action into one of survival.

The decision also meant that the Franks had to move away from the main road across the plateau, and this is where the harsh terrain in the area began to play a significant part. The roughness of the ground meant that the tight battle formation that was key to the army's survival started to break up. The organisation of the Christian army, already hard pressed because of the fierce attacks and the physical suffering involved in making the journey this far, disintegrated almost at once.

This left gaps for the enemy to exploit. They could charge into the dispersed ranks of the Frankish host much more easily now, and as a result the latter began to fall apart. Saladin could see what was happening from his vantage point in the hills overlooking the road from the south, and, realising that the Franks planned to fight their way through to the springs at Hattin, deployed his army to block the way.

The Muslim forces, spurred on by what they believed to be their imminent victory, attacked ever more fiercely. The right wing under Taqi al-Din blocked the Franks' path to water, knowing full well that this was their enemy's objective. Gökböri in the meantime led the left wing in repeated attacks on the rearguard, which must by now have begun to become isolated.

Late in the day, a request from the Templars passed through the ranks. Cocooned – or more accurately cooked – in their vast carapaces, they were fatigued to the point of collapse. They begged the King to stop so that they could rest. What purpose this would have served is a debatable point. They would still be unable to access water supplies and would allow the Muslims to position themselves wherever they wished to attack them. But incapable of resisting the injunctions of Gerard, Guy acquiesced. When he heard of the decision, Raymond – in an outburst inspired both by frustration and dejection – averred that the kingdom was surely lost.

The Templars' plea spoke eloquently of the pressure they had been under. The rearguard, of which they formed a crucial part, had suffered the most intense of attacks from the enemy. They had been irritated so much by the constant assaults of the horse archers they had at one stage tried to counter-charge them, but the much greater nimbleness of the latter meant that they could easily speed out of the way and then shortly after return to the attack once more. The tactic was highly effective: hot beneath the blazing sun, exhausted through their lack of water and their morale plummeting, the Templars would go no further.

But Raymond's response was surely right. The desperate need was for water. The army's only hope of getting this commodity was to carry on, however awful the cost might be. The decision to stop was catastrophic. It meant both a longer time without water and also gave the enemy time to tighten their grip around the army. It was also completely contrary to the aggressive policy advocated by the Templars in the short campaign up to now. Nothing could have spoken more powerfully of the disintegration of Frankish morale.

By this time, sometime in the afternoon of 3 July, the Franks were on the plateau above Hattin, within a few miles of Lake Tiberias, close to the springs at Hattin and relief to an extent from their sufferings. Between the army and the lake stood a small hill with two summits, known as the Horns of Hattin. The army set up camp at Lubieh, where there was theoretically access to water. But the well there was dry. And beyond the hill, between the Franks and the water, stood the bulk of Saladin's army, encamped in a lush green valley that amply demonstrated the quantity of water in the vicinity.

The need for water was bitterly felt. A Muslim account tells how

devastated by a thirst fed by fiery fuel, they stood patiently, steadfastly, obstinately: then struggling, rabid with greed, they drank what water their flasks contained. They lapped up whatever was held in the surrounding man-made wells, exhausting even the source of their tears as they teetered on the brink of calamity.[10]

Perhaps the army of Outremer was already past the point of no return, but at this stage the only hope of salvation lay in launching an attack on the Muslim army and smashing through to the lake. Ironically, at the very moment that they should have gone on the offensive, they stopped instead, as if God Himself would come to their rescue and do all their work for them.

As they stood stock still, like a giant, overheated tortoise incapable of anything but the most cumbersome of movements, they were surrounded in a noose that was so tight that men said that a cat could not have slipped through it. Their escape was cut off, probably by the left wing under Gökböri, while Saladin brought up 400 loads of arrows to replace the vast quantity that had been expended during the attacks earlier on.

And so the sun went down, not just on the day but on the dream that was the Kingdom of Jerusalem. Within the Franks' camp, men collapsed where they stood, throats parched with thirst, spirits overwhelmed with fear. The divine protection offered by the priests seemed more necessary than ever now. Men lay in the dust, unwilling to sleep yet forced to do so by sheer numbing exhaustion. Others stood to, on the alert for any night-time attack that might be launched on the camp. For many, it would be their last night on earth, or at least their last night as free men in the whole of their lives. But it was more than that. For this was the last night of Outremer.

It must have been particularly hard for those – the majority – whose permanent home was in Outremer, be it indigenous soldiers or those who came from families who had moved from the West. As early as 1125, Fulcher of Chartres, one of the great chroniclers of the First Crusade, and a man who lived in Outremer subsequently, wrote that:

Westerners, we have become Orientals. The Italian and the Frenchman of yesterday have been transplanted and become men of Galilee or Palestine. Men from Reims or Chartres are transformed into Tyrians or citizens of Antioch. We have already forgotten the land of our birth; who now remembers it? Men no longer speak of it.[11]

Fulcher went on to describe how men had married local women, Syrians or Armenians, rather than Western brides. He had got used to speaking the languages of the country. Most of all,

The colonist has now become almost a native, and the immigrant is one with the inhabitants. Every day relatives and friends from the West come to join us. They do not hesitate to leave everything they have behind them. Indeed, by the grace of God, he who was poor attains riches here. He who had no more than a few deniers finds himself here in possession of a fortune. He who owned not so much as one village finds himself, by God's grace, the lord of a city.[12]

Outremer had been a place of dreams for those first pilgrims, a fantasy that had transformed itself into a nightmare during their journey east. One suspects that the chronicler indulges in a few fantasies of his own: there were not enough cities to go round for everyone to own one. For most, to use the words of a much later chronicler, this was a country where blood, sweat, toil and tears were required to make any sort of life.

But for many, Fulcher's words were true, at least in part. This was no colony, no overseas posting, this was quite simply home. And it was a home that was now quite clearly about to disappear. Not just men would die on the morrow, so too would a way of life. The position was desperate and seemingly left the trapped army with no hope of escape. No doubt fighting to defend the Kingdom of Jerusalem seemed an honourable, even a noble cause, when considering the idea in the taverns of Jerusalem. When the wine had been flowing, or indeed when the priests had been preaching, the prospect of sacrifice seemed no great hardship to people who often had little to give up and to whom the thought of death, and the near certainty of hellfire, was an everyday companion.

Euphoric decisions to go to war made in the heat of the moment quickly changed in the cold light of day. A contemporary poet wrote thus:

> When men are hot with drinking wine
> And idly by the fire recline,
> They take the cross with eager boast
> To make a great Crusading host.
> But with first glow of morning light
> The whole Crusade dissolves in flight. [13]

Three decades earlier, when Louis VII led his armies in the ultimately futile Second Crusade, a French crusade song encouraged men to follow the King by saying that 'anyone who now accompanies Louis will need have no fear of hell, for his soul will be in paradise with the angels of our Lord'.[14]

These words were stirring and reassuring at the beginning of the march, but one wonders just how consoling they were to a poorly armed Frankish infantryman whose lowly status would give him no ransom value on the morrow and whose capture, and certain death or enslavement, now seemed close at hand.

Beyond their ranks, the encircling Muslims were already in ecstasy at the thought of the imminent victory that they knew was already theirs. Their prayers were of joy and of gratitude to Allah, who had delivered the enemy up to them. They realised that there would still be bloodshed and loss, but those who died in the faith were assured of paradise. Their chanting and dancing went on through the night. No need of sleep for them, drunk on the intoxicating thought of a triumph that was now inevitable.

As dawn approached, a fire started (the accounts are unclear as to exact timings, some placing it in the morning, some during that awful night). It was not clear whether this was a deliberate act or not, but it quickly took hold of the scrub surrounding the Frankish camp. Some accounts claim it was started on the orders of Saladin, and this is perhaps the most probable story. It would have been an ideal task for the *muttawiyah* to perform. Acrid, choking smoke billowed into the camp, further terrifying the poor souls within who could now hear the exultant enemy but not see him. The hours of darkness were long, and the Franks rested as best they could beneath the ominous wings of the Angel of Death. But terrible as the night was, the day that was to come would be far, far worse.

TEN

Requiem

And there were voices, and thunders, and lightnings; and there was a great earthquake, such as was not since men were upon the earth, so mighty an earthquake and so great.

Revelation 16: 18

Aday of great significance for the Western world in modern times, 4 July was equally important for medieval Islam for reasons that were altogether different. On this day, in the year 1187 in the Christian calendar, the Crusader conquest of Jerusalem was avenged. At the end of the battle that was about to be fought, the Holy City was still in Christian hands, but its loss was inevitable.

At daybreak, Saladin launched a psychological assault against the trapped army of the Franks. Caravans of camels loped up from Lake Tiberias, carrying pitchers full of water. When in sight of the Christian army, Saladin ordered the water to be tipped out onto the ground, driving his enemy almost mad with thirst. But the Muslim army had plentiful supplies of the life-sustaining liquid. He had ordered that reservoirs for water should be set up in his camp and they were kept topped up by a procession of camels ferrying in supplies from the lake.

At the break of this momentous day, one of Guy's knights came up to the King and said to him that 'now is the time for you to make the *polains* with their beards dear to the men of your country'.[1] '*Polains*' was the collective name given to the second- and third-generation settlers in Outremer. It was a derogatory term, which roughly translated means 'runt'. A song current at the time of Guy's accession used the words '*Maugré li Polain, Avrons nous roi*

191

Poitevin' – 'despite the *polains*, we shall have a Poitevin king'. It is safe to say that not everyone in Outremer was enamoured of the more recent arrivals from the West.

Within the Christian army's ranks, there were those who argued forcibly that they should fight its way out of their precarious position. However, they failed to persuade the King that this was the best course of action. Morale, already low, plummeted further. Staying put like rats caught in a trap went against the grain with the more aggressive elements in the army, who wished to die fighting if they were to die at all.

The Muslims prolonged the suffering of their incapacitated victims until the sun was high in the sky.[2] They realised that its suffocating heat was a powerful ally, particularly against an enemy suffering the effects of dehydration. They also appreciated that the sun would be shining directly into the eyes of their enemy. The Muslims launched their attack when the fire had taken hold. One Islamic account tells how 'its flame bore down upon them, and its heat became intense. They, the people of the Trinity, were consumed by a worldly fire of three types: the fire of flames, the fire of thirst, and the fire of arrows. The Franks longed for release, and attempted a sortie, but in vain.'[3]

The Muslim army now began its attack. It was the centre that started the assault, led by Gökböri. It seems that fires continued to be lit as the Christian army tried its best to extricate itself from the parlous predicament it found itself in. The volunteer *muttawiya* may not have offered Saladin much in terms of fighting power, but they were ideal for collecting brushwood to build fires with, which they had enthusiastically gathered and laid out in places where it could create maximum discomfort to the enemy.

The fire formed an effective screen and made the already parched Christian army even more desperate for water. Through the choking smoke, arrows from Muslim horse archers homed in on their massed ranks, killing men and horses alike. There was no point staying there statuesque, taking all this punishment without fighting back, so on the advice of Gerard and Reynald, Guy ordered his brother Amalric, the Constable of the kingdom, to lead a charge against the enemy.

Taqi el-Din held the right, an experienced and respected commander who was trusted implicitly by Saladin. He had dispersed his troops intelligently around the area during the preceding night. Early on in the battle on 4 July, one of the most promising Muslim emirs, Manguras from Hama, was killed: this was a serious setback for Saladin. One version of his death has it that he was slain in single combat against a knight, having been thrown from his horse and dragged into the Christian lines, where he was quickly beheaded. Other accounts are more prosaic, however, saying that he was overwhelmed by superior numbers and was then decapitated.

The Christian army formed up as best it could, with Raymond in the van with the son of the Prince of Antioch, also named Raymond. At his side rode his four stepsons, presumably frantic with worry at the probable fate of their mother. In the rear were Balian of Ibelin and Joscelin of Courtenay. So downhearted were some of the army that a few of them decided to desert rather than stay where they were to await the inevitable. The names of some of these dishonoured men have survived the passage of time in a damning roll of dishonour: men such as Baldwin of Fotina, Raulfus Bructus and Laodoicus of Tabaria.

The Franks formed up with their crossbowmen protecting the cavalry, and for a time they were successful in keeping off the Muslims. But the cavalry began to suffer further serious losses among their horses, fatally weakening their offensive capacity. As a result, the nerve of the army began to crack and, with the omnipotent sun rising ever higher in the sky, some of the soldiers broke. Yet, regardless of the powerful foe before them, and entranced by the glistening waters of the lake below, large numbers of them charged headlong towards it. But they were powerless against their enemy, fresh, well-watered and eager to deal a deathblow to Christendom. Many were driven back onto a hillock, where large numbers were cut down and the remainder taken captive. Other survivors made their way up the northern hill of the Horns of Hattin.

This left the cavalry heavily exposed to the Muslim horse archers. With the infantry screen now gone, the Christian knights were hopelessly exposed and their horses began to fall in large numbers. The Turkish archers could fire rapidly, and could wreak havoc amongst the relatively unprotected horses.[4]

Perhaps one should not be too hard on the infantry, the unsung men in the army – who later centuries would call 'cannon fodder'. There was great variation in the equipment of the foot soldiers. Some infantrymen would be almost professional soldiers, with iron cap, a form of armour or perhaps a quilted jacket, a shield and a bow. But others would be men who had hardly ever borne arms, of limited experience, who only rarely campaigned when called upon to do so by the king, involved in this battle perhaps because they believed in the righteousness of their cause, because they hoped to earn a few coppers or because they had been carried along on a spirit of adventure.

The poorer soldiers were virtually unarmoured and were without quality weapons, perhaps a basic spear or a bow at most. It is especially easy to understand how, after the traumas of the previous 24 hours, they could take no more and broke. They left no tales, they were not important enough for the chroniclers, those who related the deeds of great men, to comment on. Thousands of them would have lost their lives or their freedom, lamented only by the families they left behind – the fate of the infantry over the centuries.

Morale was now collapsing fast. The army believed that nothing save defeat was possible; and that made such a defeat inevitable. With the collapse of the infantry, it was left to the knights to offer the last effective vestige of resistance. The knights were well protected. Their equipment was generally of a higher standard than the other horse soldiers, and they were also proud members of a high social class: both these advantages enabled them to carry on fighting despite enormous odds against them. And pride spurred them on to do so.

The Christian knights indeed fought magnificently, in what was nevertheless a closely fought battle. A Muslim biographer, Ibn Khallikan, noted of Gökböri and Taqi al-Din that:

> they both held their ground although the whole army was routed and driven back. The soldiers then heard that these two chiefs still

resisted the enemy, whereupon they returned to the charge and victory was decided in favour of the Muslims. [5]

His words should be treated with some caution, as he was trying to glorify the two Muslim leaders who were his biographical subjects by playing up their valour, but there is no reason to doubt that the battle was fierce. Although under pressure, the Muslims counter-attacked. Wave after wave of Muslim onslaught was fought off, but at great loss in terms of energy expended if not of numbers.

It was now, at the height of the battle, that a hugely controversial event occurred. Reputedly at the King's orders, Raymond led his knights in a charge to break free. The knights had two principal weapons, the lance and the sword. Now his men lowered the former and charged as fast as their steeds would carry them head on at the enemy. Their left arm holding shield and reins, and the lance cushioned under their right, the knights of the Count of Tripoli charged for death or glory – or at least an opportunity to escape.

It must have been a fearsome sight, horses straining at the bit, gagging for air as their riders dug their spurs in to generate maximum velocity. But the enemy had a time-honoured tactic to counter the charge, developed after decades of facing up to these terrifying foes. As Raymond's men spurred their horses towards the encircling ranks of the enemy led by Taqi al-Din, the latter simply stood aside. But when the Christian forces were in their midst, like a wave covering the shoreline, they closed ranks on them and struck many of them down with, in one account, only about a dozen knights escaping.

It was this manoeuvre that led to later accusations of treachery. Yet in trying to escape Raymond was following the only sensible option. The continuator of William of Tyre, on whose accounts the narrative above is based, suggests that, unlike the description in some versions, Taqi al-Din did not meekly let Raymond escape. Rather, by drawing his troops to one side he was simply taking some of the momentum out of the charge of the Frankish horse – the shock of which was renowned throughout the Muslim world – only to crush it when most of their potential impact was spent.

It was, as one contemporary writer noted, merely an example of an oft-seen tactic when 'the Saracens parted and made a way for them as was their custom'.[6] The Count of Tripoli escaped with his four stepsons and Raymond of Antioch. Towards the end of the battle, Balian of Ibelin and Reynald of Sidon made a successful bid to break out. Few other men of note were so fortunate.

Raymond of Tripoli made his way to the coast. Allegations of treachery against him increased in strength and he would not live for long after this disastrous day, dying in the same year of pleurisy. He appears to have lived for those few short months a bitter and disenchanted man who felt that the world had treated him too harshly. His men had lost large numbers in the fight and those who broke out were incapable of returning to the fray once they had smashed through the steel ring surrounding them. Even so, the defeat at Hattin left an indelible stain on Raymond's reputation.

Topography played its part too. When Raymond and his knights broke through they charged down a narrow and steep track towards Hattin village. To return to the fray would be very difficult. Taqi al-Din had closed the gap formed where the Count had escaped and the Crusader knights would have had to charge uphill against overwhelming odds if they wished to rejoin the battle – hardly an appealing prospect.

But Raymond also seemed to have lost all interest in the fight. His conduct towards his wife was less than gallant. Although accusations of treachery may go too far, one is left with the unmistakable conclusion that Raymond had no stomach for the conflict and simply wished to get away as quickly as possible. If his motives should not be questioned, maybe his courage should. He made no attempt to relieve his wife in Tiberias and effectively abandoned her to her fate. He had good reason to believe, given Saladin's reputation and their former excellent relations, that this fate would be a gentle one and so it proved. But his actions following his escape did nothing to improve his standing or reputation.

Shortly after Hattin, the writer of the *Itinerarium Regis Ricardi* wrote in acerbic terms of Raymond's escape, saying that at the precise instant that the fighting began, Raymond III, Count of Tripoli, left the spot, feigning flight. The story is that he did this by pre-arrangement, so that our troops should scatter, apparently stricken by terror at the desertion of one who should have been their support, while the spirits of the enemy were raised.[7]

According to this version, Raymond's flight was nothing short of abject treason, the result of a pre-arranged plan with Saladin: true or not, it was all too believable given Raymond's alliance with Saladin shortly before the campaign. If Raymond had lived long after the battle, it was unlikely that his prestige would ever have recovered from the hammer blows dealt it at Hattin.

The claim that Raymond was ordered to escape by the King ought to be considered. Any attempt to lead a breakout would normally be led by the Templars. They were famed for their ability to charge in a wedged formation, a gigantic arrowhead of death that would shatter any opposition foolish enough to stand in its path. It was said that when they charged they were so close that a man would be unable to throw an arrow between them without it hitting either man or horse. This charge was normally the spearhead of the assault. Through the gap that the Templars would create in the enemy ranks, it was expected that the other cavalry, the secular knights and the Turcopoles, would pour. By so doing, they would widen the breach and turn the battle into a rout.

It is easy to imagine why Guy did not call upon the Templars to do this in the current situation. Several reasons suggest themselves. First, the general disorganisation of the Crusader army in the parlous situation they found themselves may have meant that the Templars were cut off from the main part of the force. They had, after all, been in the rearguard on the previous day. They might also have lost much of their offensive capability as a result of the attrition that had taken place, certainly in terms of horsepower if not of men. Their white mantles made them a prime target for the Muslim enemy, who were very well aware of their fighting prowess. It might therefore not have been possible for them to lead a general breakout.

This might explain why Raymond was delegated to do so instead. His men were after all in the vanguard and would be best placed for this tactic. The argument is persuasive save for one very important point: there is no evidence that there was any attempt by any other party of Frankish knights to escape, which surely would have been the case if the Count of Tripoli had been tasked with leading a general breakout. If he had been asked to undertake such an act, why for example did not Guy charge with him?

If Guy believed that the day were lost, then it might not be gallant for him to save his skin but he could argue persuasively *post ante* that he believed it was his duty to survive to lead the kingdom through the terrible days that must follow. But there is no evidence that Guy tried to follow Raymond and, if he were close enough to give him orders, then he was certainly close enough to charge with him should the occasion demand it.

Even more tellingly, it appears that the True Cross, most venerated totem of all to the kingdom, was close by. Guy was close enough to see it fall at the conclusion of the battle. Why was the task of leading this most crucial of all symbols to safety not delegated to Raymond, in the same way that a British infantry regiment of later centuries might see its colours carried away when a battle was on the verge of being lost? The thought of this most venerated of objects being lost to the Muslims was anathema to Christians and, given the way that the battle was going, it would surely have been logical to give Raymond the Cross to carry with him.

It is reasonable to assume then that, if Guy told Raymond to break out, it would have been part of a wider assault which would enable as many men as possible to escape the carnage, and also that the True Cross would be with him when he did so. The absence of any evidence to either effect suggests that the Count was acting on his own initiative. Believing that the battle was already lost, it seems he believed it was his duty to save his own skin. *Sauve qui peut*, in other words. Neither glamorous nor glorious. Not treasonable, but weak.

Without Raymond's contingent, the Christian cavalry was at the foot of the hills and the disintegration of the infantry left them in a dangerously exposed position. Frantically, and without success,

Guy begged the infantry to return. The latter refused, their bodies desperately weakened by thirst and their spirits by the hopeless position they appeared to be in. The King, who had ordered tents to be erected (though only three had been put up) was left with no option but to retreat up to the hilltops.

By now most of the knights were fighting on foot. This made them next to useless. As Saladin's biographer, Baha al-Din, noted

> a Latin knight, as long as his horse was in good condition, could not be knocked down. Covered by a mail hauberk from head to foot the most violent blows had no effect on him. But once his horse was killed, the knight was thrown and taken prisoner.[8]

Those knights who remained were forced inexorably back on to the plateau. They ended up on the southern Horn of Hattin, fighting on across the flat-topped hill where they sought to protect the King's bright-red tent, its ominous blood-hued fabric standing out vividly in the dry landscape. While the Muslim infantry fought enthusiastically with those who were left of their Christian counterparts on the northern hill, Saladin ordered Taqi al-Din to lead his cavalry against what remained of the Christian cavalry atop the southern Horn. The Frankish infantry were overwhelmed, exhausted and broken, and those who were not struck down surrendered.

The slopes of the southern Horn were too steep to allow cavalry to charge up them without great difficulty. Therefore, it was probably from the western slopes, which rose gently enough from a saddle that connected the northern and southern Horn, that the Muslim cavalry attacked the Frankish knights. Wave after wave of Muslim cavalry broke against the Christian ranks and was rebuffed, but each time another wave arrived and reached higher up the hill. When King Guy was forced onto the hilltop the battle still raged. Two spirited counter-attacks created doubt in the Muslim ranks even at this late stage of the battle. One came close to Saladin himself. Anxiously he tugged at his beard and shouted encouragement to his men: 'Away with the Devil's lie!'[9]

It was perhaps now that the Templars, those whose horses were still standing, made their final charge though they might also have been completely cut off from the King by this stage and isolated. The sight must have been poignant. A contemporary observer of the Templars in battle noted how they would call on God Himself for help in the fight:

> When they make the decision that it would be profitable to fight and the trumpet sounds to give the order to advance, they piously sing the psalm of David: 'Not to us, Lord, not to us but to your name give the glory', couch their lances and charge into the enemy. As one body, they rampage through the enemy, they never yield, they either destroy the enemy completely or die.[10]

It was a magnificent code by which to live and die, but it was now futile. The Psalm went unanswered: there was to be little glory in this abattoir. The knights were exhausted and most of their horses were dead. Many of them were taken alive. It was not quite time for them to die.

The Muslims pushed deeper onto the Horns. Al-Afdal, son of Saladin, told how he now believed that the battle was won; but his father was still uncertain, afraid that even at the eleventh hour his prize would be snatched from him. He tugged at his beard and rebuked his son angrily at his assumption that the battle was over. Not until the King's pavilion fell, he said, was the victory complete. At that very moment the tent was overrun.

At this sight, Saladin dismounted and bowed to the ground with tears in his eyes. The symbolism of the moment had a dramatic effect on the Crusader defence, which now collapsed. Victory indeed belonged to Saladin and with it, unless there was to be an unforeseen and unforeseeable change in fortune, the destruction of Outremer was assured as its army had been wiped out. The Sultan's place in posterity was there for the taking. But before that there was to be a time of retribution.

The Bishop of Acre had died in the fight and the fragment of the True Cross, which was under his protection, had been taken. To some writers, this momentous event led to the immediate collapse of morale in the Christian army, al-Imad noting that, 'when they knew that the Cross had been taken from them, none desired to escape from peril'.[11]

When Guy saw the Cross taken, he was overcome with emotion: 'He rushed forward and flung his arms around the Cross, hoping to snatch it back, if God so willed, or at least to die beside it.'[12] But it was in vain, and both the precious talisman and the abject monarch were seized. The Cross was taken into Muslim captivity, an appalling and perhaps irrecoverable blow to the morale of Outremer.

That at least is the most widely accepted account. But some chroniclers offer an alternative.[13] Some say that a Templar brother came to the King of Jerusalem, Henry of Champagne, a few years after the battle (Henry reigned from 1192 to 1197). The Templar told the King that he had been present at the battle, and rather than let the True Cross be taken he had hurriedly buried it on the field. Henry lent him an escort and they rode out in some danger – for the country round about was then in Muslim hands – to the awful field of Hattin. But although they dug for three days they could not find the Cross. Maybe it lies there still.

There is a much more prosaic story about the relic. Other writers[14] state that future Muslim rulers of Jerusalem were concerned that the revenues of the city had declined alarmingly as a result of the much smaller numbers of pilgrims visiting it when it was once more in Islamic hands. They therefore returned the Cross to Jerusalem as a way of attracting more Christian visitors to the city. The love of money it seems was a great motivator for men of all religious persuasions.

Many of the Frankish leaders survived the battle. Their armour had protected them against the sting of Muslim arrows, but also contributed to their state of complete physical collapse. This suggests that most of the archers had fired from a distance with a view to maiming or killing horses rather than their riders (tests in modern times show that arrows could penetrate chainmail if fired close up but not at a distance).[15] Exhaustion, superior numbers and tactics had won the day. Everywhere Christian knights lay dejectedly on the ground, incapable of raising their swords in anger. The most important were dragged off to the tent of Saladin to await judgement at the hands of the conqueror.

This dejected group were led into Saladin's pavilion. Among them were Amalric, the Constable of the kingdom, William of Montferrat, Reynald of Chatillon, the Masters of the Templars and Hospitallers and Humphrey of Toron. At their head was the King, Guy of Lusignan, a man who would soon be a monarch without a realm.

Graciously, Saladin welcomed the King and bade him be seated at his side – a clear hint that Guy would be well treated. Seeing his thirst, Saladin commanded that a golden goblet of iced water be given to him. This was the clincher. It was unthinkable that a man treated in this respectful manner would subsequently be harmed: to do so would go against some of the most fundamental rules of Muslim etiquette.

Having drunk from it, Guy passed the goblet to Reynald of Chatillon – a symbolic affirmation of the close links between their respective fortunes. But now the mood turned. Saladin told his interpreter to inform those present that it was not he who had given the cup to Reynald, a clear inference that the troublesome baron was in danger. Warming to his task, Saladin began to berate Reynald for his frequent breaches of the peace and his repeated insults to Islam.

It would have been wise for Reynald to hold his tongue. But he could not stop himself. He stood up to Saladin with his customary haughtiness, trading insult for insult. He refused to drink from the goblet and his demeanour was as arrogant as ever. He was at least consistent. But in the process he forgot – or maybe he did not care – that, in Saladin's tent, he had no power, no protection. Infuriated by the ongoing vanity of Reynald, Saladin seized a sword and ran him through.

A party of Muslim soldiers ran over and struck off Reynald's head. In a gory gesture of vengeance Saladin took some of Reynald's blood and sprinkled it over his temple. The dishonour that Reynald had brought by his actions was expunged by the shedding of his blood. The head of the once proud Reynald was eventually taken to

Damascus and dragged along the ground as a symbolic affirmation of Saladin's triumph.

Guy looked on in horror, fearing that he would be the next. Sensing his terror, Saladin reassured him. 'A king does not kill a king,' he said gently. And, he might have added, a king also does not throw away a great bargaining chip such as Guy, King of Jerusalem.

The barons too would be well treated, held for ransom against the future conquest of the Kingdom of Jerusalem. For the knights of the Orders though, no such mercy would be given. Hagiographers of Saladin frequently emphasise his compassion, but such a quality clearly did not extend to the Templars and the Hospitallers. Saladin ordered that almost to a man they should be slaughtered. They were a fearsome foe, sworn to fight the enemies of Christ and debarred from negotiating their release via ransom. They could not be allowed to live. They were therefore taken off to Damascus to await their cruel fate.

A terrible scene was played out in that city on 6 July, one that does little credit to Saladin's reputation (there is not unanimity as to the location of the terrible events that followed, some placing them partly in Tiberias and partly in Damascus). Those of the Orders who survived Hattin were given a choice between conversion to Islam or death: no choice at all for most of the knights who had sworn sacred vows and given their lives to the glory of Christendom. The fate of most of these knights was sealed. For the record, it must be noted that a few of the knights did opt to convert and there are records of a Templar of Spanish origin commanding the garrison at Damascus in 1230, though if he were a survivor of Hattin he must have been aged as this was nearly half a century into the future. But the remainder, some 230 knights, were doomed.[16]

The location of this macabre ceremony is much more than a minor detail. There was a history of captive Crusaders being humiliated over the years as a way of emphasising the triumph of Islam as well as maximising the propaganda benefits of rulers who thereby demonstrated their power and success to their people. Nur ed-Din had paraded Crusader captives in full armour through the streets of Damascus in 1157 and some of those captured after Reynald's raids earlier in the 1180s had been beheaded in Mecca.

Given this, surely the executions took place in Damascus, where the citizens could rejoice first hand in the glory of the Muslim triumph and the strength of Saladin? It was an outstanding public relations coup for the Sultan and, shrewd politician that he was, he would have milked it for all it was worth. This would help to cement his position in the affections of his people – a trick he is unlikely to have missed. It did not perhaps accord with the image of the gallant warrior that he was fostering, consciously or otherwise, but chivalry it seems had its limits.

Saladin's actions in effectively attempting to use force to coerce his captives to convert to the Muslim religion were essentially un-Islamic. Such tactics were against the tenets of the faith. The most likely explanation for Saladin's motives is that he meant to humiliate the Orders, again emphasising the triumph of Islam. He probably felt that he could offer them the choice because he believed that none would avail themselves of it. Those who did choose to become Muslims would be outside the communion of the Order forever and would be permanently disgraced. But he did at least give them what many of them aspired to, martyrdom for their faith, a death of supreme honour that would redound to their glory and help to smooth their passage into Heaven.

There was one man exempted from the slaughter to follow, the Templar knight most deserving of martyrdom. Almost certainly, Saladin recognised that Gerard de Ridfort's weakness, his cowardice in the face of defeat, meant that he could be used to gain an advantage – as indeed turned out to be the case. So the man who had been at the heart of the coup that had effectively disenfranchised and alienated Raymond of Tripoli, who had led his knights so recklessly into the slaughter at Cresson and had repeated the trick at Hattin, was allowed to live, to be given the opportunity of leading his knights into yet more disasters in the future.

Saladin gave the task of despatching the less fortunate knights of the Orders to a group of religious Sufis, holy men largely untrained in the arts of war. Some of them took six or seven attempts to sever the heads of their victims. Ironic cheers went up when a head came off after one blow. However justified the death of these men might have been in military terms, the cruelty and indignity of their death did Saladin no credit whatsoever. It was an act of violence, almost barbarism, which Saladin's apologists have all too frequently glossed over.

According to the *Itinararium Regis Ricardi*, many of the Templars sought martyrdom, rushing forward to embrace death. In a bizarre scene, this version states that there was virtually a race to see who could be killed first, which was only just won by a Templar named Nicholas. Following the slaughter, it was claimed that miraculous scenes could be witnessed. It was said that for the three nights that the bodies of the slain lay unburied a stream of heavenly light shone down upon them.

For many of the Turcopoles there would be no mercy either. Traitors in the eyes of the Muslim army, they were put to death. For the ordinary foot soldier or camp follower too – that is, the bulk of the Christian army – the future was hardly less bleak. They were also taken, along with the captured barons, to Damascus. But whereas the latter would by and large soon return to lives of relative comfort, their freedom purchased by extravagant ransom, for the poor a life of slavery and hardship beckoned. Their numbers were so great that a bizarre economic effect occurred – extensive deflation for the price of a slave. In one case, a Muslim captor decided that his prisoner was worth so little that he was exchanged for a pair of sandals.

Some men escaped the slaughter, however. Not only the rich and famous, such as Raymond, Balian and Joscelin of Courtenay, managed to extricate themselves from the battle but as many as 3,000 others survived,[17] suggesting perhaps that the Muslim noose was not as tight as it might have been or that the battle had been hard fought – or indeed both. The survivors made their way back to the great cities of Outremer, Acre, Tyre, Jerusalem and elsewhere, carrying stories of imminent disaster in their wake. Despite their escape, there were too few of them left to fight against Saladin's massive army. There can have been little doubt in their minds that Armageddon was at hand.

Hattin was now a field of death, the corpses of the slain scattered across the desolate hills and valley floor, the bodies of men and horses providing a feast for the vultures and other beasts of carrion who tugged greedily at the decaying flesh putrefying in the oven-like environment fired by the sun. The stench of death hung everywhere. Across the field of battle, the bodies of the Muslim slain were gathered up for a decent burial. It was a religious duty to bury the fallen on the day of death. Shrouds were carried by many soldiers on campaign to enable this to take place with all due dignity.

The ceremonials around burial were extremely simple, in keeping with the uncomplicated, austere ritual of Islam. The deceased would be reminded of the answers they should give when approaching paradise. For the enemy, no such honour was permitted. They would either be left to rot or thrown into hastily dug ditches. On occasion, there were instances of some of the Turkish forces keeping the heads of their enemy as a gruesome trophy of war, though whether or not this happened at Hattin is not mentioned by the chroniclers. It is likely that, given the fact that there was no pressing need to bury the Crusader dead as the battlefield was not close to habitation, they were just left to rot where they fell.

As much as it was a place of doom for the Christian rulers of Outremer, and despite its resemblance to a particularly disturbing Hieronymus Bosch landscape, it was also a field of glory for the Muslims. The victory won there owed much to the tactical acumen of Saladin. His troops had shown themselves to be far more manoeuvrable than the enemy. They had been well handled and well led. The terrain had been carefully chosen to maximise the advantages of the Muslim army. They had fought in a coordinated and disciplined manner. The execution was not flawless though: some of the enemy had escaped. But such criticisms are churlish when compared to the scale of the triumph.

In contrast, the leadership of the Christian army was far from exemplary. The decision to march without proper provisioning was a catastrophic blunder. It should have been clear that Saladin had laid a trap, but instead of recognising this, the Franks obligingly placed their head in the noose. The frailties of the structure of Outremer played themselves out in the battle. In contrast to Saladin, Guy did not have absolute authority. He had to negotiate with his barons and his control was weak at best. He was not a great tactician – but many men would have struggled to lead an army as disunited as his. Only a man with genuine top-class leadership qualities could have succeeded in uniting the army through the force of his personality and vision, and Guy was no such individual.

He was in a difficult position. He was bound by the laws of Jerusalem to aid a vassal attacked by Muslims and this legally compelled him to rush to the rescue of Eschiva in Tiberias. There were other reasons that could be used to excuse his tactics, too. He had been criticised for negative tactics in the past and now, at the head of the largest army ever raised in Outremer, his stock may have plummeted if he refused to fight. It should be remembered that not long before, some of the leading barons of the kingdom had allegedly encouraged Sibylla to divorce him rather than have him as their leader.

The position of the King vis-à-vis Raymond also needs to be considered. During the succession crisis of the previous year, Raymond had been bitterly opposed to Guy's usurpation of power. His interests had been badly damaged by the accession of Sibylla and Guy. It would have been all too easy for a powerful personality like Gerard of Ridfort to convince the King that Raymond was trying to discredit him.

All this is true and those who point out that Guy was in a difficult position present a rational case.[18] But a large part of the responsibility for Hattin must rest with him, nonetheless. His role was to offer leadership and on this occasion he failed to provide it. In part, this was the natural conclusion of a series of events that had seen the progressive decline of the status of the King of Jerusalem. All these problems were exacerbated by the weaknesses in Guy's personality, his lack of tactical nous and his inability to resist the manipulation of stronger men. A brave man, no doubt, but a good king, or a capable strategist, he was not.

Some commentators advocate caution about taking the accounts in support of Raymond of Tripoli's tactical advice before the battle at face value.[19] It has been said that these narratives have been written with the benefit of hindsight and attempt to make the Count out to be some kind of prophet. Of course, this can never be proved one way or the other. What follows must therefore be an opinion, one based on evidence, but subjective nevertheless.

Clearly, Raymond was no romantic: if he had been so, he would have attempted to reach Tiberias after his escape, but he did not do so. It is notable that those who know the region well remark that Raymond's route, his efforts to break through the Muslims guarding the path to the village of Hattin, gave him the opportunity to move on to Tiberias if he broke through.[20] In the event, he made no attempt to do so.

He was, instead, a hard-headed character, who made his decisions based on an analytical assessment of the situation rather than on instinctive emotional reactions, as for example Gerard would have done. He was lord of the land through which the army was marching. He knew how short of water the terrain that the army was to cross would be at this time of the year for the simple reason that he lived there.

He was also an experienced warrior who knew Saladin first hand. He was therefore well aware of his enemy's prowess and also of Muslim battle tactics. Knowing the country, knowing the enemy, knowing his tactics, surely it was all too obvious to Raymond that a trap was being laid and the army was marching straight into it. From this perspective, Raymond's cautionary attitude on the eve of battle rings true.

Yet he was a bitterly disappointed man. It is easy to talk of military strategies and of the policies of the kingdom, but the Hattin campaign was a human story too, of men with flaws and weaknesses as well as virtues and strengths. Raymond had spent much of his life in prison and had then sampled the intoxicating taste of power. He had seen that power snatched from him in the space of a year by some of the men who were in the very same army as him, such as Guy, the King, Reynald the marauder and Gerard, most fierce of rivals. He had been deprived of all the trappings of power, a loss that had left him angry and disillusioned – so much so that he had been prepared to take up arms against his noble brothers in the kingdom. What loyalty could he really feel to men such as these?

As he left the field of Hattin, abandoning both his comrades in arms on the field and his wife in Tiberias, he rode towards an uncertain future, not knowing that he had just a few months to live. One thing must have been abundantly clear to him given the size of the defeat: there was little point in thinking about who would rule Outremer in the future because there was little likelihood that it would continue to exist. One can only speculate as to the emotions he felt; regret, certainly, but perhaps more than a little guilt and shame. We know little of his short life post-Hattin but it does not seem unreasonable to assume, in the light of this denouement, that the Count of Tripoli was a broken man.

Raymond though had good reason to advocate caution during the Hattin campaign: one argument in particular was convincing. This was the fact that, just a few years earlier, the Crusader army had adopted a defensive posture when Saladin had invaded. Guy, leader of that army also, had suffered much criticism for his inaction on that occasion but no one could argue against the results of this passive resistance. Saladin had, in the end, gone away. For Raymond, such a result was enough. For men like Reynald and Gerard it was not. Nothing but crushing victory would suffice.

But Guy's previous experiences were not the only precedent to draw upon. The Crusaders were well used to fighting defensive actions and, indeed, could use them to claim a tactical advantage that might in the end lead to a decisive victory. If Saladin took Tiberias then he might well have been inspired to drive on towards the Crusader army. If he did so, then he would have borne the risk of water shortages and extended lines of communication. His army weakened, his supplies uncertain, the Franks might then have launched a counter-attack against a worn-out foe.

Considering all the options, there was really only one correct decision that could be taken: to stay on the defensive. For the risks were great and the price of failure extortionate. If Saladin had lost at Hattin, then he would have gone away to lick his wounds and perhaps have tried again later. If the Franks lost the battle, then they would lose their kingdom. These were ridiculous odds to take on when the benefits of victory could only be limited and the costs of defeat were enormous. Hattin should never have been fought. Or, as one of the great pioneers of military history, Sir Charles Oman, said of it in the nineteenth century:

> The whole battle, therefore, was unnecessary, and the details of Guy's bad generalship are comparatively small blunders when compared with the enormous initial mistake of fighting at all.[21]

The Franks had battled gallantly, even heroically, but then their courage was never really in question. Even Nur ed-Din had said of them that they were 'the bravest people of earth'.[22] It was their judgement that was at fault. As one commentator has succinctly put it, Hattin was won by Saladin because 'he got his enemies to fight where he wanted, when he wanted and how he wanted'.[23]

It was for Saladin the defining moment of his life, a victory that brought him enormous kudos throughout the Muslim world, for it effectively opened up the gates of Jerusalem. Imad ad-Din soon after said of Saladin and Hattin that 'were no other merit his than that of this day, in majesty and valour Saladin would still stand out above all the kings of former times let alone of this age'.[24]

Inspired by the religious significance of his great triumph, and wishing to give the honour to Allah, Saladin ordered a monument to be erected on the battlefield, known as the Dome of Victory. Here, on the southern Horn where the King of Outremer had stubbornly erected his tent in a last gesture of defiance, a testament to the victory of Islam surveyed the field of Hattin. It has long gone now, witness to the transience of human glory and the frail uncertainties of our existence. Nothing lasts forever, as the Kingdom of Jerusalem was about to find out. As one writer eloquently said of Hattin, 'this fateful battle was fought on 4 July 1187. In that short space of time, all the glory of the Kingdom of Jerusalem was shattered and destroyed.'[25]

With the loss of the army, Outremer, even Jerusalem, lay bare before the Muslim conqueror. No viable garrisons remained to defend the cities and citadels of Christendom. It was all just a matter of time, and it was unlikely to be very long before the Dome of the Rock was once more in Muslim hands. Defenceless and demoralised, all the people of Jerusalem, Acre, Tyre and the other great places of Outremer could do was watch and wait like a flock of sheep, frozen into a state of hypnotised terror, as a pack of wolves charged down the mountainside towards them.

ELEVEN

Last Rites

And I heard a great voice out of the temple saying to the seven angels, Go your ways, and pour out the vials of the wrath of God upon the earth.

Revelation 16: 1

Saladin had won a great victory. However, the destruction of the army of Jerusalem, important though it was, was not an end in itself. Rather, it was the means by which the Holy City itself could be taken. To achieve that objective, time was of the essence. He must push on to ensure that al-Quts was now recovered for Islam.

The reasons for these time pressures had little to do with the enemy, who were poorly equipped to defend the kingdom. The garrisons of Outremer had been stripped bare to man the army of Jerusalem. Most of the soldiers in that army were now either bleached bones on the field of Hattin or they stood in chains in the slave markets of Damascus. The emaciated garrisons that remained would not be enough to hold off Saladin.

As far as reinforcements were concerned, it would be weeks before the West even heard of the outcome of the battle. It would be months, probably years, before new Crusading armies could be raised and transport arranged to move them eastwards – the latter in itself a monumental undertaking. By the time they arrived, Jerusalem would be long lost – provided that Saladin moved quickly.

Neither was the Byzantine Empire likely to intervene. The halcyon days of Manuel Comnenus were but a dim and distant memory. Since his death, the Empire had declined rapidly. Those who now ruled in Constantinople were far too busy watching their backs dealing with the next would-be usurper to worry about foreign adventures. Even if they had had the desire, they lacked the wherewithal to make any meaningful move on Saladin to protect the Franks' kingdom. And the truth was that they did not have any motivation to assist Outremer, for the Western powers had done little for the cause of Byzantium in the region. Rather, their presence in the Levant had served to emphasise the disunity of Christendom between East and West. The Crusades had done Byzantium little good.

No, the real reason for the need for speed was not the strength of the remaining garrisons of Outremer, it was not the West, it was not Byzantium. It was rather Saladin's own, mostly volunteer army that was the problem. No doubt morale was at unprecedented levels and, given the spiritual nature of the *jihad* most of the army would want to complete the task and conquer Jerusalem. But the campaign could not be long and drawn out. Otherwise, the fervour would wane, the enthusiasm diminish and morale would sink. Should this happen, men would start to desert the army and return to their homes, to bask in the reflected glory of the triumph of Hattin if not the capture of Jerusalem.

Such emotions were hardly surprising, particularly when some of the army came from as far away as Iraq. The harvest was due for reaping and landowners would need to return to their territories to ensure that all taxes due were collected. It has even been suggested that some of the men were worried because under Muslim law if a man were away for more than four months then his wife could divorce him.[1]

Saladin therefore moved with alacrity. First to fall, predictably enough, was Tiberias, now beyond hope of succour. Saladin treated the Lady Eschiva with honour, allowing her to go free and make her way unmolested to the coast. The rest of Galilee fell soon afterwards. Count Raymond's lands (or to be legally accurate his wife's) were lost to Christendom forever. If the Count were indeed a traitor, then he appears to have been singularly poorly rewarded for his treachery by Saladin.

The port of Acre was even more critical to the survival of a viable Outremer than the Holy City. Within three days of Hattin, Saladin had despatched Taqi al-Din to see if he could seize it. The city was under the command of the Seneschal of the kingdom, Joscelin of Courtenay, who had played such a key and dishonourable role in the election of Guy as king. It was too much to expect that Joscelin would put up much of a fight. He had in any case seen far too much of the Muslims in recent days. He had been involved in the battle and had escaped along with Balian of Ibelin. He knew better than most the power of his enemy.

What followed was shameful. Saladin arrived outside Acre on 8 July, a day after an army under Taqi al-Din had arrived and invested the city. Joscelin sent an envoy, by the name of Peter Brice – a member of a Venetian family long associated with Acre – to negotiate for the city's surrender. Joscelin sent him, along with the keys to the city, and asked for a safe conduct for the leading inhabitants, and of course their possessions, in return.

In Acre itself, many were horrified at this cowardice and riots broke out in protest. Fires were started by some of the inhabitants, who said that they would burn the city rather than let it fall into Muslim hands. When Saladin arrived outside the walls he was so shocked at the sight of the fires that he promised to treat the citizens with kindness and courtesy if they would put them out.

On 10 July, less than a week after Hattin, Acre was lost without the semblance of a fight. Those who wished to remain could do so on condition that they paid the tax traditionally charged on all non-Muslims in Muslim states. Those who did not wish to stay would be escorted to a safe place from where they could make their way to wherever they wished. In the event, few of the citizens opted to live under Muslim rule. One Christian did benefit though. The brother of the Byzantine Emperor had been imprisoned by the Franks. He was now released and sent to Constantinople by Saladin. This act further strengthened relations between Byzantium and the Sultan, but it hammered yet another nail into the coffin of Byzantine and West European relations.

The people of Acre were given forty days to put their affairs in order before they left. Great riches were captured in the port when the Muslims moved in, and these were distributed generously among the army as payback for their service so far. One group to benefit from the capture of the city were the Muslim slaves inside its walls, some 4,000 in all. It has been estimated that the conquest of Outremer released 20,000 Muslim slaves in the country while 100,000 Franks were theoretically taken captive in return, though a number of these would surely have been released at some point.[2]

The capture of Acre gave the Muslims a port on the Mediterranean coast in Outremer for the first time since the fall of Ascalon in 1153. Saladin ordered ten galleys up from Alexandria to use Acre as a base for maritime operations. Possession of the port meant that Saladin had access to the wealth that came from the Western merchants who used the port for access to the region (and would continue to do so) but, more importantly in the short term, deprived Crusaders from the West of the chance to use it as the launch-pad for a counter-attack into Outremer.

Saladin now despatched forces to mop up resistance in Samaria and Galilee, while his brother, al-Adil, brought up an army from Egypt to lay siege to Jaffa, another important port on the coast. Here, the city resisted, but in vain. It was stormed and most of the population sold on into captivity. Sidon followed on 29 July – again without a fight – and Beirut changed hands on 6 August. This was not so much a military campaign, more a triumphant processional.

Two days of shame followed, one at Ascalon, another at Gaza. The Egyptian fleet had blockaded Ascalon, cutting off its lifeline across the sea. A hard fight ensued in which several of Saladin's more prominent emirs were killed. The city was strongly fortified and capable of putting up stern resistance. When the defence proved to be stubborn, Guy of Lusignan was brought up from Damascus.

On arrival at Ascalon, Guy was offered his freedom if he could persuade the city to surrender. The King approached the walls and shouted up the terms he had been offered. In fairness to him, he told the citizens that if they felt they could hold the city against Saladin they should not give up; but if on the other hand they were not confident they could do so then he asked them to surrender. Believing that they could not hold out, they decided to take the terms on offer provided that they were allowed to go free along with their possessions.

Saladin complied with the terms and also promised to release nine of the senior knights in his possession. Despite the generosity of the terms, the fact remained that Ascalon had fallen without a fight. It appeared that the people of Outremer now believed that the demise of the kingdom was inevitable. The point was hammered home soon after at Gaza, which with Ascalon formed the forward defences to Outremer on the road from Egypt. It was a specific part of the Templar code that a knight could not bargain for his ransom. The code was clearly something that either the Master had not read or, if he had, he had decided that it did not apply to him. He instructed the garrison of Templars to surrender so that he might be freed. The deal was done, and Gerard was released.

Guy was kept for a while longer. His imprisonment does not appear to have been harsh and his queen, Sibylla, was allowed to join him. They were set free in 1188, something of a masterstroke by Saladin as it caused yet more problems for the rump of the kingdom because of the political difficulties that the presence of the discredited monarch created.

Saladin's strategy so far was clear enough. To borrow a botanical analogy, he hoped that by digging up the roots the fruit would wither on the vine. In other words, Jerusalem – and Outremer – could not survive without the castles and cities that protected it. By eliminating as many of these as possible, Jerusalem would be indefensible and would fall meekly into Saladin's lap. Jerusalem could not stand alone, a strategic reality that Richard the Lionheart would have to deal with a few years later: it was a problem that he never overcame.

Saladin took a calculated gamble that he could delay the attack on Jerusalem for a short while and still keep his army together. If he were to besiege the city first, then there was a small risk of a counter-attack from the vastly depleted Latin forces left in the kingdom, but a much greater one that his army would dissolve once the city fell. This would leave the job half done. Much better to take the other important cities first and still leave the prospect of Jerusalem as the ultimate lure to keep his army in the field.

The rapid mopping up of so many cities in Outremer meant that the problem of morale did not arise. Triumph followed triumph as surely as summer follows spring. Nothing interfered with the relentless advance of Islam. And so it was that, at last, preparations for the assault on Jerusalem were made. While at Ascalon, Saladin received a delegation from the Holy City. In a moment of wonderfully apposite symbolism, while they talked an eclipse of the sun plunged the place into darkness in the middle of the day or, as one account vividly put it, 'the sun moved in such a way that at the hour of nones it seemed like night'.[3]

Saladin did not initially want to take the city by force. As a religious man, he had no desire to damage the sacred buildings of Jerusalem in an assault, so instead he came up with an offer. He would give the citizens money to fortify the place and would leave them unmolested until next Pentecost. If by that time a relieving force had not come to their aid, then they would surrender the city to him.

But the citizens were not as timid as some of their compatriots. They would not, they said, surrender the place where Christ had died to his enemies. Saladin's mood then became much sterner. So be it, he responded. If they would not surrender the city to him under these very reasonable terms then it would be a fight to the death.

The defiance of the citizens appeared to be predicated more on their contemplation of martyrdom rather than any military prospect of success. They did not even have anyone of reputation to organise the defence. The Master of the Temple was in captivity, the Master of the Hospital had died. Reynald had been decapitated and the King was in Saladin's hands. Raymond, whose reputation had been badly damaged, was back in Tripoli while most other knights of standing were dead or captured.

But with a fortunate sense of timing, Balian of Ibelin had recently arrived in Jerusalem. He had been in Tyre, then one of the few remaining places in Latin hands, and had successfully sought a safe conduct from Saladin to fetch his wife, the former Queen Maria, and their children who were trapped in the city. Saladin consented only on condition that he spent just one night there and he bore no arms. Balian agreed to do so, swearing on the Bible to confirm his oath. But when Balian arrived he found the city in a state of chaos, despite the best efforts of Queen Sibylla and the Patriarch Heraclius to organise a defence.

Many of the people begged Balian to stay. He was a man of good repute, tried and tested in arms and with a sound military record behind him – just the sort of person to organise the city in the face of the imminent Muslim attack. As Balian was about to leave, the pleas of the populace grew frantic. Heraclius approached him, and absolved him of his oath. Balian felt that he had no choice but to comply. Anxious at the moral dilemma facing him, he wrote to Saladin explaining the reasons for breaking the terms of his safe conduct. In response, Saladin recognised the difficulties facing Balian and forgave him to such an extent that Queen Maria and her children were allowed to leave unmolested for Tyre with all the possessions that they could carry.

The population of the city had grown enormously as refugees from the tidal wave that had swept Outremer had sought security within the doubtful safety of its walls. This put huge pressures on already depleted supplies. Only two knights were present in the city, so Balian knighted every male over 16 with a noble background. He then set about organising a form of government in the besieged city. Practical considerations were not forgotten and gold was stripped from the roof of the Holy Sepulchre so that the new knights could be paid. As much food as possible was garnered, and the funds that the Hospital had received from King Henry II of England were sequestered to help pay for the defence.

The Muslim army lumbered inexorably towards the Holy City, unstoppable and seemingly assured of triumph. Frantic preparations were made by the inhabitants to prepare their city to resist the foe. For some, it was already too late. The monks of the Premonstratensian house of Montjoie had tried to erect defences to rebuff the Muslims, but the place was overwhelmed before they could complete their work.[4] But, like a cornered animal, the defenders of the city could still produce a fierce bite. The fortified abbey at Bethany was taken, but in the aftermath one of Saladin's emirs, assuming that the fight was over, advanced carelessly and paid for his slovenliness with his life. The defenders had scoured as much in the way of possessions from the surrounding countryside as they could. Not everyone sought glory though. Within the walls were thousands of defenceless and terrified civilians. But there were enough zealots to ensure that Jerusalem would produce its fair share of martyrs.

The Muslim army duly prepared for its attack. The tactics to be used had been honed through decades of practice. The standard technique was for lightly armoured infantry to launch the attack while the heavier siege engines were moved into position. Engineers would erect palisades to protect the encircling army, behind which trenches were built. Miners would also be used if appropriate, but this was a tactic used more by the Muslims than the Latins[5] and was a tried and tested technique (witness for example the fall of Edessa a few decades earlier).

A wide range of siege engines was available. It has become the norm to think of these as massive constructions capable of hurling huge boulders at the walls with astonishing velocity. But destruction of masonry was not their only task. They were also employed to keep the battlements clear of archers and others hurling missiles at the besieging force.

Sieges could be long and protracted affairs. They would normally commence with an offer to the besieged to surrender on good terms. Saladin had already effectively made this offer at Ascalon. Once an assault had been decided upon, the attackers needed to ensure that they were protected against a sally from out of the besieged city. This was an option seriously considered by the defenders of Jerusalem, even though the odds against success were prohibitively high. From the besiegers' perspective, once a breach had been created, another offer of surrender might be made.

Often the outcome of a siege was decided not by warfare but by starvation or disease (sometimes as much of a problem for the attackers as for the defenders). Such sieges could be very protracted and were a trial of nerve and determination as much as of strength. The attackers' camp could be extensive. At the counter-siege that Saladin laid around the Franks besieging Acre in 1190 there were some 7,000 shops patrolled by Saladin's own police force. Bathhouses were set up to look after the cleanliness of the attackers (and in the process reduce the possibility of disease).[6]

But such protracted sieges were to be the exception rather than the rule in this campaign. There were many reasons for this. For one, the Franks had lost many of their garrisons at Hattin. The Muslims therefore had overwhelming force on their side. Latin morale was also low and leadership generally poor. Further, Outremer was an enclave, an anomalous island in the midst of a Muslim sea. The difficulty in reinforcing the cities of the kingdom with provisions and men meant that Saladin's advantage was generally decisive. Only in one case did this prove to be untrue, significantly at Tyre, on the coast, a city that could be reprovisioned from the sea.

Many people had taken refuge inside Jerusalem's walls but few of them were fighters by profession. Refugees had streamed in from across Outremer, including some from cities now lost such as Ascalon and Gaza. Some of the usual afflictions of a siege would be spared the defenders since there was, at least, water. As Fulcher of Chartres, a chronicler of the First Crusade, had noted of the city at the beginning of the twelfth century:

the city of Jerusalem is situated in a mountainous place, lacking streams, woods and springs, with the sole exception of the spring at Siloam, which is a bowshot from the town, in the bottom of the valley under Mount Zion. However, there are many cisterns in the city holding plentiful water, which are reserved for the rains of winter.[7]

These cisterns were invaluable.

But even if supplies were available to sustain the defence, the prospect of attack from the huge army without the walls was nevertheless terrifying. Moreover, the city was heavily overcrowded.

It was compact at the best of times, never a kilometre across at its widest point and never more than 800 metres from north to south. Within this cramped area, with its warren of alleys, a terrified population prepared itself for the worst. It was a fearful, febrile atmosphere.

Saladin needed to find a weak spot. There were five main gates and up to eight posterns,[8] frequently interspersed at regular intervals with towers. Some of them, such as the Templar Gate in the southern part of the city, were massive. It was the north-west that appeared weakest, overlooked by higher ground, and it was here that Saladin decided to make his initial move.

The attack began on 20 September. The first assault was against the north-west corner of the city walls between the David and St Stephen Gates. The fighting was fierce and caused grievous injuries to many of the defenders. One of them, the anonymous writer of *De Expugnationae Terrae Sanctae*, mentions that he was hit in the nose by an arrow, stating that 'the metal tip has remained there to this day'.[9]

The Muslim siege engines hurled their deadly load against the city, hammering into walls and battlements, sending up choking clouds of dust and rubble and crushing skulls and limbs beneath them as they pinned their unfortunate victims to the ground. The defenders had their own engines on the Towers of David and Tancred and they spewed out their defiance, exacting their own toll in revenge. The defence was fierce and determined. Heroic sallies from within the city drove the attackers back.

Breaches made could not be exploited. The Muslims were troubled by the sun shining brightly in their faces, so much so that they delayed their assaults to the late afternoon when the sun was low in the sky and more of a problem for the defenders. To add to the discomfort of the gallant army manning the walls, mangonels were loaded with sand in an attempt to blind them while Muslim troops attempted to climb siege ladders. But a number of days' attack achieved no tangible gain for Saladin: against the odds, the initial attack had been repulsed. After Hattin, all appeared lost, but it was clear that the defenders of Jerusalem, trapped and with nowhere else to run, would exact a heavy price for their city.

When Saladin moved camp on 25 September some of the defenders believed that the siege had been lifted and that they had achieved a miraculous victory; but the optimists were disabused of this misguided idea on the following day when the army appeared again and set up camp in a different position. From his new base near the Mount of Olives, Saladin set about the city with renewed vigour. His cause was helped as there was only one place where the defenders could sally out and attempt to drive him back. Then, by the second day of this second phase of the assault, he brought up his siege engines, petraries and mangonels. He used his infantry to set up a shield wall, from behind which his archers could fire on the defenders desperately seeking cover behind the wall's machicolations. They unleashed clouds of arrows, shooting 'so quickly that it was like rain'.[10]

The attack was focused against the walls of the northern sector of the city, to the east of where the previous attack had been directed. The north-east angle of the city where the Syrian quarter was placed was the weakest part of the defences. It was here that the Crusaders had made their critical breach when taking the city in 1099. At one stage in the battle, a boulder from one of the petraries scored a direct hit on the wooden hoarding shielding one of the towers, causing it to implode with a massive crash. So great was the noise that the defenders thought that the whole wall had come down, while those besieging the city believed that a huge counter-attack was being launched against them. But neither was right.

As so often in medieval warfare, it was not the great ballistae, the mighty battering ram, or precipitous siege towers that won the day but the skills of humble miners. Three battalions of engineers advanced to the base of the walls. Protective devices were put up over them while they dug away at the outer wall, to shield them from the deadly arrow-storm that rained down. They worked in conditions of suffocating claustrophobia. They were helped no end by the fire from their own archers, which was so heavy that the defenders dared not show their faces above the parapet. Scraping away for hour after hour in the airless, oven-like tunnels that they had chiselled painstakingly into the earth, their efforts began to bear fruit within a few days. One tunnel ran for 30 metres. The roof was propped up with timbers and, when the time was right, these were set ablaze. As flames consumed the timbers the wood disintegrated and the roof crashed down, bringing the walls above with it.

By 29 September, sections of the wall had started to collapse outwards into the ditch and the city was poised on the brink of a terrifying chasm. Disaster loomed for the defenders. Sorties were launched from Jerusalem, only to be driven back by Saladin's cavalry, which he had kept at hand in case of such an eventuality. Realising that the end was nigh, some of the more fanatical zealots inside the city proposed that everyone should make one final sortie from within. Such an attack would be doomed, unless God saw fit to provide a miracle, and would be more an act of collective martyrdom than a military exercise. The population included a disproportionate number of women and children, while true fighting men were in very limited supply.

Glorious though the defence had been, it now seemed doomed to fail. It seemed as if even God had now deserted the defenders and left them to their cruel fate:

> The citizens put up what barriers they could but everything our people tried was fruitless and unsuccessful. In vain they wielded catapults and slings. It was as though both weapons and engines were clearly proclaiming the wrath of the Lord and foretelling the doom of the city.[11]

Both Heraclius and Balian believed that these proposals for a sortie were madness. To engage in such an act would be to invite the Infidel to slay all the men and lead the women and children off to a life of slavery. Heraclius chose the moment to offer up the observation that, by their martyrdom, those who wished to fight to the death might save their own souls but condemn those of their kith and kin to perdition. Far better to try to negotiate some kind of deal.

It was hardly a glorious position for the Patriarch to take but it was at least pragmatic. In addition, if either Balian or Heraclius were in touch with some of the key constituencies in the city, they may also have been aware that there was an enemy within. Saladin had apparently already made contact with some of the Orthodox Christians in the city who were prepared to open the gates to him. Ironically, they felt that they would receive more religious freedom under Muslim rule than they currently enjoyed under their Catholic brothers.

The imagery of the last few hours of Jerusalem was almost apocalyptic. The women brought out huge basins, setting them up by the hill on which Christ's crucifixion had taken place. Immersing their children up to their necks, they then shaved their heads. Their daughters were stripped naked and washed in cold baths in public at Calvary – a mark of shame that showed that no indignity was too great if only such actions bought divine aid to save Jerusalem. All the priests and nuns in the city walked barefoot around the perimeter of the walls as they carried another portion of the True Cross (described as a 'Syrian' variant: not to be confused with that taken at Hattin) and praying for salvation.

Their prayers went unanswered. According to one of the chroniclers, 'the stench of adultery, of disgusting extravagance and of sin against nature would not let their prayers rise to God. God was so angered at the people that He cleansed the city of them.'[12]

Here we have a sideswipe at those who had settled in Outremer and adopted a sensible 'live and let live' philosophy. The people of the West sometimes saw their fellow Christians in Outremer as a soft and morally loose breed, who adopted too many of the customs of the locals and even – especially despicable – sometimes intermarried. In their simplistic worldview, there was no room for accommodation with the perceived enemies of Christ – not just Muslims or Jews, but even Christians of the 'wrong' persuasion, Orthodox or Syrian. These two views of the world had fought each other, a battle between the hawks like Reynald of Chatillon and Gerard of Ridfort and those who sought accommodation like Raymond of Tripoli.

Saladin took the moral high ground when Balian of Ibelin approached him to discuss surrender terms soon after. He had sworn to take the city by the sword, partly to avenge the massacre that the Crusaders had visited on the city when they had first captured it in 1099. He was already in secret discussions with the non-Frankish elements within the city, who, as we have seen, were happy enough to see a Muslim victory. One of Saladin's close confidantes was an Orthodox Christian named Joseph Batit, whose co-religionists inside Jerusalem were ready to open a gate into the city and let the enemy in. Even as they spoke, a Muslim flag appeared on the walls; but it was quickly thrown down again. Why should he negotiate?

Balian's response was blunt but realistic. If the defenders were forced to fight to the death then they would take as many Muslims as possible with them. Further, there were some of the most sacred sites in Islam within the city walls. Balian would have no compunction in raising them to the ground unless terms were offered. In short, if Saladin were not prepared to negotiate then all he would gain when he conquered the city would be a heap of rubble and a pile of corpses.

Subtle the argument was not, but it was convincing. Saladin had no wish to take possession of a ruin. He therefore proposed that the population should ransom itself at the cost of ten dinars for a man, five for a woman and one for a child. Balian calculated that there were about 20,000 poor folk in the city who could not afford such a sum. The city was full of people from the surrounding areas who had made their way into the city to seek protection. Now their refuge had become a prison.

Saladin agreed that the poor could all be released for a lump sum of 100,000 dinars. There was no prospect of all this money being raised, so a sum of 30,000 dinars for the release of 7,000 of these unfortunates was agreed. These terms may seem harsh, but were better by far than they could have been. And there was, in truth, no alternative for Balian; so the deal was struck.

The Franks came perilously close to a bloodbath. The awful treatment meted out to Jerusalem when it had first been taken by them in 1099 had seared itself into the Muslim consciousness. There is conclusive evidence in a letter to the caliph written after the event that Saladin had intended to exact highly priced retribution when he took the city. He says that, when Balian sought terms

> we refused point blank, wishing only to shed the blood of the men and to reduce the women and children to slavery. But they threatened to kill the prisoners, and to ruin and destroy crops and buildings. We granted them the aman in return for a ransom equal to their value if they had been made prisoner and reduced to slavery. Those who did not pay the ransom became slaves.[13]

In other words, Saladin had intended to expunge the horrors of the original sack of Jerusalem by inflicting his own. By his skills as a negotiator, whether or not he was indulging in an outrageous bluff as to his intentions, Balian had saved the lives of thousands of people.

Friday is a holy day for Muslims, and 2 October marked a particularly resonant moment for Islam, this being the anniversary of the occasion when the Prophet Mohammed had been transported to the city in his sleep and taken up to Heaven. So there was no better day on which Saladin could have entered the city in triumph.

On that day in 1187, the gates of Jerusalem were opened to Saladin the Conqueror. His troops filed in in their thousands, overwhelmed by the significance of the moment and the place that it bought them all in history. There was by most accounts no violence. No treasure was taken, no women dishonoured, no one slain in bloodthirsty revenge for acts committed long ago. Saladin's guards patrolled the streets more to protect the Christians than to bully them. Right from the outset, Saladin posted two Muslim knights and ten sergeants on each street to ensure that no one did harm to the captured population.

The discipline and restraint of Saladin's soldiers could not disguise the fact that thousands were faced with an imminent loss of freedom unless their ransom could be found. The 30,000 dinars was found with some difficulty, and the money recently sent by Henry II of England to fund a new Crusade was now used instead to buy the freedom of many of the 7,000 poor whose release Balian had negotiated. The funds were those that had been deposited with the

Hospitallers: as we have already seen, those sent to the Temple had been spent on hiring troops for the Hattin campaign. It proved easy to convince the Hospitallers to give up these funds as the brothers believed that Saladin would seize the money in any case.

There was a precise rate of exchange for the prisoners. Two women or ten children were equated to one man in terms of the numbers released. Those freed should keep their arms to protect themselves against bandits, although the Muslim army would watch over them for the first part of their journey to freedom.

On the day of the takeover, the keys to the main gate were taken out to Saladin and the city handed over formally. He then posted his guards on the exits from the city, so that none might escape without first of all paying their ransom. Magnanimity in victory clearly only went so far. Those wishing to buy their freedom should present themselves with their ransom at the Tower of David. They had to depart within fifty days because those left in the city after that period would be deemed to be Saladin's slaves.

When the time for purchasing freedom came, the actions of the Patriarch Heraclius were shocking. He paid the ten dinars for his own release and presumably for those of his servants whom he needed and then left the city accompanied by as much of the Church's wealth as he could carry. While a line of carts carrying the possessions of the wealthy lumbered towards the coast, laden down with their possessions, another line composed of weeping, distraught, terrified fellow Christians prepared to march into a life of slavery in a strange and alien culture.

Even the Muslims were shocked at this lack of compassion and insisted that the rich should be deprived of their wealth. But Saladin had an image to protect. A deal was a deal and he had only insisted that a ransom be paid in return for freedom. It would be dishonourable to change the terms of surrender once the city was his.

The Sultan was also living up to an ancient code of conduct, the *siyar*, which governed the rules of war in the Islamic world. This emphasised in particular the importance of keeping one's word. Women, children, the elderly, non-military slaves or religious officials should not be harmed, and any destruction visited on a conquered city should only be commensurate with military necessity. Men could be killed but again only if this was unavoidable. It was an ideal, of course, and it was breached many times by Muslim commanders (for example, Zengi at Edessa forty years before). But the fact that such rules existed at all was an advance on what was on offer from Christendom at the time, and in this instance at least it appears that they were generally complied with.

There were rumours that Saladin might have released more prisoners were it not for the subterfuge of one man, allegedly an Englishman. This individual, an apparently poor man, was heading out of the city carrying a gourd on a stick. He was spotted by some Muslim Sufis, or holy men, who assumed that there was wine in the pitcher. As drinking was anathema to them (though not to many other Muslims, who drank widely, for example a form of beer called *buzah*),[14] they grappled with the man for the gourd, intending to dispose of the alcohol. But, as they struggled for the gourd it fell from the stick and shattered into smithereens. Rather than wine, it was a torrent of gold coins that fell to the ground. Believing that wealth was being illicitly smuggled out of the city, Saladin let no one else go free without a ransom.

Two groups of Franks now left Jerusalem, one headed for freedom, the other for captivity. Many of the Muslims were overwhelmed at the pathos of the situation. Saladin's brother al-Adil asked that he might be given a gift of 1,000 of the slaves for his own use. Saladin agreed, upon which al-Adil released them all there and then. Heraclius, shocked into action, asked for 700, which was granted; and Balian received 500. Saladin announced that all the elderly slaves should also be released.

Further compassionate acts followed. The captive husbands of any woman released were freed, while widows and orphans received gifts from Saladin's own treasury. But despite these grand gestures, praiseworthy and meaningful though they were, many remained to be carried off into a life of drudgery and exploitation. Up to 11,000 people made their way off to new and frightening existence in an unknown land.[15] To educated Christians who witnessed these scenes, perhaps the words of the New Testament felt especially poignant: 'And they shall fall by the edge of the sword, and shall be led away captive into all nations: and Jerusalem shall be trodden down of the Gentiles, until the times of the Gentiles be fulfilled.'[16]

Three columns moved the other way towards the coast. The Templars led one, the Hospitallers the second and Balian and Heraclius the third. Fifty Muslim knights would escort them to safety in Christian-held lands. As any stragglers fell by the wayside, the escort would pick them up and carry them to safety, ensuring that losses were kept to an absolute minimum. When the party reached a defile where an ambush from bandits was possible, the escort ensured that all the Latin men-at-arms took up their weapons so that any assault could be successfully beaten back.

Where to go was more of a problem. Tyre, still under siege, refused to admit anyone except fighting men. As those that remained moved on, they were subject to attack from unscrupulous warlords whose lands they passed through. Tripoli did not have enough resources to feed them all, and so again many were left outside the gates. Raiding parties from within the city fell on unguarded sections of the sorry host and robbed them of the few possessions they had managed to retain. A safe haven was found only on reaching Antioch.

Those parties in the south of the country were more fortunate. Many of them made their way to Alexandria, where they were housed in makeshift stockades to ensure that none escaped. Apart from this loss of liberty, they were well treated. When ships arrived from the West in the spring, the prisoners were embarked and taken to Christian lands overseas. While they were in the city, the elders of Alexandria supplied them with gifts of wine, bread and money.

By March it was time for them to depart. Many ships from the Italian city-states had wintered in the port. Now they wished to leave, but because they would not be paid for carrying the human cargo (and neither did they have supplies for them) they had no desire to take the prisoners with them. The governor of Alexandria had previously taken away the oars of the ships so that they could not steal away without paying the port taxes due. When he heard that the Italian ships did not want to take the captives with them, he asked them bluntly how they would steer without oars – he refused to give them back unless they took the prisoners back to safety.

The attitude of the Muslim governor, desirous that Saladin's reputation should not be sullied, contrasted markedly with the behaviour of the sailing-masters of the Christian ships. But in the end the latter had no choice. They could not leave without the prisoners, and before they went they were all made to swear sacred vows on the Bible that they would look after their charges meticulously and do all that they could to ensure that they came to no harm.

In Jerusalem itself, the Orthodox and Syrian Christians mostly remained in the city. Some of the wealthier members of the population bought the properties vacated by the Franks when they left. Latin churches were largely handed over to other Christian groups for use as their own places of worship. Jews and Muslims were also encouraged to settle in the city to help seal the Islamic reconquest through social, rather than military, measures. For all but the Franks, Saladin's triumph was widely welcomed.

The attitude of the native Christians had largely been shaped by the way in which the Latin Church had conducted itself since the First Crusade of 1099. Latin clergy had been established in the cities that had been conquered and Greek bishops had not been allowed to return, which naturally infuriated the Orthodox Church. Syrian Christians had been permitted to retain their churches but there was no doubt that the Latins provided the dominant ecclesiastical force in the kingdom, a predominance that had been emphasised by the arrival of a number of monastic orders. Given an opportunity to redress the balance, it is no real surprise that local Christians took advantage of the situation.

But care needs to be taken that this view of the Muslims as liberators among non-Latin Christians does not become a cliché. Not all of the inhabitants felt this way. A Syrian Christian writing of the capture of Jerusalem leaves an account strikingly at odds with the picture of the smooth transfer of power that is often portrayed, saying that:

> words cannot describe the crimes we saw committed in the town; nor could any books contain them; how the sacred vessels were

sold in the town's markets to men of various races; how the churches and the altars became stables for the horses and cattle and places of debauchery, drinking and singing. Added to which was the shame and derision of the monks, of noblewomen, of pure nuns who were delivered to impurity with all sorts of people, of the boys and girls who became Turkish slaves and were dispersed to the four corners of the earth.[17]

In other words, there are alternative views to consider, which suggest that some shameful acts did take place after the capture of the city though not, it must be said, on anything like the scale that had attended the Crusaders' conquest in 1099.

According to some, not all the Franks left. It was rumoured that there were two aged men in the city, one called Robert of Coudre, who had journeyed to Jerusalem with Godfrey of Bouillon, and the other called Fouchier Fiole, who had been born in the city soon after its conquest in 1099. They asked Saladin if they could stay and see out their lives in Jerusalem. He was happy to agree to their requests and so they stayed on. The story may seem fanciful. Robert must have been in his 90s even if he was a young boy in Godfrey's entourage. But it is just possible that it is true. And in many ways one hopes that it is.

Neither was this the only story to suggest that not everyone left Outremer. Some thirty years after Hattin, a traveller, Thietmar, was lost and asked a French widow who still lived at Montreal the way to Mount Sinai. The fact that a relic of the Frankish era was still living in such an out of the way place, far removed from any other human beings of her race, suggests just how magnetic was the attraction of the Holy Land to those who believed that it was a place of special spiritual significance.

There was one more serious act whose full significance would only become apparent nearly twenty years later. Isaac Angelus, the Emperor of Byzantium, wrote to Saladin congratulating him on his victory and asking that the holy Christian places of Jerusalem should be returned to Orthodox hands. Saladin took a while to make a decision, but eventually fell in with the request. At some point, a Greek patriarch would return to the city.

For the Franks, Isaac's actions were despicable treason. They came as the final straw in a series of initiatives emanating from Constantinople that were regarded by the Franks as perfidious. Seventeen years later, in 1204, a Crusade ostensibly on its way to Egypt diverted to Constantinople and sacked the city, setting up a Frankish Empire within Byzantium itself. As the inhabitants of Constantinople woke up to the devastation that had scarred their city beyond repair, as they wandered through the ashes of whole sections of the city that had been consumed in flames, as they looked on in disbelief as some of the holiest treasures in Christendom were grabbed for their scrap metal value and as they averted the gaze of hundreds of their violated womenfolk, then some of them may have thought that Isaac's sycophantic missive to Saladin was no less than an ill-advised suicide note.

All that was still in the future though, and when Saladin worshipped for the first time in the newly rededicated al-Aqsa Mosque on 9 October 1187, it was a moment of supreme triumph, both for Saladin and the faith that he fought for. It was the second time that Islam had captured Jerusalem from Christians and, as on the first occasion half a millennium earlier, its conquest had been followed by scenes that were largely peaceful, although one should not underestimate the sense of devastation felt by those who faced a lifetime of slavery or those Christians in the city who believed that the loss of Jerusalem was a terrible blow for Christendom.

For the priests, those who could read the Bible, the words of Revelation may have touched particularly tender emotions:

> And he carried me away in the spirit to a great and high mountain, and showed me that great city, the holy Jerusalem, descending out of heaven from God, having the glory of God: and her light was like unto a stone most precious, even like a jasper stone, clear as crystal.[18]

The vision of a new Jerusalem that had inspired the First Crusade was now dying, though for some centuries afterwards men would still aspire to rebuild it anew. But it had been obvious from the start that the city of God was little more than a dream. The kingdom of which it was the capital had the same frailties as all other earthly realms: it was governed by men who were ruled by human ambition, with the same weaknesses of character as the rest of mankind. Now, the light that was the Christian city, and kingdom, of Jerusalem had been extinguished, perhaps forever.

There were some unexpected corollaries of the loss. The written laws of the Kingdom of Jerusalem were stored within the city walls, and were not recovered when the city fell. During the thirteenth century, the lawyers of the shrunken Christian state had something of a field day arguing about various aspects of the legal system. They became well known for their argumentative nature and their technical legal arguments. They were perhaps one of the few Christian groups to benefit from the loss of the city, though it is doubtful that few outside their profession took much pleasure in this.

For the victors, religious euphoria was the predominant emotion. Muslims as well as Christians believe in the last days, Armageddon, when a great leader, the Mahdi, will appear and usher in an everlasting era of triumph, including the capture of Jerusalem, Constantinople and Rome. It was said that Christ Himself would descend from heaven (Christ holds a place of high honour in the Muslim hierarchy), destroy the Cross and call on all to follow the teachings of Islam. The sun would set in the east, the trumpet would sound and the dead would be raised. Islam and Christianity share more than is sometimes realised. Now, perhaps some of the more thoughtful Muslims believed that the Last Days were imminent.[19]

But it is easy to concentrate solely on the religious aspects of the Muslim triumph and to forget that this was also a very human story. For the ordinary soldier, whose experience is largely untold by the chroniclers, this was a day of great pride. Those who had lived through the campaign could go back to their homes to regale their families with accounts of how they had won the Holy City for Islam once more. A great Muslim chronicler, Usama Ibn Munqidh, who in later life advised Saladin, told how he met a swordsman, Jawad, who had retired some years before Hattin: 'I saw him in

Damascus. He had become a dealer in fodder and was selling barley and hay. He was old and looked like a worn-out water-bag, too weak even to keep the mice away from his fodder – much less keep away people.'[20]

But at least these soldiers could now look back with increasingly rose-tinted vision on this great day as it retreated into the world of memory. They might grow frail and their powers might diminish as the years advanced, but they could always say with honour that, in their youth, they had fought and won at Al-Quts.

For Saladin, it was a great personal triumph, but, if his biographer is to be believed, it was not the end of his ambitions. Just a couple of years later, according to Baha al-Din ibn Shaddad, the great Sultan said that

> when by God's help not a Frank is left on this coast, I mean to divide my territories, and to charge my successors with my last commands: then, having taken leave of them, I will sail on this sea to its islands in pursuit of them, until there shall not remain on the face of this earth one unbeliever in God, or I will die in the attempt.[21]

This statement reads like the dream of Alexander told in a spiritual key; but the Sultan, too, would lose the fight against the greatest enemy, death, and die an unfulfilled man.

Saladin sent for his sister, who had previously been captured by Reynald of Chatillon, and told her to join him in Jerusalem. They were to re-enter the al-Aqsa Mosque and reconsecrate it to Islam. She brought with her rose water, carried by twenty donkeys, in order to purify the place from the unbelievers who had been ejected. The site could not have been more poignant, since for the past sixty-nine years it had been the headquarters of the Templars. Now all trace of their unwelcome occupation had been removed. The ancient and sacred stones were washed clean and the building was formally rededicated to the service of Islam.

The purification was an important part of the ritual 'reclaiming' of Jerusalem for Islam. The ceremonies employed were described by

Terricus, acting commander of the Templars, in a letter sent to King Henry II in 1188:

> After Jerusalem had been captured, Saladin had the Cross taken down from the Temple of the Lord and, beating it with clubs, had it carried on display for two days throughout the city. Then he caused the Temple of the Lord to be washed with rose water, inside and out, above and below, and, with an astonishing commotion, had his law acclaimed from on high in four places.[22]

Close by stood the Dome of the Rock, on the very site of Solomon's ancient and hallowed temple. When the Franks took the city, a cross was raised over it, as a sign of the triumph of Christendom over the forces of the Infidel. Now the cross had gone and the universal symbol of Islam once more stood in its place. Outside the David Gate, it was broken into pieces and mocked by some of the Muslims. The Dome, over the place where the Prophet had once stood, was now clear of all signs of Christian occupation.

For Christians of the time, the loss was unbearable. The *Itinerarium* stated boldly that 'a muezzin climbed the high mount of Calvary and there, where Christ on his Cross put an end to the law of death, the proclamation of a bastard law rang out'.[23] Nothing could contrast more with the mood of the victors and in particular the adulation that now showered down upon Saladin. His face lit up with joy as he lavished gifts on those who had fought alongside him.

And in victory he had, at least, shown mercy, not just to the Christian inhabitants of the city but also to that which they valued most highly in Jerusalem. He had cleared all signs of their presence from much of the city. But, despite the admonitions of some of his advisers, he refused to destroy the Church of the Holy Sepulchre. There was some damage though: the aedicule, for example, may have been dismantled at his command, although according to Imad al-Din, Heraclius was responsible for some of this, as he stripped out its gold plating and precious artefacts before leaving the city.

Saladin took time to review the future of the Holy Sepulchre. He handed it back to the Greek rather than Latin clergy, and introduced certain restrictions: in future Christian pilgrims could enter the city by only one route and were forbidden access to other parts of the city. Pilgrims who were allowed to visit would also have to pay a tax to enter the church. It therefore remained accessible after a fashion to Christian visitors, while at the same time providing a useful form of income to the Muslim rulers of Jerusalem.

Despite this, the city suffered a significant economic decline as a result of Saladin's conquest. Pilgrims came, but in smaller numbers than before. After a few years, the tax paid to enter the Sepulchre was withdrawn, one of the conditions of the truce that Saladin agreed with Richard I at the conclusion of the Third Crusade. Jerusalem did not have the same drawing power for Muslims as Mecca or Medina, and it was certainly substantially less important as a place of *hajj* than it was to the Christians as one of pilgrimage.

These developments, however, were in the future and did not diminish Saladin's well-deserved pride in his achievements. Even his bearing was remarkable:

His expression shone, while giving off a sweet perfume. The sense of triumph descended on him, garlanding him in a moonlike halo. The Koran reciters sat reading and repeating sections of the Book, poets stood reciting their verses. Pennants were raised and unfurled, as pens inscribed the news. Out of joyous emotion, tears welled up in eyes, and hearts were overcome by the rapture of victory; and lips invoked God in prayer.[24]

Al-Quts belonged to Islam once more. The crescent was truly ascendant.

TWELVE

The End of an Age

*And God shall wipe away all tears from their eyes: and there shall
be no more death, neither sorrow, nor crying, neither shall there be
any more pain: for the former things are passed away.*

Revelation 21: 4

The fall of Jerusalem should really have spelt the end for
Outremer, and in some ways it did. Nothing would ever be the
same for the kingdom, and the state that had been created with the
conquest of Jerusalem eighty-eight years earlier was gone, never to
return. But the end was not quite as definitive as it should have
been. The fact that Outremer survived at all was something of a
miracle, but it was a miracle created by human hands. The reasons
can be summarised as the contrasting fortunes of two men: one a
newly arrived Western adventurer and the other Saladin himself.

With Jerusalem captured, it appeared that the last acts of the
drama were being played out. Admittedly, the cities of Tripoli and
Antioch had survived unscathed (though many of the lands around
them did not), but to Saladin these were not the major objects of
his attention. Within the Kingdom of Jerusalem proper, very little
remained to be done. There were a few castles to take, and on the
coast the port of Tyre was proving to be more obstinate than
expected; but it was surely just a matter of time before these fell into
Saladin's hands.

No immediate help could be expected from the West. The news of
Hattin would have taken weeks to arrive from across the
Mediterranean and it would then be months, perhaps years, before a
relieving force was despatched. In fact, there was no certainty that

one would ever be sent. In the event, the shock of the devastating tidings from Outremer, first brought by Genoese merchants, was so great that, on 20 October 1187, Pope Urban III died, reputedly of grief. A new Pope, Gregory VIII, was quickly elected to succeed him, and by the end of October he had despatched letters to the great men of the West urging them to raise an army. But on 19 December he too expired. This was a bad year for Outremer: it was little better for the Papacy.

Before his death, Gregory had sent out a moving message to the rulers of Europe, known as *Audita tremendi*, which still speaks across the centuries with unsurpassed eloquence of the terrible shockwaves that inundated Europe, causing the Continent to tremble in fear and castigate itself for the sins that had been responsible for the disaster. For it was the West as much as anyone that was responsible for the loss of the Holy Land. As Gregory had said: 'Faced by such great distress concerning that land, moreover, we ought to consider not only the sins of the inhabitants but also our own and those of the whole Christian people.' He went on to lay on the guilt even more thickly:

> It is, therefore, incumbent upon all of us to consider and to choose to amend our sins by voluntary chastisement and to turn to the Lord our God with penance and words of piety: and we should first amend in ourselves what we have done wrong and then turn our attention to the treachery and malice of the enemy.[1]

The loss of Jerusalem was bitterly felt in Europe. Laments went up across Christendom. One anonymous cry stated that:

> neither counts, dukes nor crowned kings can escape from death: when they have amassed a great treasure, great the grief when they have to abandon it. Alas, unfortunates, we have laboured so hard to satisfy the pleasures of the flesh which are so soon lost and past. That is why it is better to gain paradise where all services are doubly repaid. We have too long delayed going to God's assistance to win back the land from which he was chased

and exiled because of our sins. There each one will accomplish his desire, because he who sets aside his riches for God will in truth win paradise.[2]

Secular poets such as Gaucelm Faidit joined in the lament too, their verses aimed at some of the highest echelons in society:

for the false race who do not believe in him are disinheriting him and insulting him in that place where he suffered and died. It behoves everyone to consider going there, and the princes all the more since they are highly placed, for there is not one who can claim to be faithful and obedient to him if he does not aid him in this enterprise.[3]

The West prepared its response, having been firmly reminded that first of all it must repent, but it is interesting to note that not everyone accepted guilt; for some, it was those who had lived in Outremer who should be held accountable. Particularly after the failed Second Crusade, for which many held the local barons of Outremer responsible, a significant number of people in the West viewed the rulers of the kingdom with disdain. One writer, Ralph Niger, said in 1188 that the devastation visited on the people there was 'well deserved by their guilt' and that the loss was 'hardly surprising as that land was certainly more dissolute than any other'.[4]

It was said that Saladin himself believed that Outremer had fallen because of the evil of those governing the country. When he looked over the abattoir that was Hattin and saw the captives being led away in terror and the bodies of the slain strewn across the battlefield 'he raised his eyes to heaven and thanked God for the victory, as he always did when things went well for him. One of his most frequent remarks was that our wickedness, not his power, gave him this victory, and the turn of events bore him out. On this occasion however we were not with the Lord nor He with us.'[5]

In the meantime in Outremer, Reynald's old haunt, Kerak, held out. His widow, the Lady Stephanie, offered to exchange it in return for her son, Humphrey of Toron, the reluctant king of just a year ago, though it seemed like another age – as indeed it was. However, something of the intransigence of their old master had clearly rubbed off on the garrison, who refused to fall in with the scheme. Saladin had already handed over Humphrey on trust, and when the castle refused to give in Stephanie handed him back into captivity. Such honesty received its just rewards when a few months later he was released unconditionally. This was a strange play of morality between the Sultan and the dowager, whose husband Saladin had executed only a few weeks earlier.

These exchanges merely delayed the inevitable, but the defence that followed at Kerak was truly heroic. It lasted for over a year, not falling until 1189, and the garrison stubbornly refused to surrender despite their increasingly parlous state and the fact that no relief seemed possible. They were reduced to eating their horses and only when the last one had been consumed did they give up. Those who roundly condemn the Franks for some of their excesses – justifiably so – should also remember their frequent gallantry.

Other castles fell, mighty fortresses such as Safed and Belvoir, a key Hospitaller base. Saladin laid siege to the castle at Montreal and demanded its surrender, but the defenders stoutly refused. It was said that provisions were in such short supply that the garrison had to resort to selling their wives and children to buy more food. There was also a severe shortage of salt, which caused many of the men to go blind. Despite offers of safe passage and money from Saladin, they simply refused to give up. The Sultan was therefore forced to move on to other challenges and leave Montreal to be starved out. The garrison at Montreal fought on until 1188.

At Beaufort the end was delayed for a while by the trickery of Reynald of Sidon. Reynald was renowned for his interest in Islamic affairs and approached Saladin with an unusual request. He wished to retire to Damascus, but before giving up his lands he wanted three months to settle his affairs. Saladin was pleased at the offer and agreed to it. Unfortunately for him, Reynald had no intention of going to Damascus and instead used the time he had bought to reinforce the castle defences.

Why, in the face of all these losses, did those who were left to defend the kingdom not just give up? There are two answers to this question. The first is that they hoped that by buying time relieving forces from Western Europe could be despatched, and by holding on for as long as possible and retaining as much force as they could, some basis for a counter-attack would still be available. The second can be found in one word: Tyre.

This city had been one of the last to fall to the Latins: it was not taken until 1124, with the aid of Venetian ships. Significantly, it was not for want of trying, two previous attempts to take it having failed because of the resilience of the defenders. It is doubtful whether Tyre still surpassed 'all other cities of Syria and Phoenicia in size and renown'[6] as it did in the time of Alexander the Great, but it remained an impressive refuge. It was to here that most of the men of substance and power who had survived the denouement of Outremer gravitated, as if attracted by a magnetic force. The position though seemed hopeless as Saladin had brought up his troops to assault the town. The commander of the port, Reynald of Sidon, was on the point of surrendering when a ship hove into the harbour.

On board was a most unlikely hero in the making. Conrad of Montferrat had important connections with Outremer it is true. His brother, William, was the former husband of Queen Sibylla and had lived for only a very short time after his marriage to her. He was, as a result, also the uncle of the late boy king, Baldwin V. On these grounds at least it was not a complete bolt from the blue when Conrad arrived. But his reputation as a ruthless adventurer made him an odd kind of Christian hero. The reason he came at all was that he had been implicated in a murder in Constantinople and was seeking to escape the possible repercussions by heading to Outremer on pilgrimage.

The timing of his arrival could hardly have been worse from the point of view of fulfilling his pilgrim vows, but for the defenders of Tyre it seemed an inspired and inspiring moment. Conrad was totally unaware of the catastrophes that had befallen Outremer when he arrived off Acre a few days after Hattin. It was the custom of the day that a bell would be rung when a ship arrived from abroad, demonstrating that this was still a relatively uncommon event – sailings to the East traditionally took place at two times of the year because of the difficulties of the trip and the frailties of the craft involved. But when no bell sounded, the captain of the vessel launched the ship's boat and sent it into the harbour to find out what was amiss. Only when a Muslim port official hailed them did they realise that Acre had fallen. The official shouted to them that they were welcome to land, but they rushed back to the ship instead. Conrad fled from Acre as fast as he could and made his way up the coast to Tyre, arriving on 14 July.

Conrad must have had some inspirational qualities, for the people of the city appointed him to lead the defence, which he organised with ruthless efficiency. There were rumours that Reynald of Sidon had been in league with Saladin with a view to betraying the city. This was an exaggerated accusation: Reynald had in fact organised the first defence in the city and he probably now surmised that the fall of Outremer was inevitable and wished only to ensure that the best possible terms were negotiated for such an eventuality. Such defeatism, though, was not acceptable in the changed climate. Conrad ejected him and turned his attention to beating off the Muslim attack.

Reynald returned to his castle at Beaufort where, as we have seen, he entered into negotiations with Saladin for the castle's surrender while at the same time surreptitiously strengthening its defences. He discussed the possibility of exchanging his castle for a pension in Damascus, giving the impression that he would happily adopt a life in Muslim lands in return for fair treatment. But in fact he was merely being duplicitous and buying time. It is quite possible that this, too, had been his strategy at Tyre and that he had no intention of giving up the city, merely stalling Saladin while he built up his strength.

Conrad's cause was helped by the advent of three Pisan ships shortly after his arrival, laden with both supplies and men. According to one account, Saladin approached the city soon after expecting Reynald to meekly hand it over. Indeed, Reynald had even taken his banners inside the city to be planted on the walls as a sign that the city was now in Muslim hands. When Conrad found the banners he flung them into the moat as a sign that, if Saladin wished to take the city, he would have to fight for it.[7]

Conrad realised that he would be much better placed to fight off the attackers if he had help from elsewhere, and so a ship slipped out of port under cover of darkness seeking aid from Tripoli. Ten galleys were despatched in response, but a fierce storm drove them back from whence they had come – fortunately without damage – when they were not far from Tyre. Tyre and Conrad were, for the time being at least, on their own.

Saladin's strategy was to launch a multi-pronged attack from both land and sea. Siege engines were hauled over from Damascus to bombard the walls from the landward side. But given the narrow approach to the port across the sinewy causeway the sea provided perhaps an even more important line of attack. So Saladin ordered the Egyptian fleet to set sail and lay siege to the city from the water.

On approaching the walls Saladin was horrified at the unexpected tenacity of the defence: this was not the meek surrender he had expected. On learning of the identity of the man in charge of the defence, he brought the captive Marquis of Montferrat, Conrad's father, from Damascus and threatened to kill him unless the city was surrendered. He also brought with him some of the captives from Jerusalem to add further moral pressure. Conrad's reply to these threats was unequivocal. When faced with the prospect of responsibility for his father's life or death, he shouted from the walls – one hopes more in an act of bravado rather than a statement of real intent – an extremely uncompromising answer: 'Tie him to a stake and I will be the first to shoot him . . . For he is too old and hardly worth anything.'[8] His father, equally defiant, told Conrad to guard the city well. Then Conrad took a crossbow and fired a bolt at his father, narrowly missing. Saladin, horrified at the Count's intransigence and outraged by his actions, realised that Tyre was going to be no easy target. When the defence continued as vigorously as ever, Saladin left the port under siege and moved on to Ascalon.

The medieval world was well aware of the exploits of Alexander the Great, a leader highly regarded by the Muslims for his military deeds. It would have served Saladin well if he had turned to the histories of Curtius, which would have told him how even the great conqueror had been held up for nine months at that city. The problem for Saladin was that the port was connected to the mainland of Outremer only by a narrow causeway. Indeed, the causeway itself was one of Alexander's greatest achievements as, before he had ordered it to be constructed, Tyre lay on an island 600 yards offshore. The narrowness of the causeway allowed the Muslims only very limited access to the approaches to the city, and its position, jutting out into the sea, allowed the port to be resupplied. Saladin's siege engines, fourteen in number, made little impression on the walls.

The defenders were vigorous in their attempts to drive Saladin away. They frequently sallied out in force. Particularly prominent among them was a Spaniard, Sancho Martin. He wore green arms, hence his nickname, the Green Knight. To add to the effect of this distinctive display, he wore antlers on his helmet: he must have made a striking sight indeed. Certainly many of the attackers made a point of seeking him out just to have a glimpse of him.

This was no static defence. Conrad had small craft fitted out and protected with animal hides. These vessels, called *barbotes*, were manned with crossbowmen. Because of their manoeuvrability and shallow draft the Muslim ships could not fight them off, and so they could sail up and down, close inshore, doing great damage to the besieging force.

Conrad was cunning. He had a useful ally inside the city, an important young Muslim who had recently fallen out with his father and defected to the Christians as a result. Conrad involved him in a plan that was intended to do considerable harm to Saladin's cause. The first stage involved the disaffected youth shooting an arrow from inside the city walls into the ranks of the besiegers. The message attached to the arrow was that the defenders were planning to flee from the city en masse that very night: if Saladin did not believe this, then he should listen to the noise emanating from the port area as it grew dark.

The message, which of course was a trick, was duly delivered to Saladin, who had a number of galleys made ready to swoop down on the fleeing Latin vessels as they left the harbour. But Conrad had stationed a number of men hidden away close to the harbour walls while he had others make the requisite commotion to convince the Muslims that the defenders were indeed making ready for a hasty getaway.

The harbour entrance was guarded by a chain, which was stretched across its mouth. This had been lowered and as the Muslim ships approached at dawn – the time they assumed the Christians would try to sail away – they could see that the harbour appeared to be wide open to them. Driven on by hopes of glory, some of the ships' captains charged into the seemingly unprotected harbour with all the reckless abandon of young stallions sensing a prize nearby.

Once five of them were inside, the trap was suddenly sprung. The chain was raised with all the speed that could be mustered. The concealed men then fell upon the cornered galleys. Every single man on board was struck down. The vessels that were taken were turned to future use in the service of the Christian cause.

That future service was not long in coming. The next day, again at dawn, Conrad's small fleet set sail from the harbour and fell on the residue of the Muslim armada. The Latin ships were well stocked with mighty warriors, eager to strike a blow for their cause. They quickly threatened to overwhelm the Muslim ships, which headed for the shore in an attempt to escape. As men jumped from them trying to escape, those onshore frantically tried to help them. Horsemen spurred their mounts into the water in a desperate attempt to come to their aid. Soon the sea was churned up by the beating of hooves and the sky was riven with the shrieks of the dying while the blue-green waters of the Mediterranean turned a vivid shade of crimson.

At the end of this ferocious struggle, five Muslim ships ran aground while two others escaped towards Beirut, where they would cause great damage. These two surviving ships anchored in the shadow of the hills guarding Beirut harbour, from where they would act the part of privateers, attacking passing Christian traffic and taking ships, men and goods in abundance. It was said that these two ships were responsible for the enslavement of 14,000 men, not including those killed as a result of those manning the galleys.

Tyre soon reached a crisis point. On New Year's Day, it appeared that the city was at last on the brink of falling. Saladin's men broke through the outer defences. Ladders were perched precariously against the walls by the trembling hands of those whose task it would be to scale them and fight the defenders in vicious hand-to-hand combat atop the battlements. But the walls were too high and the defenders too determined, realising that for them the only options were death or glory. In the heat of battle, after such a stubborn and costly defence, they could expect no quarter should they be taken.

Seeing that the attack was stalled, Saladin again turned to his sappers and gave them the task of bringing down the walls. This was a tactic much more difficult for the defenders of Tyre to counteract, and the work of the miners soon began to tell. The walls began to crumble and the Muslim assault expected in its aftermath began to form up in eager anticipation of a breach being opened up.

Realising that the defence was on the verge of a precipice, the defenders decided to take destiny into their own hands. They would charge forth in one last defiant gesture and either drive the Muslim army back or die a martyr's death in the attempt. And so, at this climactic moment, the defenders of Tyre poured out of the city gates towards the waiting host of the enemy, crashing against the defensive line of the Muslim army, which quickly began to disintegrate. Exultant, the defenders chased the broken enemy all the way back to the mainland.

Shortly after this reverse, Saladin's officers prevailed on him to raise the siege. Help had already begun to arrive from the West. William II, King of Sicily, had despatched a fleet, which brought provisions for Tyre. The fightback was already under way. Saladin reluctantly agreed to the pressure to abandon the siege and soon after moved off, leaving the burning hulks of his abandoned siege engines and galleys in his wake.

In his view, there was no other option. It was the middle of winter, not the most clement of seasons even in the Mediterranean, and the men were tired and wished to return home. So Saladin let them go, assuming that the fall of the city had only been delayed. But he was wrong. Tyre was indeed the springboard from which a Latin revival of sorts was launched.

Historians customarily explain that Saladin's failure to take the city was his greatest blunder, and perhaps it was. But Saladin did not have that great gift of hindsight that historians possess. His achievements had already been great and his army was in all probability approaching a state of exhaustion. They were mostly volunteers after all, and if they wished to desert it would be difficult to stop them.

In addition, one should not overlook the strains on Saladin himself. He had been critically ill just a couple of years earlier and some of the vigour of his younger years had gone. In fact, he had just a few more years to live and the pressure of six months of constant campaigning had taken its toll. He, too, was glad to go home, although in his case he had pressures of a different kind to worry about in Damascus – politics, patronage, personalities.

Whatever the failings he may have exhibited at Tyre, he would always be known as the man who had retaken Jerusalem for Islam. After nearly a century, the al-Aqsa Mosque echoed again to the soft footsteps of the faithful, while pilgrims once more visited the Dome of the Rock in hallowed awe. Merchant caravans travelled again in peace from Damascus to Cairo. No longer did the traders look up in fear as they passed beneath the shadow of Kerak. Reynald of Chatillon, *Arnat* as he was known to the Muslims, was no more, and the way of life that he had represented had died with him. Allah be praised. And also Salah as-Din Yusuf, his faithful servant, whose position of honour in the Islamic world was now secure.

Saladin had ventured into both Antioch and Tripoli after his triumphs in Jerusalem. Many towns and castles fell to him, until all that was left were these two cities, whose neutral stance did them little good, and St Symeon, the port of the former. Elsewhere a few castles remained, including the most famous of all, Krak des Chevaliers, the mighty desert base of the Hospitallers, which towered over the surrounding area.

This was a tremendous change in fortunes for the kingdom in the space of just a few months, and it appeared that the decline of

Outremer was unstoppable; but it was not. Within two years of Hattin, a great Crusader army arrived from the West under Philip, the King of France, and Richard I, King of England. It is ironic that the defeat at Hattin had at last forced Henry II's hand in taking the sign of the cross as tangible evidence of his intention to lead a Crusade; but he died shortly afterwards, to be succeeded by his son Richard. On arrival in Outremer, Philip and Richard joined a siege of the great port of Acre that had been initiated against seemingly hopeless odds the year before.

Richard was financed largely by taxes that had been raised by his late father, including a special form of tax known as the Saladin Tithe. This required that everyone should give one-tenth of their wealth towards the recovery of the holy places of Christendom. Special teams were set up to ensure that each man paid his due, each one including a representative from the Templars and the Hospitallers. Those who attempted to escape the tax were to be excommunicated. Only clerics or knights who had taken the cross were to be granted exemption.

King Philip mirrored Henry's example, but opposition to the tax was so widespread in France that he was forced to confirm that this was strictly a 'one-off' measure and would not act as a precedent for the future. There was no doubt, though, that this was seen to be a spiritually significant time. When Henry and Philip took the cross together at Gisors, it was said that a cross also appeared in the sky.

There were other miracles, too. The Archbishop of Canterbury, Baldwin, set out on a journey around Wales to preach a Crusade. He was joined by Gerald of Wales, who wrote an account of the mission. As a result of a speech Baldwin delivered at Haverfordwest, many rushed to take the cross, despite the fact that he spoke in Latin and French, which most of the audience did not understand. Among his listeners was an elderly blind woman who had asked her son to stand close to the Archbishop and bring back some form of miracle cure. The son duly dug out a scoop of soil from the very spot where the Archbishop had preached, and when he rubbed it on her eyes her sight was miraculously restored.

Such stories may seem to us incredible, but they are important nonetheless. They mark out the spiritual euphoria that could affect people so strongly at that time, strongly enough for them to risk life and limb for the sake of their cause. It was religious motivation such as this that acted as a catalyst for those who were to join the forthcoming Crusade, and this was the reason why so many from England and Wales took up their posts at the great siege that had been laid around Acre.

Most curious of all was the identity of the man who started the siege at Acre. When Saladin released Guy of Lusignan in 1188, he was effectively sending back a king who no longer had a state to rule. He may even have hoped that Guy's presence would cause dissension in the Crusader ranks, which it certainly did. What he would not have reckoned on was Guy's decisiveness when the citizens of Tyre refused to recognise him as their king. They had decided that Conrad was a much better leader, so they sent their would-be ruler away with insults ringing in his ears. With his position now hopeless, Guy marched with a small army to lay siege to Acre. It seemed nonsensical: the garrison was much larger than the besieging force and it appeared that Saladin could attack him from the rear and destroy him at any time. It seemed as pointless an exercise as a flea trying to pierce the hide of an elephant.

But despite counter-attacks launched against him, Guy stood firm, and as he persisted stubbornly, support for him grew. Amazingly, the weak and insipid king of old had metamorphosed into an inspiration for others to follow; and so when new recruits arrived from the West in their thousands it was to Acre that they journeyed. Having borne a large part of the responsibility for the loss of the kingdom he now played a key role in its rebirth.

Some of the survivors of Outremer joined him, too. Gerard of Ridfort brought the remainder of his Templars up to join Guy. The Templars had vast resources in the West, and although it would take time for new recruits to arrive to replace those lost at Cresson and Hattin, arrive they would. An attack led by the Templars was repulsed by the Muslims, but even though he stood alone Gerard refused to retreat. It was yet another foolish act on the part of this obstinate and errant Grand Master, but it was to be his last. His captors decided that even they had had enough of him, and so had him executed – a fitting end considering that his errors had been the cause of so many lost lives.

Acre eventually fell to the Crusaders, and with it a new kingdom became viable. But Guy would never again be its king. Richard 'the Lionheart' nominated him to assume control of the restored and reshaped kingdom (Guy's family were tenants in the lands that Richard held in France as part of his inheritance in Aquitaine), but to his genuine surprise none of the local barons supported the decision. Instead, the hero of Tyre, Conrad of Montferrat, was elected king. But for him, too, the crown was a poisoned chalice. Within weeks of his election, he was dead, slain by an assassin's knife.

The murder showed just how unstable the kingdom was and how far removed from the ideal of a heavenly kingdom. It could do nothing to improve the image of Outremer in the West, badly damaged as it already was. And it is indeed important to realise just why the Third Crusade was launched. It was not to help the rulers of Outremer, who were largely discredited: it was, rather, to avenge the insult that the defeat at Hattin and the loss of Jerusalem was perceived to have delivered to Christ Himself.

The major expeditions in the twelfth century came in response to great losses – the Second Crusade in response to the fall of Edessa and the Third to that of Jerusalem. In its way, this shows how difficult it was to summon up enthusiasm for a major Crusade in a European environment that was beset with its own internal difficulties and that had become disillusioned by the effort and cost involved in Crusading for ever diminishing returns. Only a great defeat could remind the West of the importance of Outremer. Even the appeal of Jerusalem, though still at this stage strong, was not as powerful as it had been, certainly in the build-up to the First Crusade.

Despite Conrad's death, it was right that Guy should not rule – and his claims had been damaged severely on the death of Sibylla, through whom he had originally held his position, in 1190. As compensation for his loss of a greater kingdom, Richard gave Cyprus to Guy in 1192, at about the same time that Conrad was declared king. There was no going back to the old days now. Outremer would never be the same as it had been previously and it needed new kings with new ideas. The kingdom's confidence had been shattered by Hattin and much of the hinterland was gone for ever.

A few decades after Hattin Jerusalem was, for a short time, handed back to the Crusaders when it was given to the German Emperor, Frederick II. But the outlying towns that were the key to the city remained in Muslim hands. As a result, the Holy City was only regained on sufferance, falling for good to the attack of Khwarismian forces displaced by the terrible advance of the Mongols across Asia in 1241.

By that time, Jerusalem was a sullied prize. Following the death of Saladin, the Sultan's kingdom fell apart and civil war blighted the landscape of the Islamic Levant. The city had been handed to Frederick as a bribe from one Muslim warlord for his help against another. It was a tawdry deal and it did Frederick no good. At the moment that he was given the city he was an excommunicate. No prelate in Jerusalem would crown him. As an improvised coronation took place in the Church of the Holy Sepulchre, outside the city walls a Catholic bishop hurled insults at the would-be king of Jerusalem. Jerusalem, once the city of God, had become the city of schism.

The declining power of Jerusalem to draw Crusaders eastwards was reflected in an increasingly cynical mood. It was by no means all-embracing – there would be occasional flare-ups of enthusiasm in the thirteenth century that could still draw men to the cross. The change reflected not just the losses in Outremer perhaps, but also an increasing uncertainty as the Crusading movement was diverted, for example to Constantinople or to the Cathar lands in the south of France. A poem written in about 1228 bitterly exclaimed, 'the cross saves the people but causes me to go mad, the cross makes me sorrowful and praying to God does not help me. Alas, pilgrim cross, why have you destroyed me in this way?'[9]

Despite this declining interest, the emaciated rump of the kingdom clung limpet-like to the coast, sometimes struggling, sometimes thriving. It was not until 1289 that Outremer was lost for good in a truly apocalyptic battle for Acre. Templars and Hospitallers, frequently at odds with each other in everyday life in Outremer, fought and died side by side as brothers in arms.

At the end of the siege one of the last bastions remaining was the Accursed Tower, in which the last of the defenders fought fiercely with their Muslim foe in a battle that was truly hopeless. The intensity of the fight and the siege that preceded it had weakened the tower irreparably. As men fought each other to a standstill, the foundations of the edifice collapsed, bringing down a deluge of masonry on the men below, Muslim and Christian alike. It was a fitting finale to the Kingdom of Outremer.

But this was a different Outremer from the one that had existed before 1187. On the hills of Hattin, men fought and died for a concept that they believed in passionately, however hard we might find it to understand nowadays. The great and not so good, like Reynald of Chatillon, shared a common grave with those of humble background who died in their hundreds. Loss of life in battle is a sad inevitability, but what distinguished Hattin from many other confrontations over the ages was that it was one of the decisive battles of history, in which not just men passed away, but an idea also. And a dream, keenly felt but now gone forever, was blown away like a fallen leaf in the path of a sandstorm.

Notes

PROLOGUE

1. Definition of 'colony' in R. Allen (ed.), *New Penguin English Dictionary*, Penguin, 2001.
2. Quoted in E. Hallam (ed.), *Chronicles of the Crusades*, Weidenfeld & Nicolson, 1989, p. 22.

CHAPTER 1

1. J.J. Saunders, *A History of Medieval Islam*, Routledge, 1996, p. 49.
2. From Robert the Monk, *Historia Hierosolymitana*, in Hallam (ed.), *Chronicles of the Crusades*, p. 90.
3. *The Economist*, 15 April 2006.
4. Z. Oldenbourg, *The Crusades*, BCA, 1998, p. 42.
5. In Hallam (ed.), *Chronicles of the Crusades*, p. 63.
6. Joshua 6, *passim*.
7. In Hallam (ed.), *Chronicles of the Crusades*, p. 93.
8. Joshua 6: 21.
9. Revelation 19: 11–15: see also C. Tyerman, *The Crusades – A Very Short Introduction*, Oxford University Press, 2005, p. 68.
10. Not all historians agree that Godfrey assumed this humble title though it has often been claimed that he did. See for example J. Riley-Smith, *The Crusades – A Short History*, Continuum, 2001, p. 40.
11. For further analysis of the political structures of the state of Outremer, see J. Prawer, *Crusader Institutions*, Oxford University Press, 1998.
12. C. Daniell, *Death and Burial in Medieval England*, Boydell, 1998, p. 81.
13. *Ibid.*, p. 73.
14. J. Gillingham, *The Life and Times of Richard I*, Weidenfeld & Nicolson, 1973, p. 125.
15. See J. Riley-Smith, *Oxford Illustrated History of the Crusades*, Oxford University Press, 1995, p. 27.

Notes

CHAPTER 2

1. See Prawer, *Crusader Institutions*, p. 31.
2. S. Runciman, *A History of the Crusades*, vol. 2, Penguin, 1990, p. 298.
3. The 'Attire of Antioch', silk and brocade, was particularly sought after and is specifically mentioned in surviving customs texts from Acre. See J. Prawer, *The Crusaders' Kingdom*, Phoenix Press, 2001, p. 393.
4. For further discussion of his life see G. Regan, *First Crusader*, Sutton, 2001.
5. See M. Barber, *The New Knighthood – A History of the Order of the Temple*, Cambridge University Press, 1998, pp. 34–5.
6. *Ibid.*, p. 38. It should be pointed out that in its early days the Order was for both healthy and leprous brothers.
7. *Ibid.*, p. 69.
8. For further discussion of the uncertainties surrounding the evidence, see *Ibid.*, pp. 74–5.
9. *Ibid.*, p. 99.
10. For further information see W.B. Bartlett, *The Assassins*, Sutton, 2001.
11. See Barber, *New Knighthood*, p. 51.
12. *Ibid.*, p. 60.
13. There is no unanimity concerning the date of the events about to be described. Runciman, *History of the Crusades*, implicitly dates it to around 1173 (vol. 2, p. 406) while Barber, *New Knighthood*, p. 109, dates it much later in 1180.
14. Runciman, *History of the Crusades*, vol. 2, p. 406, offers the information that he believes from the price paid, 10,000 besants, that she weighed about 10 stone.

CHAPTER 3

1. Quoted in D. Nicolle, *Hattin – Saladin's Greatest Victory*, Osprey, 1998, p. 16.
2. See for example J. Richard, *Saint Louis, Crusader King of France*, Cambridge University Press, 1999, p. 191.
3. Hallam (ed.), *Chronicles of the Crusades*, p. 154.
4. *Ibid.*, p. 156.
5. H. Mayer, *The Crusades*, tr. John Gillingham, Oxford University Press, 1990, p. 125.
6. In Nicolle, *Hattin*, p. 16.
7. *Ibid.*, p. 17.
8. *Ibid.*
9. See p. 34.
10. Daniell, *Death and Burial*, p. 76.
11. Mayer, *Crusades*, p. 123.
12. In H. Nicholson and D. Nicolle, *God's Warriors*, Osprey, 2005, p. 187.
13. Richard, *Saint Louis*, p. 193.
14. See A. Jotischky, *Crusading and the Crusader States*, Pearson, 2004, p. 98.

CHAPTER 4

1. See p. 46.
2. See Runciman, *History of the Crusades*, vol. 2, p. 420.
3. See R.C. Smail, *Crusading Warfare 1097–1193*, Cambridge University Press, 1996.
4. *Chronique d'Ernoul*, in P.W. Edbury, *The Conquest of Jerusalem and the Third Crusade – Sources in Translation*, Ashgate, 1996, p. 151.
5. *Ibid.*, p. 152.
6. *Ibid.*, p. 152.
7. Edbury, *Conquest of Jerusalem*, p. 149, describes Guy as coming from 'a reasonably prominent French provincial seigneurial family', while William of Tyre says dismissively that he was 'noble enough'.
8. *Chronique d'Ernoul*, in Edbury, *Conquest of Jerusalem*, p. 150.
9. William of Tyre, in Edbury, *Conquest of Jerusalem*, p. 150.
10. Roger of Howden, in *ibid.*, p. 150.
11. William of Tyre's Continuator, in *ibid.*, p. 44.
12. Riley-Smith (ed.), *Oxford Illustrated History of the Crusades*, p. 163.
13. J.J. Norwich, *A Short History of Byzantium*, Viking, 1997, p. 291.
14. From the bull *Cor nostrum* quoted in Richard, *Saint Louis*, p. 202.

CHAPTER 5

1. A.J. Boas, *Jerusalem in the Time of the Crusades*, Routledge, 2001, p. 35.
2. *Ibid.*, p. 35.
3. *Ibid.*, p. 103.
4. *Ibid.*, p. 106.
5. *Ibid.*, p. 102.
6. *Ibid.*, p. 109.
7. Norwich, *Short History of Byzantium*, p. 292.
8. Nicolle, *Hattin*, p. 11.
9. Hinted at for example in Jotischky, *Crusader States*, p. 99.
10. The Continuator of William of Tyre, in Edbury, *Conquest of Jerusalem*, p. 11.
11. In Hallam (ed.), *Chronicles of the Crusades*, p. 162.
12. It is estimated that during the 1180s there were 500,000 people living within Outremer's borders of whom about 120,000 were of Frankish origin. See Nicolle, *Hattin*, p. 7.
13. In Prawer, *Crusaders' Kingdom*, p. 206.
14. H. Kennedy, *Crusader Castles*, Cambridge University Press, 1994, p. 45.
15. See J. Bradbury, *The Medieval Siege*, Boydell, 1998, p. 252.
16. See Daniell, *Death and Burial*, p. 204.
17. See Mayer, *Crusades*, p. 127.
18. Daniell, *Death and Burial*, p. 204.

Notes

CHAPTER 6

1. M. Erbstösser, *The Crusades*, David and Charles, 1978, p. 155.
2. C. Tyerman, *England and the Crusades 1095–1588*, University of Chicago Press, 1996, p. 39.
3. Richard, *Saint Louis*, p. 204.
4. Tyerman, *England and the Crusades*, p. 45.
5. *Ibid.*, p. 38.
6. Included in their number was William Marshal, destined to become one of England's greatest knights.
7. The exact date of Gerard's promotion is unclear but Malcolm Barber (in *New Knighthood*) dates it to early 1185.
8. From the Continuator of William of Tyre, in Edbury, *Conquest of Jerusalem*, p. 14.
9. *Ibid.*, p. 15.
10. Oldenbourg, *Crusades*, p. 402.
11. Mayer, *Crusades*, p. 132.
12. From the Continuator of William of Tyre, in Edbury, *Conquest of Jerusalem*, p. 15.
13. In Norwich, *Short History of Byzantium*, p. 294.
14. Mayer, *Crusades*, p. 125.
15. From the Continuator of William of Tyre, in Edbury, *Conquest of Jerusalem*, p. 24.
16. From B.S. James (tr.), *The Letters of Saint Bernard of Clairvaux*, Sutton, 1998, p. 295.
17. See the chapter 'Northern Europe Invades the Mediterranean', in G. Holmes (ed.), *The Oxford Illustrated History of Medieval Europe*, Oxford University Press, 1991, p. 221.
18. In J. Riley-Smith, *Hospitallers – The History of the Order of St John*, Hambledon, 1999, p. 21.
19. From the Continuator of William of Tyre, in Edbury, *Conquest of Jerusalem*, p. 26.
20. Oldenbourg, *Crusades*, p. 406.
21. In Edbury, *Conquest of Jerusalem*, p. 154.
22. *Ibid.*, p. 155.

CHAPTER 7

1. From the Continuator of William of Tyre, in Edbury, *Conquest of Jerusalem*, p. 28. Many commentators now believe the story to be untrue, but it added to the picture of the villainous Reynald that had grown up around him.
2. *Ibid.*, p. 29.
3. In Tyerman, *Crusades*, p. 1.

4. Nicolle, *Hattin*, p. 57.
5. From the Continuator of William of Tyre, in Edbury, *Conquest of Jerusalem*, p. 134.
6. Smail, *Crusading Warfare*, p. 105.
7. Translated in Edbury, *Conquest of Jerusalem*, p. 157.
8. *Ibid.*
9. From the Continuator of William of Tyre, in *ibid.*, p. 33.
10. In Oldenbourg, *Crusades*, p. 408.

CHAPTER 8

1. Estimates from Runciman, *History of the Crusades*, vol. 2, p. 455.
2. In Tyerman, *England and the Crusades*, p. 37.
3. From the account by the Continuator of William of Tyre, in Edbury, *Conquest of Jerusalem*, p. 36. Such statistics should be treated with caution; Riley-Smith, for example, estimates that the force had about 1,500 knights and 15,000–18,000 foot: see his *Hospitallers*, p. 40.
4. In Nicolle, *Hattin*, p. 47.
5. Riley-Smith (ed.), *Oxford Illustrated History of the Crusades*, p. 101.
6. Nicolle, *Hattin*, p. 52.
7. See Nicholson and Nicolle, *God's Warriors*, p. 159.
8. *Ibid.*, p. 172.
9. A. Hyland, *The Medieval Warhorse: From Byzantium to the Crusades*, Sutton, 1996, p. 152.
10. *Ibid.*, p. 149.
11. *Ibid.*, p. 140.
12. *Ibid.*, p. 165.
13. See Riley-Smith (ed.), *Oxford Illustrated History of the Crusades*, p. 190.
14. In Nicholson and Nicolle, *God's Warriors*, p. 129.
15. In Hallam (ed.), *Chronicles of the Crusades*, p. 189.
16. Nicholson and Nicolle, *God's Warriors*, p. 58.
17. The Continuator of William of Tyre, in Edbury, *Conquest of Jerusalem*, p. 36.
18. *Ibid.*, p. 36.
19. Prawer, *Crusader Institutions*, p. 486.
20. Oldenbourg, *Crusades*, p. 412.

CHAPTER 9

1. Prawer, *Crusader Institutions*, p. 491.
2. Riley-Smith (ed.), *Oxford Illustrated History of the Crusades*, p. 232.
3. In Nicholson and Nicolle, *God's Warriors*, p. 103.
4. *Ibid.*, p. 117.

5. This fascinating but seemingly improbable story comes from the Continuator of William of Tyre, in Edbury, *Conquest of Jerusalem*, p. 40.

6. In Hallam (ed.), *Chronicles of the Crusades*, p. 158.

7. In Nicholson and Nicolle, *God's Warriors*, p. 183.

8. Timings are as per Prawer, *Crusader Institutions*, p. 493.

9. In Nicholson and Nicolle, *God's Warriors*, p. 125.

10. Imad ad-Din in Hallam (ed.), *Chronicles of the Crusades*, p. 158.

11. In Oldenbourg, *Crusades*, p. 209.

12. *Ibid.*

13. French poem from 1266 by Rutebeuf, in R.W. Southern, *The Making of the Middle Ages*, Pimlico, 1993, p. 55.

14. Riley-Smith (ed.), *Oxford Illustrated History of the Crusades*, p. 98.

CHAPTER 10

1. From the Continuator of William of Tyre, in Edbury, *Conquest of Jerusalem*, p. 45.

2. There is no consensus on the time that the battle on 4 July started, some believing that it commenced at around 9 a.m. – e.g. Prawer, *Crusader Institutions*, p. 496 – but others pointing to a start at midday.

3. Imad ad-Din, in Hallam (ed.), *Chronicles of the Crusades*, p. 158.

4. Smail, *Crusading Warfare*, p. 81.

5. In Nicholson and Nicolle, *God's Warriors*, p. 66.

6. In Edbury, *Conquest of Jerusalem*, p. 160.

7. In Hallam (ed.), *Chronicles of the Crusades*, p. 156.

8. In Nicolle, *Hattin*, p. 89.

9. From al-Afdal, son of Saladin, quoted in Runciman, *History of the Crusades*, vol. 2, p. 459.

10. In Nicholson and Nicolle, *God's Warriors*, p. 184.

11. In Oldenbourg, *Crusades*, p. 414.

12. From *Itinerarium Regis Ricardi*, in Hallam (ed.), *Chronicles of the Crusades*, p. 157.

13. From the Continuator of William of Tyre, in Edbury, *Conquest of Jerusalem*, p. 47.

14. See Boas, *Jerusalem in the Time of the Crusades*, p. 19.

15. See Nicholson and Nicolle, *God's Warriors*, p. 35.

16. See Nicolle, *Hattin*, p. 79.

17. *Ibid.*, p. 79.

18. See for example Smail, *Crusading Warfare*, p. 195.

19. *Ibid.*, p. 191.

20. Prawer, *Crusader Institutions*, p. 498.

21. C. Oman, *A History of the Art of War in the Middle Ages*, vol. 1, 1924, p. 333.

22. In Richard, *Saint Louis*, p. 191. Nur ed-Din was writing a letter justifying his seizure of Mosul so he may have had an ulterior motive for saying it. But it supports views of the Franks stated by many others.
23. Nicolle, *Hattin*, p. 88.
24. In Hallam (ed.), *Chronicles of the Crusades*, p. 159.
25. *Itinerarium Regis Ricardi*, in Hallam (ed.), *Chronicles of the Crusades*, p. 157.

CHAPTER 11
1. See Nicolle, *Hattin*, p. 82.
2. *Ibid.*, p. 81.
3. The Continuator of William of Tyre, in Edbury, *Conquest of Jerusalem*, p. 54. The hour of nones was at 3 p.m. This is possibly a piece of poetic licence: it also grew dark when Jesus died at 3 p.m.
4. Boas, *Jerusalem in the Time of the Crusades*, p. 15.
5. See Nicolle, *Hattin*, p. 35.
6. *Ibid.*, p. 35.
7. In Hallam (ed.), *Chronicles of the Crusades*, p. 92.
8. For a detailed description of the fortifications of Jerusalem, see Boas, *Jerusalem in the Time of the Crusades*, chapter 7.
9. Nicolle, *Hattin*, p. 82.
10. The Continuator of William of Tyre, in Edbury, *Conquest of Jerusalem*, p. 574.
11. *Itinerarium Regis Ricardi*, in Hallam (ed.), *Chronicles of the Crusades*, p. 160.
12. The Continuator of William of Tyre, in Edbury, *Conquest of Jerusalem*, p. 59.
13. In Richard, *Saint Louis*, p. 210.
14. See Nicholson and Nicolle, *God's Warriors*, p. 106.
15. The Continuator of William of Tyre, in Edbury, *Conquest of Jerusalem*, p. 63.
16. Luke 21: 24.
17. In Richard, *Saint Louis*, p. 211.
18. Revelation 22: 10–11.
19. See Riley-Smith (ed.), *Oxford Illustrated History of the Crusades*, p. 217.
20. In Nicholson and Nicolle, *God's Warriors*, p. 116.
21. In Riley-Smith (ed.), *Oxford Illustrated History of the Crusades*, p. 236.
22. In Barber, *New Knighthood*, p. 114.
23. In Hallam (ed.), *Chronicles of the Crusades*, p. 160.
24. Imad ad-Din, in *ibid.*, p. 161.

CHAPTER 12
1. In Riley-Smith, *Crusades*, p. 109.
2. In Hallam (ed.), *Chronicles of the Crusades*, p. 161.
3. Riley-Smith (ed.), *Oxford Illustrated History of the Crusades*, p. 108.
4. In Tyerman, *England and the Crusades*, p. 38.

Notes

5. *Itinerarium Regis Ricardi*, in Hallam (ed.), *Chronicles of the Crusades*, p. 157.
6. From Tania Gergel (ed.), *Alexander*, Penguin, 2004, p. 52.
7. See the Continuator of William of Tyre, in Edbury, *Conquest of Jerusalem*, p. 53.
8. *Ibid.*, p. 54.
9. By Rinaldo d'Aquino, in Riley-Smith (ed.), *Oxford Illustrated History of the Crusades*, p. 105.

Select Bibliography

There are a large number of texts available on the Crusades. Rather than give a comprehensive bibliography, which many of the publications mentioned below offer, I refer to those with particular importance to the writing of this book.

Barber, M., *The New Knighthood – A History of the Order of the Temple*, Cambridge University Press, Cambridge, 1998

Bartlett, W.B., *The Assassins*, Sutton, Stroud, 2001

Boas, A.J., *Jerusalem in the Time of the Crusades*, Routledge, London and New York, 2001

Bradbury, J., *The Medieval Siege*, Boydell, Woodbridge, 1998

Bronstein, J., *The Hospitallers and the Holy Land*, Boydell, Woodbridge, 2005

Daniell, C., *Death and Burial in Medieval England*, Routledge, London and New York, 1997

Edbury, P.W., *The Conquest of Jerusalem and the Third Crusade – Sources in Translation*, Ashgate, Aldershot, 1996

Erbstösser, M. (tr. C.S.V. Salt), *The Crusades*, David and Charles, Newton Abbott, 1978

Gillingham, J., *The Life and Times of Richard I*, Weidenfeld & Nicolson, London, 1973

Hallam, E. (ed.), *Chronicles of the Crusades*, Weidenfeld & Nicolson, London, 1989; Bramley Books, Godalming, 1996

Holmes, G. (ed.), *The Oxford Illustrated History of Medieval Europe*, Oxford University Press, Oxford, 1991

Hyland, A., *The Medieval Warhorse – From Byzantium to the Crusades*, Sutton, Stroud, 1996

James, B.S. (tr.), *The Letters of St Bernard of Clairvaux*, Sutton, Stroud, 1998

Jotischky, A., *Crusading and the Crusader States*, Pearson, Harlow, 2004

Kennedy, H., *Crusader Castles*, Cambridge University Press, Cambridge, 1994

Mayer, H. (tr. John Gillingham), *The Crusades*, Oxford University Press, Oxford, 1990

Murphy-O'Connor, J., *The Holy Land – Oxford Archaeological Guides*, Oxford University Press, Oxford and New York, 1998

Nicholson, H. and Nicolle, D., *God's Warriors*, Osprey, Oxford, 2005

Nicolle, D., *Hattin – Saladin's Greatest Victory*, Osprey, Oxford, 1998

Norwich, J.J., *A Short History of Byzantium*, Viking, London, 1997

Oldenbourg, Z. (tr. Anne Carter), *The Crusades*, BCA, London, 1998

Oman, C., *A History of the Art of War in the Middle Ages*, vol. 1, Greenhill, London, 1924; repr. 1991

Prawer, J., *Crusader Institutions*, Oxford University Press, Oxford, 1998

——, *The Crusaders' Kingdom*, Phoenix Press, London, 2001

Read, P.P., *The Templars*, Phoenix, London, 2003

Regan, G., *First Crusader*, Sutton, Stroud, 2001

Richard, J. (tr. Jean Birrell), *Saint Louis, Crusader King of France*, Cambridge University Press, Cambridge, 1999

Riley-Smith, J., *The Crusades – A Short History*, Continuum, London, 2001

——, *Hospitallers – The History of the Order of St John*, Hambledon, London, 1999

—— (ed.), *The Oxford Illustrated History of the Crusades*, Oxford University Press, Oxford, 1995

Runciman, S., *A History of the Crusades* (3 vols), Penguin, London, 1990

Saunders, J.J., *A History of Medieval Islam*, Routledge, London and New York, 1996

Smail, R.C., *Crusading Warfare 1097–1193*, Cambridge University Press, Cambridge, 1996

Southern, R.W., *The Making of the Middle Ages*, Pimlico, London, 1993

Tyerman, C., *England and the Crusades 1095–1588*, University of Chicago Press, Chicago and London, 1996

——, *The Crusades – A Very Short Introduction*, Oxford University Press, Oxford, 2005

Index

Index

Index

Index

Index